drowning in laws

Labor
Law and
Brazilian
Political
Culture

drowning in
laws

John D. French

The University of North Carolina Press
Chapel Hill and London

© 2004 The University of North Carolina Press

All rights reserved

Manufactured in the United States of America

Designed by Heidi Perov

Set in ITC Charter and Serifa by Keystone Typesetting, Inc.

Portions of this book have been reprinted with permission, in some-
what revised form, from John D. French, "The Origin of Corporatist State
Intervention in Brazilian Industrial Relations, 1930–1934: A Critique of the
Literature," *Luso-Brazilian Review* 28 (Fall 1991) : 13–26; John D. French,
"Drowning in Laws but Starving (for Justice?) : Brazilian Labor Law and the
Workers' Quest to Realize the Imaginary," *Political Power and Social Theory* 12
(1998) : 177–214, © 1998, reprinted with permission from Elsevier; and Joan L.
Bak, "The Man of the Book: 'This Is My Bible,' " in John D. French, *Afogados
em Leis: A CLT e a Cultura Política dos Trabalhadores Brasileiros* (São Paulo:
Fundação Perseu Abramo, 2001).

The paper in this book meets the guidelines for permanence and durability of
the Committee on Production Guidelines for Book Longevity of the Council on
Library Resources.

Library of Congress Cataloging-in-Publication Data
French, John D.
Drowning in laws : labor law and Brazilian political culture /
by John D. French.
    p. cm.
Includes bibliographical references and index.
ISBN 0-8078-2857-2 (cloth : alk. paper)
ISBN 0-8078-5527-8 (pbk. : alk. paper)
1. Labor laws and legislation—Social aspects—Brazil.
2. Industrial relations—Brazil. I. Title.
KHD1792.F74 2004
331.2'0981'09045—dc22

                2003025753

cloth   08 07 06 05 04   5 4 3 2 1
paper   08 07 06 05 04   5 4 3 2 1

DR. JAMES BRUCE FRENCH (1921–2002),
a man of principle and hater of empires,

and DR. JAN HOFFMAN FRENCH,
companheira de luta e sonhos

contents

Preface   *xi*

Abbreviations *xvii*

Introduction   *1*

one Brazilian Labor Legislation and the Origins Debate:
Gifts Bestowed and Fascist Impositions   *10*

two The Scholarly Politics of Brazilian Labor Law   *23*

three The CLT in Practice: A Generosity Akin to Fraud   *40*

four For the English to See? The CLT in Foreign
and Domestic Perspective   *54*

five The Enigma of Brazilian Labor Law: Vargas and the
Government's Bureaucratic *Trabalhista* Empire, 1950–1954   *73*

six Labor Law through the Prism of Subjectivity: Legal
Consciousness, Grievances, and Class Mobilization   *97*

seven The Politics of Aphorism: The Social Question
as a Police Matter (*Caso de Polícia*)   *122*

conclusion Drowning in Laws and Starving (for Justice):
Workers and the Quest to Realize the Imaginary   *151*

appendix The Man of the Book:
"This Is My Bible," by Joan Bak   *155*

Notes   *159*

Glossary   *203*

Bibliography   *205*

Index   *227*

illustrations,
tables, and figures

ILLUSTRATIONS

President Getúlio Vargas greets workers in São Paulo,
May Day, 1944   *13*

Government-sponsored May Day rally in São Paulo, 1939   *16*

Union members at a government-sponsored labor rally,
ca. 1941–42   *17*

Monument celebrating ten years of Vargas's rule,
Rio de Janeiro, 1940   *18*

Vargas on the labor laws   *27*

Workers march in a government-organized celebration
of ten years of Vargas's rule, 1940   *28*

Underage child at work at a cobbler's bench, ca. 1941–42   *50*

A group of adolescent boys in São Paulo on strike against the
Irmãos Gasparotti factory, 5 March 1964   *51*

Rally celebrating Adhemar de Barros's election as governor
of the state of São Paulo, São Paulo, 11 March 1947   *68*

Vargas meets with José Gonçalves, president of the Port
Service Workers' Union in Santos, 1952   *79*

1953 communist cartoon expressing skepticism about
João "Jango" Goulart   *87*

Observance of Vargas's death on 24 August 1954 at the
headquarters of the Port Service Workers' Union in Santos   *93*

Philadelpho Braz's diary entries for 20–21 July 1961   *108*

Philadelpho Braz as a trade union leader   *110*

Philadelpho Braz as a trade union bureaucrat   *110*

Metalworkers gather outside union headquarters during a strike at the Pirelli factory in Santo André, 1961 *112*

Communist labor leader Marcos Andreotti, 1982 *113*

Adelço de Almeida, leader of the Chemical Workers' Union of São Paulo, congratulates a worker who won a case in the labor courts before 1964 *115*

Rally at Pacaembu stadium in São Paulo, May Day, 1944 *142*

1953 communist cartoon criticizing the McCarthyite repression that characterized the Dutra and Vargas administrations *146*

Philadelpho Braz and Luis Inácio "Lula" da Silva, 1982 *149*

TABLES

1 Comparison of Labor Provisions of the Estado Novo Constitution of 1937 and Mussolini's Carta del Lavoro of 1927 *15*

2 Comparison of Preparatory *Bilhete* and Final Text of Getúlio Vargas's 1952 May Day Speech *80*

3 *Dissídios Individuais* Filed in the State of São Paulo as a Percentage of the National Total, 1944–1976 *103*

FIGURES

1 Typical Procedure for a Grievance Solved by a Formal Court Hearing, 1972 *101*

2 The Law (CLT) Is My Bible *152*

preface

This book is a study of the work that language and culture does in human societies. In methodological and historiographical terms, this volume moves away from a straightforward social history of labor toward a processual cultural history of labor law enactment, worker mobilization, and political culture in Brazil. In particular, it reflects my personal engagement with the theoretical debates that came to be known as the discursive turn and postmodernism. Within this context, *Drowning in Laws* advances a convincing materialist approach that incorporates questions of discourse and culture directly into the explanatory fabric of causal analysis. Unlike older approaches, my model does not substitute postulated class interests and behaviors for the words through which they are expressed (discourse). At the same time, this approach does not treat those words as self-sufficient but rather as weapons that are deployed to achieve the objectives of those who use them and that, in turn, shape those objectives. In this sense, my book recognizes the role that discursive universes play in shaping politics within a given national reality but does not use discourse analysis as a substitute for empirically grounded causal explanation. Finally, this work avoids treating the subjectivities and discourses of historical actors in strictly internalist and individualistic terms and thus ignoring how these subjectivities and discourses are patterned by society, culture, and history. (Social being precedes consciousness.)

The book starts from two premises: (1) that all conflicts that emerge from socioeconomic realities must eventually find expression through speech acts, and (2) that law is a particularly powerful locus for discourse that comes to be shared across and between lines of socioeconomic and role differentiation. In analyzing the discourse that has arisen around the Consolidation of Labor Laws (Consolidaçao das Leis do Trabalho, or CLT), as well as Brazilian law in general, I draw on a wide range of voices, including those of labor activists, rank-and-file workers, businessmen, lawyers, judges, politicians, and scholars (both Brazilian and foreign). In so doing, I reveal recurrent and readily identifiable motifs and gestures that cross differences in education, geography, socioeconomic roles, and occupational and professional specializations. This book suggests that such overlapping discourses constitute a common political culture yet reminds the reader that no truth is to be found in words themselves, only in when and how they are used, by whom, and to what end.

My 1992 monograph, *The Brazilian Workers' ABC*, dealt with workers, industrial relations, and politics in the ABC region of greater São Paulo from 1900 to 1950. A year before that book was published, I began research in Brazil, with support from the American Council of Learned Societies and the National Endowment for the Humanities, for a volume on the region's metalworkers after 1950. During that fieldwork, I discovered the 1961 diary of Philadelpho Braz, the secretary-general of the ABC metalworkers' union from 1956 to 1964. As I grappled with this unique source, a 1992 Social Science Research Council fellowship allowed me to begin a richly rewarding collaboration with Dr. Jody Pavilack, a talented young historian with whom I have worked on coding the diary. As I deepened my research at the National Humanities Center (NHC) in 1995–96, my work with the diary led to a welcome shift in focus as I concluded that my earlier work had too brusquely dismissed the importance of labor law in shaping working-class consciousness.

My original impatience with the extant historiography had been driven by its excessive concentration on legal forms and an accompanying weakness of empirical research at the grassroots. My deepening engagement with Braz's diary and interview transcripts, however, led me to realize that labor law was fundamental to the politics of worker mobilization, although not in the simple or straightforward ways imagined by earlier scholars. I had first addressed labor law directly in a 1991 historiographical piece in the *Luso-Brazilian Review*, whose traces can be seen in chapters 1 and 2 of this volume, and I broadened the geographical scope of my research while at the NHC to include Brazil as a whole. In tracking down discussions of labor law from as many points of view as possible, I owe special thanks to the NHC's energetic and resourceful librarians, Jean Houston, Eliza Robertson, and Alan Tutle. The scholarly community that crystallized at the NHC during my fellowship year, with the encouragement of the program's director, Kent Mulliken, provided the ideal environment for thinking in new ways about old subjects.

Since I joined the Duke University faculty in 1992, the development of my ideas has been accelerated by generous research and travel support polices, especially grants from the Arts and Sciences Research Council and the International and Latin American and Caribbean Studies Centers, as well as from the Consortium in Latin American Studies at the University of North Carolina at Chapel Hill and Duke University. The diplomatic and consular records at the U.S. National Archives and Records Administration in College Park, Maryland, proved most helpful, as did the extensive work I carried out in the Robert J. Alexander Papers at Rutgers University (parts are which are now available on microfilm from IDC Publishers). In 1999, a grant from the American Philosophical Society made possible a month of work in the political police records in São Paulo, an enterprise greatly facilitated by Antonio "Gino" Negro, a fellow historian of ABC's metalworkers. In 2000, I surveyed the Brazilian holdings of the International Confederation of Free Trade Unions when Jan Lucassen and Marcel Van der Linden invited me to participate in a conference on global labor history at the International Institute of Social History in Amsterdam. Helena Weis Gonçalves did a superb job of transcribing my interviews with leaders of ABC's metalworkers, while two U.S. labor studies colleagues, Kenneth Mericle and Cliff Welch, graciously provided me with data drawn from their research on the labor court system in São Paulo.

Early in this project, I received encouraging feedback from Maria Cook and the Collective Bargaining Workshop of the School of Industrial and Labor Relations at Cornell University as well as from Joan Meznar and her history colleagues at the University of South Carolina. I also received useful suggestions on its various written iterations from colleagues at the Latin American Labor History Conferences of 1996 and 1999, at conferences at Georgetown University in 1996 and New York University in 1998, and at the 1998 conferences of the Brazilian Studies Association and the Conference on Latin American History. This book's publication also marks an important point of inflection in my two-decade-long dialogue with Daniel James, co-organizer of the annual Latin American Labor History Conferences since 1984. Discussions with Jon Beasley-Murray, Paulo Fontes, Alexandre Fortes, Ivonne Wallace Fuentes, Mark Healey, Jody Pavilack, Tom Rogers, Michael Snodgrass, Fernando Teixeira, Alejandro Velasco, and Emília Viotti da Costa sharpened my thinking along the way, as did formal comments offered by my colleagues Joan Bak, Jeff Bortz, James Brennan, Michael Hall, Aldo Lauria-Santiago, Deborah Levenson-Estrada, and Barbara Weinstein. As I was undertaking the final revision, I also benefited from the perspective gained in discussions about law and the popular classes in Brazil since the late colonial period at a May 2003 conference organized by Silvia Lara and Joseli M. N. Mendonça at the State University of Campinas (UNICAMP) in São Paulo.

The first published results of my new interest in law appeared in a 1998 article in *Political Power and Social Theory*, which benefited from rigorous and stimulating comments from editor Diane Davis and two reviewers. In 2000, I received an invitation to publish a book on this subject from the Perseu Abramo Foundation of the Brazilian Workers' Party as part of the History of the Brazilian *Povo* (Common People) series initiated by Dr. Marco Aurélio Garcia, a historian at UNICAMP who served as secretary of culture in the São Paulo city administration of Martha Supplicy in 2001 and 2002. *Afogados em Leis*, which appeared in 2001, is part of the Memory and History project coordinated by Alexandre Fortes, who had primary responsibility, along with Gino Negro, for editing the shorter Brazilian version of this book. Paulo Fontes was responsible for a carefully crafted Portuguese translation, with contributions from Alexandre Fortes and Fabio Durão.

The Abramo Foundation's editorial requirements for the series played an enormously productive role in shaping this book's intellectual trajectory. As is typical of the best of Brazilian social science, the foundation sought intellectual rigor, up-to-date historiographical discussion, and political relevance. In addition, the foundation insisted that the book meet standards of clarity that would facilitate success for a publication designed to be distributed, read, and debated in both academic and nonacademic contexts. The book's publication ceremony was held in São Paulo in July 2001, with welcome support from the AFL-CIO Solidarity Center, headed by Carolyn Kasdan, and the assistance of Flamarion Maués, the foundation's publishing coordinator. The event was attended by some of my dear friends from ABC, including Philadelpho Braz, Ademir Medici, and Valdenizio Petrolli, as well as by Carlos Alberto Grana, the head of Brazil's largest trade union confederation. As secretary-general of the Central Única dos Trabalhadores, Grana's personal recollections of his trajectory within and opinions about the CLT system offered convincing proof of the need for and the fruitfulness of a dialogue between past and present in contemporary Brazil.

From the beginning, my editor at the University of North Carolina Press, Elaine Maisner, grasped the importance of this project, while the reports by Joe Love and another external reader were helpful in reshaping this much-enlarged manuscript. The final revision was completed during a fall 2002 leave generously granted by Duke Arts and Sciences Dean William Chafe and Associate Dean Karla Holloway. I owe special thanks to the staff at the University of North Carolina Press, especially assistant managing editor Paula Wald and copyeditor Ellen D. Goldlust-Gingrich, for their contributions to improving the final manuscript and moving it efficiently through production.

Every line of this book, more than a decade of work, has been profoundly influenced by hundreds of hours of intense discussion—of law, Brazil, and social theory—with my *companheira*, lawyer-anthropologist Jan Hoffman French. The rebel spirit of our children, Paul Joseph and Elizabeth Nora, will also surely be felt in these pages dealing with the complexities of the ongoing fight for a better world.

ABC   Santo André, São Bernardo do Campo, São Caetano do Sul; one administrative unit until 1945, the ABC region of greater São Paulo encompasses today's *municípios* of Santo André, São Bernardo do Campo, São Caetano do Sul, Diadema, Mauá, Ribeirão Pires, and Rio Grande da Serra

CLT   Consolidaçao das Leis do Trabalho (Consolidation of Labor Laws)

CNTI   Confederaçao Nacional dos Trabalhadores na Indústria (National Confederation of Industrial Workers), a national entity founded in 1946 and indirectly elected that was led by conservative trade unionists for all but a brief moment before 1964

DET   Departamento Estadual do Trabalho (State Labor Department), São Paulo state agency

DIP   Departamento de Imprensa e Propaganda (Press and Propaganda Department), under the Estado Novo regime of Getúlio Vargas

DOPS   Delegacia/Departamento de Ordem Política Social (Social and Political Order Department or Delegacy), a police agency founded in 1924 and abolished in 1983

DRT   Delegacia Regional do Trabalho (Regional Labor Delegacy), subordinate organ of the MTIC; headed by the *delegado regional do trabalho* (regional labor delegate)

IAPI   Instituto de Aposentadorias e Pensoẽs dos Industriários (Industrial Employees' Pension and Retirement Institute)

ILO   International Labour Organization/Office

MTIC   Ministério do Trabalho, Indústria, e Comércio (Ministry of Labor, Industry, and Commerce)

PTB   Partido Trabalhista Brasileiro (Brazilian Labor Party), founded in 1945 by Getúlio Vargas

SESI   Serviço Social da Indústria (Social Service of Industry), founded in 1946

TRT   Tribunal Regional do Trabalho (Regional Labor Court)

TSN   Tribunal de Segurança Nacional (National Security Court)

TST   Tribunal Superior do Trabalho (Supreme Labor Court)

drowning in laws

The Brazilian worker is a worker surrounded
by laws on all sides but dead from hunger. So
many laws! But we lack one to keep him from
dying of hunger.
—Minas Gerais trade union leader from
the 1950s

introduction

Since 1943, the world of Brazilian blue-collar workers, white-collar employees, liberal professionals, and those who employ them has been governed by a
"highly structured, minutely regulated labor code" that has long been characterized as the "world's most advanced labor legislation."[1] Originating during
the political and legal ferment of the 1930s under Getúlio Vargas, Brazilian
social and labor legislation was systematized in 1943 under Vargas's Estado
Novo (New State) dictatorship in the Consolidation of Labor Laws (Consolidaçao das Leis do Trabalho, or CLT). This system of labor and social security
laws, noted U.S. economist Werner Baer in 1965, was "quite elaborate and
advanced for an underdeveloped country which was just beginning to indus-
trialize"—indeed, Brazil's system was "one of the most advanced in the whole
world."[2]

Looking back over a half century, the CLT stands out as among the most
important policy initiatives identified with Vargas and his regime. As sociolo-

gist José Albertino Rodrigues noted in 1968, the CLT would come to occupy a unique status as Brazil's "most widely divulged legal document," far "better known than the federal constitution" promulgated in 1946.[3] And the CLT's mandated working papers (*carteira do trabalho*), observed Brazilian scholar Wanderley Guilherme dos Santos in 1979, emerged as far more than a legal record of a worker's employment history. In the workers' relation to the state, the *carteira* constituted a "certificate of civic birth."[4] As for the CLT itself, hundreds of editions have been published since 1943, in multiple forms, and the wider legal literature on the CLT system constitutes the majority of the published works related to labor in Brazil.[5]

In a 1942 book, *Brazil under Vargas*, political scientist Karl Loewenstein offered an acute assessment based on an exploratory trip to Brazil, a U.S. ally during World War II. The Vargas regime, he suggested, had proven capable of combining "two seemingly conflicting or overlapping policies": (1) the vigorous encouragement of "private capitalism . . . unfettered by state regimentation"; and (2) the implementation of "progressive paternalism in social policy for the benefit of the laboring classes."[6] Put in more analytical terms, Vargas moved the country decisively down the road to capitalist industrialization, shifting from the plantation (*fazenda*) to the factory as the symbol of Brazil while implanting an "advanced" program of social reform aimed at urban working people. As Brazilian historian Angela de Castro Gomes aptly put it in 1979, one of the ironies in the history of Brazilian labor legislation is the contrast between the 1920s and the 1930s. During the 1920s, urban industrialists easily stymied attempts at labor legislation despite industry's relative political marginality. In the 1930s, by contrast, these industrialists were unable to prevent labor's gains despite their emergence for the first time as important contenders for national power.[7]

Attuned to Brazil's wry form of truth telling, Loewenstein went on to offer a summary judgment of the Vargas regime that many later observers would echo. The government had the support of the rich, which was not difficult to achieve as long as their privileges were defended. The Vargas regime's special talent, however, was to have succeeded simultaneously at the "more arduous task . . . of winning the sympathy of the nameless masses of the toilers."[8] In its colloquial Brazilian variant, Vargas had positioned himself as both the "mother of the rich" and the "father of the poor."[9]

Approaches to the CLT: The State of Play

As an enduring monument to the political genius of the Vargas regime, the CLT represents a lasting challenge to analysts of modern Brazilian social and political history. A limited number of themes have served as touchstones for the "lawyers, judges, politicians, historians, political scientists, and sociologists [who] have dedicated tens of thousands of pages to analyzing . . . the CLT and its adjacent legislation."[10] Almost all these observers see this body of labor law as a singular and decisive feature of the statecraft of Getúlio Vargas, the architect of the centralizing state that stands at the core of a modernizing Brazil. Most commentators echo the *varguista* claim that the 1930s marked a symbolic shift away from liberal laissez-faire, while some see the advent of legislation as the end of an exclusively repressive handling of workers' grievances and popular demands. No longer would social agitation be treated solely as a police matter (*caso de polícia*), as was said to have been the case during the First Republic (1889–1930).

There are also recurring references to the unique style of anticipatory and co-optive statecraft that brought the new labor relations regime into effect as a gift bestowed on the Brazilian populace (*outorga*). Rightly characterizing the Vargas regime as paternalistic in posture, most observers link the CLT to the emergence of a new style of mass electoral politics that blossomed after Vargas's fall from power in 1945. This shift is most closely identified with Vargas's Brazilian Labor Party (Partido Trabalhista Brasileiro, or PTB), founded by labor ministry functionaries, which served as the vehicle for his triumphant 1950 return to the presidency "in the arms of the people." Although officially described as "laborite" (*trabalhista*), the PTB is more often glossed as populist and would grow in strength in the two decades leading up to its extinction in 1966, when the antipopulist military regime abolished the party but left untouched the CLT's fundamental structures.

Not surprisingly, many of these commonplace observations originated in the universe of self-representations and propaganda that characterized Vargas's twenty-four years at the center of national politics after 1930.[11] Other statements are more caught up in polemical controversy, although even supporters recognize Vargas's tenuous commitment to electoral democracy as such, at least in comparison to what the Estado Novo's apologists sometimes called "social" democracy. (The term had little substantive kinship with its European analogue.) When the CLT was decreed in 1943, Vargas was the outright dictator in an anticommunist regime, explicitly inspired by Portuguese, Spanish, and Italian corporatism, that had begun with a self-administered coup against elections in 1937 and ended with Vargas's ouster by the military in 1945. Even sympathizers appreciate this simplest of paradoxes: the systematization of rights and benefits for working people took place under a right-wing regime that explicitly outlawed strikes in its 1937 constitution *outorgada* and mandated jail sentences and worse for those responsible for agitation.

In discussions of the CLT, the debate over origins inevitably broadens into larger disagreements about philosophy, essence, and legacy. Although the discussion has become somewhat hackneyed from repetition, no one denies the role of foreign ideologies and corporatist discourse in the CLT's creation; there is, however, less agreement regarding their significance. Reporting on a 1958 mission to Brazil, the representatives of the anticommunist International Confederation of Free Trade Unions judged, as have innumerable others, that the CLT was "inspired by (and in some regards a faithful copy of) the Italian corporatist laws and the fascist Carta del Lavoro." The CLT was, in essence, a "fundamentally totalitarian law adapted to a democratic country."[12] The CLT's carryover through successive political regimes highlights another general sentiment: surprise at its remarkable durability. From a broader international perspective, as labor lawyer Éfren Córdova noted in 1990, few similar labor relations systems from the interwar years survived their creators. "Other regimes which had followed the corporatist system"—for example, Italy, Vichy France, Spain, and Portugal—"disappeared, but the Brazilian system remained intact. The labour systems of the other countries of the [Western] hemisphere tended progressively to resemble one another, but Brazil retained, without great change, the main lines of a very different regime." As a result, Brazil remains, even under its democratic constitution of 1988, one of the few countries in the Americas, along with the United States, not to have ratified Convention 87 on freedom of association of the International Labour Organization (ILO).[13]

The CLT's survival over the next half century is especially striking given the far-reaching socioeconomic changes that transformed an agrarian and rural country of 41 million people in 1943 into an overwhelmingly urban and industrial one. Although Brazil is known abroad only superficially, the regulatory regime and labor struggles of this medium-developed country should be of wide interest given that Brazil possesses the world's fifth-largest population (176 million in 2003) and tenth-largest economy in gross domestic product.[14] If the legal framing of class struggle in Brazil is a peculiarity of that nation's system of rule over those who work, interest should be further piqued by the country's unique political trajectory over the past twenty-five years. The rise of a powerful labor-based Left began with the popular insurgencies of the 1970s against the military dictatorship (1964–85), including a militant "New Unionism" that harshly criticized the CLT system of labor relations. In 1979, the charismatic leader of the dramatic metalworkers' strikes of 1978–80, Luis Inácio "Lula" da Silva, called for a new Workers' Party (Partido dos Trabalhadores) to bring together a wide gamut of social movements, including Catholic practitioners of liberation theology and much of the Left. Over four successive presidential campaigns, Lula and his party built a powerful leftist political appeal that brought him the presidency in 2002 with 63 percent of the national vote in the second round. The rise of Lula and the Workers' Party offers interesting parallels to class formation in Western Europe in the nineteenth century while speaking to analogous developments within other newly industrializing countries of the developing world in the late twentieth century.[15]

Going beyond the Corporatist Consensus

The CLT's anomalous origin and ubiquitousness as a legal and cultural reference within the country has prompted endless debate among participants, contemporary observers, and later scholars. Profoundly shaped by what has been called the "corporatist consensus,"[16] the many social scientists who wrote about the CLT concentrated largely on "the repressive and centralized union laws" that were thought to "set the limits and potential of working class organization and militancy."[17] With few exceptions, as Maria Célia Paoli noted in her 1988 dissertation, these scholars "seldom consider[ed] the significant role that the legal provisions designed to protect rights at work have played in the cultural and political formation of the Brazilian working class."[18] After all, the "constitution of the working class as a collective actor," as Angela de Castro Gomes emphasized in her influential 1988 book, A Invenção do Trabalhismo (The Invention of Trabalhismo), "is a political-cultural phenomenon" that articulates "values, ideas, traditions, and models of organization through a discourse in which the worker is at the same time subject and object."[19]

The emerging analytical breakthroughs that gathered momentum in the early to mid-1990s were connected to the reestablishment of civilian rule in Brazil in 1985, capped off by an advanced democratic 1988 constitution that failed to abolish the CLT system. Deeper subsequent empirical investigation has slowly but surely transformed our understanding of the history of workers, industrial relations, and mass politics in Brazil.[20] With historical distance and sufficient density of research, the time is ripe to historicize the CLT, with its many spheres, constituencies, and possible contemporary and retrospective meanings. We can now ask questions that were previously invisible and formulate more definitive solutions to older conundrums.

If the foundational myths of *varguismo* once needed repudiation, it is now abundantly clear that simple negation does not in and of itself resolve apparent paradoxes or dispel rhetorical fog, whether for or against Vargas and his legacies, including the CLT. To achieve a durable new understanding of these labor laws and practices requires engagement with the mythologies surrounding the CLT, the wider discussion within Brazilian society, and the evolving interpretations in the historiography across all disciplines, including law and sociology. Thus, chapters 2 and 3 of this volume reconfigure debates about the origins of the labor laws in the 1930s to clarify questions of causality while moving beyond simplistic ideological attributions and doctrinal discussions. Likewise, chapter 4 pays special attention to the specificity of law within the Brazilian social formation while explaining how the CLT, viewed comparatively, represents an approach to lawmaking that diverges from the norms and assumptions of North Atlantic observers.

Yet even a dynamic sociology of knowledge is insufficient without the use of different tools—those of legal history—to address the old questions in new ways. In approaching law, legal historian Cynthia Herrup notes, most scholars "give either too much or too little consideration to the interrelationship of law and society. Sometimes, social and cultural influences appear as intrusions extrinsic to an otherwise self-referential law. More frequently, authors bring their broader knowledge to bear" in such a way that "the legal setting fades to background, to an occasion which happens to produce historically relevant materials." In its attention to the grammar of the law, this book approaches the legal arena of the CLT as a frontier, an area of exchange among those who rule, those who obey, and those who lawyer. My objective, in Herrup's words, is to move back and forth between "the rule-bound unreality of the law" and "the unruliness of life" to grasp "how completely interwoven are the legal and the cultural ambiguities within the law."[21] Law must be examined, as legal historian William Forbath suggests, as language and discourse, on one hand, and as "institutional practices, constraints, and legitimated violence" on the other. In his 1989 study of U.S. labor law, he explored how "the centers of power and the language" could be directly linked to the "experiences of labor in local contexts and conflicts."[22]

Embracing a social-historical approach to the study of law, this book examines the creation and functioning of legal instruments and institutions that deal with workers as well as the words generated by and about the CLT. I ask why and how these institutions have functioned and evolved through time and explore the dynamics of social interactions with and within these institutions. After introducing the reader to the CLT and its background, the book focuses on the relatively open political era known as the Populist Republic (1945–64). In particular, chapter 3 surveys how this surprising and profoundly problematic body of law was administered—or, some would say, misadministered—in greater São Paulo, the heart of modern industrial Brazil. Using the chasm between law and reality in São Paulo as a fulcrum, the book then examines how both academics and nonacademics have discussed the CLT system while criticizing those who have sought to explain Brazilian labor law in terms of corporatism, whether understood as a cultural predisposition or a bourgeois fraud. In chapter 5, this volume also enters into debate with more recent interpretations that have sought to present the CLT as an integral part of a wider state project of nation building and inclusionary citizenship (the *trabalhista* thesis identified with Castro Gomes).

Throughout, the book takes a holistic approach that encompasses the structural as well as the conjunctural, the institutional as well as the discursive. While keeping an eye on the regularities of conduct by social actors, I focus on the discourses and practices of those who write the laws, staff the government ministries and labor courts, operate within these institutions as lawyers, or enter into those institutions as supplicants in pursuit of practical interests. Although the voices of the CLT's architects are abundantly represented, *Drowning in Laws* also pays close attention to the discourses of workers and labor activists in a country with a long tradition of protest against a labor relations system that violates union autonomy and freedom while failing to deliver on its most basic promises of rights and benefits for workers. Operating within a discursive universe not of their own making, workers internalized these dominant discourses and practices, which thus helped to shape—without unilaterally determining—the interiority, cultural, and intellectual life of a working class in formation. This process also gave birth to certain unique but characteristic forms of social critique, protest, and mobilization among workers. What is it about the Brazilian labor law system that simultaneously produce deep bitterness and cynicism on the part of working-class labor activists as well as an unprecedented hopefulness and utopian militancy?

This sustained reflection on the CLT places *varguismo* within the sweep of

Brazilian history as an integral part of long-standing traditions of rule by the dominant classes. Unlike those who focus single-mindedly on the labor law and its surrounding rhetorical penumbra, I also examine yet another vital state institution that shaped the lives and impacted the struggles of Brazilian workers: the police. To fully understand Brazilian political culture, our analysis must encompass the violent arm of the state as well as the labor laws, both of which figured into *varguista* mythology—the former as "the social question as a police matter [*caso de polícia*]" and the latter as a gift (*outorga*). The examination of the repressive interface between the state and workers will allow us to better understand the proven wariness of Brazil's working people as they interacted with an ostensibly benevolent state toward which they were expected to feel loyal and grateful, whatever its shortcomings. In wrestling with the "politics of aphorism," chapter 7 also illustrates the fundamental continuities that marked Brazil before and after Vargas's rise to power in 1930. In the end, workers had to reckon with the state as both a bestower of rights and benefits, however uncertain, and a force for the repression of worker rights and the denial of the effective enjoyment of those benefits.

The ambiguous role played by the Brazilian state that drafted such ambitious labor laws can be understood only in terms of the legal and political culture of Brazilian elites as they were shaped by an ideological inheritance of authoritarian paternalism. From the outset, the labor law was as much imaginary as real for both the government bureaucrats who drafted the CLT and the workers who sought to use the law to advance their interests. For the former, the law's visionary and even utopian promises could be tolerated precisely because they were never meant to be real. As a result, Brazilian workers developed a complicated—indeed, fundamentally conflicted—relationship with the CLT system. Working-class activists needed the law, with all its flaws, yet could not afford to entertain any illusions about the CLT, its creators, or its enforcers. In the end, the labor laws became "real" in Brazilian workplaces only to the extent that workers struggled to make the law as imaginary ideal into a practical future reality.

In offering this interpretation of the legal consciousness of Brazilian workers and labor activists, *Drowning in Laws* adds substance to Paoli's 1988 hypothesis that "the formation of the Brazilian working class cannot be understood without considering the legal intervention by the State in daily work relations, [which] served to shape workers' demands for justice [while constituting] a common cultural horizon as to what dignity and fairness in labor issues should be."[23] At the same time, this proposition in no way lessens the bitter but powerful insight offered by the trade unionist quoted at the outset of this chapter: only a limited freedom is accorded the majority of the population in a wage-dependent capitalist economy, particularly in Brazil, where basic survival is not a given for tens of millions of people.[24]

Although offering hope, Brazil's abundant and advanced labor legislation was easily perceived as a mockery by working people who saw themselves as drowning in a sea of tantalizing but ineffective and frustrating laws. Indeed, the publisher of the Brazilian version of this book simply titled it *Drowned in Laws*, as if the ocean had already claimed its victims. That title was chosen precisely because it effectively grabbed attention by speaking to an important dimension of the legal consciousness of Brazilians as a whole. So much offered, so little gained, and yet a persistent hunger to believe.

one

Brazilian Labor Legislation and the Origins Debate

Gifts Bestowed and Fascist Impositions

The 1943 Brazilian CLT has been inextricably linked to one man and two dates: Getúlio Vargas and 1930, the year of the "revolution" that brought him to power, and 1937, when he established a dictatorship to maintain that power. If 1937 links the CLT to an authoritarian and "fascist" regime of exception, the 1930 date associates the labor laws with an antioligarchical movement, led by Vargas, that decreed the secret ballot in 1932. In both cases, the state, the nation, and the man "bestowed" advanced labor laws on Brazilian workers—a generous gift given their limited numbers and minimal influence.

The CLT's relationship to 1930 and 1937 has always been a matter of polemical importance to both Vargas's supporters and opponents. In the eyes of apologists, the CLT and its predecessor legislation in the early 1930s, whatever their imperfections, were examples of enlightened and pioneering statesmanship that increased and broadened available freedoms. Critics and scholars, by contrast, have tended to see the CLT and its preceding jurisprudence as a corporatist monstrosity, a top-down imposition that limited workers' freedoms and damaged civil society by forcibly incorporating trade unions into the state apparatus. Yet a still earlier time looms behind this chronological dispute: the explosive years immediately after World War I, when a series of general strikes in São Paulo and other cities marked the social question's dramatic entrance onto the center stage of Brazilian politics. Although the political and economic establishment's continued rule was never threatened, these episodes of dramatic labor insurgency between 1917 and 1919, magnified by the reverberations of the Russian Revolution, impressed the conservative classes, those who governed on their behalf, and those who resented the conservatives' power. This chapter uses disputes over the pre-1943 origins of the CLT system to critique well-worn ways of talking about the Brazilian labor relations system that emerged between 1930 and 1945. The roots of these debates about chronology lie in alternative genealogies of legitimation and delegitimation vis-à-vis state intervention as practiced in Brazil. In dissecting the historiography, this chapter also highlights the specificities of the juridical field that will be decisive to this book's larger argument.

The Birth of Brazilian Labor Law in the 1930s

Labor law emerged as a leitmotif of Brazilian political life with the overthrow of the First Republic of 1889–1930, which opened the way for fifteen years of rule by Getúlio Vargas. In 1930, Vargas was the governor of the state of Rio Grande do Sul and agreed to serve as the presidential candidate of a loose coalition called the Liberal Alliance. The forty-eight-year-old establishment politician lost the election to a *paulista* candidate, Júlio Prestes, who had been selected by President Washington Luis, a former governor of the state of São Paulo. Having served as finance minister in Luis's cabinet from 1926 to 1928, Vargas was an unlikely and reluctant insurgent, but his rise to power in a bloodless rebellion, christened the Revolution of 1930, ousted the economically dominant state of São Paulo from national power. While deriving its credibility from powerful regionalist rivalries, Vargas's heterogeneous movement also gestured toward the political discontent of the previous decade among the country's small but growing urban population. In its 1930 platform, the Liberal Alliance took aim at the republican system of oligarchic parliamentarianism characterized by restricted electoral participation, the absence of the secret ballot, and undemocratic machine rule. Distinguishing itself from its opponents, the alliance declared in its final platform that "one cannot deny the existence of a social question in Brazil, as one of the problems that must be faced with seriousness on the part of government [*poderes públicos*]. . . . Both the urban proletariat and the rural," it went on, needed protection.[1]

When a junta of top military generals turned over power to Vargas in November 1930, labor laws quickly received a prominent place in the politics of symbols and gestures that would come to be indelibly associated with Vargas's name. Three weeks after being sworn in as provisional president, Vargas named the author of the alliance's platform to head a newly created Ministry of Labor, Industry, and Commerce (Ministério do Trabalho, Indústria, e Comércio, or MTIC). As chief of what he grandiosely hailed as "the ministry of revolution,"[2] *gaúcho* journalist Lindolfo Collor issued a flurry of decrees on labor and other social issues, including unionization. Although Collor resigned in 1932 in a split with Vargas, the social and labor legislation that began during Collor's sixteen months in office was followed by a torrent of additional laws over the next two years.[3]

The social question's new status was confirmed in 1934 when a constitution was drafted in response to a violent but unsuccessful 1932 rebellion by the state of São Paulo. Whether allied for or against Vargas, status quo politicians joined with those of a more reformist bent to directly incorporate these concerns into the new Magna Carta.[4] Thus, when the assembly elected Vargas to serve as constitutional president through 1938, he ruled under a constitution that accorded legal recognition to unions, sanctioned a system of labor courts, and granted a wide array of social and economic rights to workers. Charged with overseeing elections that would pave the way for democratic alternation in power, Vargas maneuvered with cunning during the rest of the 1930s, which were marked by worldwide geopolitical and ideological ferment. Vargas shrewdly used flashy but shallow mass mobilizations by the Brazilian ramifications of the international Popular Front and fascism (the integralist movement). In 1935, he seized on a barracks revolt led by communist military rebels to eliminate the Left through a massive wave of repression that imprisoned at least five thousand people from all walks of life.

Stoking the fires of anticommunism, Vargas proceeded to rule under a repeatedly renewed state of siege, approved by a supine congress, as the presidential elections of 1938 began to take shape. (He was not a candidate.) Trumpeting a fabricated "Cohen plan" for communist revolution, Vargas surprised the nation on 11 October 1937 by canceling elections, dissolving Congress, and establishing a dictatorship called the Estado Novo (New State).

Riding in an open car, President Getúlio Vargas greets workers at Pacaembu stadium in São Paulo, May Day, 1944. (Courtesy Iconographia/Cia. da Memória/Brazil)

Backed by the military and supported at first by the integralists (who were crushed after a revolt the following year), Vargas struck down the electoral ambitions of his opponents and "bestowed" a new constitution (*constituição outorgada*) that was modeled after those of European fascist and strong-arm regimes.[5] On hearing the news, recalled Vargas's daughter, Alzira, one of the newly unemployed congressmen rushed over to see her at the presidential palace: "Little Alzira, I know that the boss [*patrão*] is right. But this is not done, not without advance notice [*aviso prévio*]," he complained. "What about the labor laws? Why even my floor waxer has the right to a month's warning before being fired."[6] (This wry joke shows that the labor laws had already emerged as grist for Brazil's brand of cynical political humor.)[7]

Vargas had placed himself above "juridical formalisms," and his charter for the Estado Novo was quickly dubbed the "Polack Constitution" (*constituição polaca*), a deprecatory reference that was by no means restricted to his opponents.[8] The designation evoked an authoritarian Polish constitution that the Estado Novo's jurists were said to have copied as well as the foreign Jewish prostitutes of Rio de Janeiro known as *polacas* (hence, the name also referred to the prostituted constitution). While humor could be found at the expense of the regime's fragile constitutionalist pretensions, far more serious matters were at stake, including the abolition of all political parties, the establishment of rigorous censorship, and a radical move to centralize power in the national government. On 29 November 1937 Vargas officiated at a well-publicized ceremonial burning of the flags of the Brazilian states. From this day forward, he declared, there would be only Brazil and there would be "no more intermediaries between the government and the people."[9] Few failed to note, of course, that in the vein of France's Louis XIV, Vargas was declaring "L'État c'est moi" (I am the state) under this explicitly authoritarian new dispensation; indeed, when Vargas fell from power in 1945, two years after decreeing the CLT, his rule had been unconstitutional under even the 1937 charter because he had never held the national plebiscite that was mandated to ratify the constitution.[10]

The Politics of Chronology I: The Fascism of the 1937 Estado Novo Dictatorship

As many observers have emphasized, the Brazilian corporatist labor system has remained fundamentally unchanged since its piecemeal establishment over the course of the 1930s and its consolidation into systematic form in the 1943 CLT, despite many subsequent shifts in political regime.[11] Thus, every discussion of labor in later decades inevitably turned back to the radical shifts in state policy that occurred in the 1930s. Oddly enough, the literature did not agree on whether this decisive transformation occurred in 1930–31 or in 1937. One group of scholars, including U.S. industrial relations specialist Kenneth Mericle and distinguished Brazilian labor lawyer Evaristo de Moraes Filho, contends that the decisive shift toward a corporatist labor model took place only after the 1937 proclamation of the Estado Novo dictatorship.[12] In the words of political scientist Amaury de Souza, the labor legislation's original inspiration and first steps forward in the 1930s "were run over, halfway there," not so much by labor ministry decrees as by the 1937 constitution.[13]

The 1937 date has the advantage of directly associating the state's interventionist role with the height of authoritarian, corporatist, and fascist influence on Brazil.[14] Proof of the "Mussolini-esque inspiration" of Vargas's "fascist labor system" could be found in Vargas's "bestowed" charter of 1937.[15] The Estado Novo constitution not only included an even more extensive list of social and labor benefits than did the 1934 document[16] but also contained two complete articles—and numerous phrases—that were taken, almost word for word, from Mussolini's 1927 Carta del Lavoro.[17]

TABLE 1: Comparison of Labor Provisions of the Estado Novo
Constitution of 1937 and Mussolini's Carta del Lavoro of 1927

Constitution of the Estado Novo, Brazil, November 1937	Mussolini's Carta del Lavoro, Italy, April 1927
Article 136: Labor is a social duty. Intellectual, technical, and manual labor has the right to protection and special solicitousness by the state.	Article 2: Labor in all forms—intellectual, technical, and manual—is a social duty. In this sense, and only in this sense, it is protected by the state.
Article 138: Professional or syndicate organization is free. But only the syndicate regularly recognized by the state has the right to legally represent those who participate in the production category for which it is constituted and to defend their interests before the state and other professional organizations, draw up obligatory collective labor contracts for all its members, impose contributions on them, and exercise delegated functions of the public power.	Article 3: Trade or syndicate organization is free. But only the syndicate regularly recognized and placed under the control of the state has the legal right to represent the entire group of employers or of workers for which it is constituted, to guard their interests before the state or other organized economic groups, to draw up collective labor contracts, obligatory on all those belonging to the same group, to impose contributions on them, and to exercise delegated functions of public interest relating to them.

Sources: Brazil, Constituições, 1:217–18; Haider, Capital and Labor, 88.

The backbone of the Estado Novo's authoritarian discourse was a highly accentuated ideological antiliberalism and anticommunism. The disordered individualism and rampant materialism of liberal capitalism, authoritative voices declared, had bred atheistic communism and threatened the basis of private property, public order, and Christian civilization. "Corporativism kills communism," declared Justice Minister Francisco Campos in 1940, "just as capitalism generates communism." Campos, the jurist who had drafted the 1937 charter, argued that corporatism staved off the "decomposition of the capitalist world foreseen by Marx as a result of liberal anarchy."[18] In 1938, Vargas would declare to a São Paulo workers' rally, "The Estado Novo does not recognize rights of individuals against the collectivity. Individuals have no rights, they have duties: Rights pertain to the collectivity!" Turning to the social question, he thundered that his "state does not want, does not recognize, class struggle." The labor laws, he insisted, were laws of social harmony that replaced the negative concept of class struggle with that of class collaboration.[19]

Government-sponsored May Day rally in the Praça da Sé in São Paulo, 1939. Banners highlight the various trade union delegations present. (Courtesy Iconographia/Cia. da Memória/Brazil)

During the Estado Novo, few discontented workers were unaware of the consequences liberally meted out to those with unsound ideas of "class conflict." While tens of thousands were bused to May Day rallies to honor Vargas for his latest "gifts," thousands of malcontents were spied on, picked up, arrested, and sometimes tortured by the state, while still others were condemned to prison terms by the National Security Court (Tribunal de Segurança Nacional, or TSN).[20] As union institutions resurrected themselves after the repression of 1935, their affairs were conducted in a submissive way, at least in part because only individuals with an official police "certificate of ideology" could hold office.[21] Moreover, these groups had to provide authorities with advance notice of public meetings so that the police could officially monitor the gatherings for suspect activity.

Given such right-wing discourses and repressive practices, few would deny that Brazilian corporatism, as institutionalized during the Estado Novo, contained a pronounced authoritarian—even fascist—dimension, especially prior to Brazil's entry into the war against the Axis, which somewhat eased the ideological atmosphere. Yet it would be wrong, as most scholars have concluded, to see Brazil's state-linked labor system as derived exclusively from European fascist, corporatist, and right-wing Catholic sources. Rejecting the invocation of Mussolini (no one cites Hitler and the Nazis as precedents), Brazilian scholars have rightly emphasized that the "corporative union structure did not originate as a copy of fascism . . . transposed to our country."[22] Although an understandable polemical expedient, the "fascist" label fails to capture the intellectual and legal origins of the social and labor legislation that preceded 1937.

Union members at a government-sponsored labor rally, ca. 1941–42. The sign reads, "Stevedores Union of Rio de Janeiro. United for Brazil." (Photograph by Genevieve Naylor/Courtesy Reznikoff Artistic Partnership)

The Politics of Chronology II:
The Progressivism of the Revolution of 1930

For the overwhelming majority of scholars and even the Vargas regime, the decisive moment of transition in state-labor relations remained the Revolution of 1930. As many students of Brazilian labor history point out, corporatist control of unions began not in 1937 but in March 1931, with Collor's unionization law, which is thought to have given birth to "a trade unionism subordinated to the state."[23] Decree 19,770 not only proclaimed unions, for the first time, to be "consultative organs" of the state but is generally accepted to have "laid the bases of our model of corporativist unionism."[24] The preference for this dating reflects, in part, a concern with identifying the original sin of the Brazilian labor movement, the moment of its loss of innocence vis-à-vis the

Monument celebrating ten years of Vargas's rule, Rio de Janeiro, 1940. The top of the monument says, "Work is a social duty." The left side of the tablet reads, "Promises of the Candidate. 1930 Platform. 'One cannot deny the existence of a social question in Brazil, as one of the problems that must be faced with seriousness by the public powers.' 'It also behooves us to assist the proletarian with measures that assure him of relative comfort and stability and to sustain him in sickness and old age.' " The right side reads, "Accomplishments of the president. Decade of 1930 to 1940. I. Ministry of Labor, Industry and Commerce. II. 8-hour workday, protection of labor conditions during work at night and in unhealthy industries, Sunday and holiday rest," and a long list of government decrees. (Courtesy Iconographia/Cia. da Memória/Brazil)

state. Yet legal commentary and serious scholarly research reinforce the notion of an essential continuity of thought and design before and after the 1937 coup d'état, even as Vargas's discourse turned decisively to the right.[25] With few exceptions, the essential features of Brazil's social and labor legislation were promulgated before 1937, especially during the revolutionary (1930–34) and, to a lesser extent, constitutional (1934–37) phases of Vargas's rule.[26] As Michael Hall and Marco Aurélio Garcia have concluded, the essential traits of state control were already visible in 1931, although the system attained its final form only during the Estado Novo regime.[27] Rather than introducing new legal innovations, the centralizing corporatist regime after 1937 largely perfected, systematized, and, most importantly, created the structures that could be used to enforce measures already on the books.

The choice of 1930 as the key turning point also introduces a more sympathetic origin story because the 1931 legislation was drafted by the Brazilian First Republic's most outstanding radical lawyers. This turn of events stemmed from the challenges facing Collor as the head of the new Ministry of Labor after the Revolution of 1930. Collor had no personal background in or specialized knowledge about the social question,[28] so he needed knowledgeable men who could educate him in these matters. Yet as a "revolutionary" leader, he also needed men marked with the excitement of the new who were uncompromised by allegiances to the old regime, thus ruling out anyone who worked for the employers. He met the challenge by approaching the handful of lawyers with direct involvement in political opposition and social agitation before 1930, starting with Maurício de Lacerda, a combative former federal deputy from Rio who had championed social legislation after World War I. Lacerda turned the invitation down, he would later claim, because Collor's approach was corporatist rather than socialist.[29] Collor had more success with younger lawyers, including Joaquim Pimenta and Agripino Nazareth, who had played individual roles in the postwar insurgencies. The minister's most important hire by far was a courageous people's advocate, Evaristo de Moraes, an early socialist from Rio de Janeiro's vibrant world of popular politics. A self-made mulatto lawyer, Moraes had a thirty-year record of outstanding legal advocacy, support of striking workers, and defense of labor radicals such as anarchist Edgard Leuenroth in 1918.[30] Indeed, the labor ministry's early legal measures, including 19,770, were clearly foreshadowed in Moraes's pioneering 1904 book, *Apontamentos do Direito Operário* (*Notes on Labor Law*).[31]

In terms of intellectual genealogies, in other words, Vargas's earliest labor legislation can be traced to the semisocialist ideas of this coterie of dissident intellectuals. During the First Republic, as Gisálio Cerqueira Filho has re-marked, the labor issue had not been "inscribed as a [legitimate] question within the dominant thought" of the agrarian oligarchies whose rule set the contours of intellectual and political life. Rather, the topic found its home as a concern of "marginal thinkers and publicists, in addition to socialist activists proper, who elaborated their own way of thinking" that gave special priority to the social question.[32] Many of these individuals—including Moraes, Pi-menta, Nazareth, and Lacerda—had briefly belonged in 1921–22 to the Bra-zilian affiliate of the international antiwar movement Clarté (Lucidity or Clar-ity), founded in 1918 by Romain Rolland and Henri Barbusse, writers who sympathized with the Russian Revolution. Perhaps, as Michael Hall and Paulo Sérgio Pinheiro have wryly observed, nowhere else in the world did this call for a "thinkers international" have such "a strange and ironic outcome" as in Brazil, where many radical leaders of the "Revolution of the Spirit" ended up, in less than ten years, as high-level functionaries of a corporativist labor ministry, where a number of them stayed for decades.[33]

The involvement of such reformist elements in the birth of this new branch of Brazilian law, even if only briefly in the case of Moraes (who left in 1932 with Collor), helps explain why the "fascist" label has not stuck without qualification for Brazil's corporatist system of interest representation. In the case of the 1931 unionization decree, for example, the most important study of Collor's ministry (Rosa Maria Barbosa de Araújo's *O Batismo do Trabalho* [*The Baptism of Labor*]) concluded that 19,770 was substantially Brazilian and reformist in origin, with evidence of foreign—but by no means exclusively Italian or right-wing—influences.[34] Rebutting the charge of copying the Ital-ians, Pimenta observed in 1934 that similar principles appeared in the con-temporary labor legislation of revolutionary Russia after 1917 and Chile be-tween 1924 and 1925. All of these initiatives, he pointed out, preceded the Carta del Lavoro.[35]

The profound geopolitical and ideological crises after World War I and the Russian Revolution of 1917 popularized ideas and policies that could be deemed corporatist and were common across the political spectrum.[36] In 1917, for example, a newly emerging Mexican revolutionary regime was the first to directly incorporate labor rights into its constitution, followed in 1919 by Germany's new Weimar Republic.[37] Although Brazilian jurists and politi-cians seldom cited Mexico and its revolution, the 1919 Treaty of Versailles, which proposed the inclusion of labor rights in law, was ubiquitous in these writings.[38] Indeed, Brazil was one of the first countries to join the newly founded ILO, thus linking enlightened Brazilian elites directly to a civilized European precedent that used such labor legislation for the conservative end of combating communism and revolution.

Progressive Conservatism and the Juridical Field

The progressive orientation of the labor ministry's functionaries in 1931–32 has long been widely recognized, as has the highly negative association between the post-1937 labor jurisprudence and Francisco José de Oliveira Vianna (1883–1951), an authoritarian corporatist ideologue who held sway from 1932 to 1940. To many observers, wittingly or unwittingly, the story of labor policy appears to be symbolized by the transition from Moraes to Oliveira Vianna, a forty-nine-year-old mulatto lawyer appointed in 1932 as the ministry's second juridical consultant. Author of foundational texts in Brazilian sociology, Vianna published various works on the labor laws and corporatism, and his departure from the labor ministry was followed by his appointment in 1942 to the federal Court of Audits (Tribunal de Contas).[39]

Yet such a left-to-right interpretation, invoking the 1930/1937 contrast, distorts the processes at work in this pioneering area of law. Every year after 1930, a widening array of lawyers was drawn into the elaboration, reelaboration, and administration of social and labor legislation. Former socialists like Pimenta labored together in the ministry's ranks with Vianna, a corporatist theorist possessed of an authoritarian but utopian vision. Both coexisted with avowed integralists like Paulo Burlamaqui as well as traditionalist Catholics like Bezerra de Menezes, who would later serve as president of the Supreme Labor Court (Tribunal Superior do Trabalho, or TST) from 1946 to 1953.[40] Even Eugênio Gudin, who would emerge as Brazil's most famous economic liberal, served in the labor ministry during the early 1930s, albeit briefly, while Moraes's anti-*getulista* son, Evaristo de Moraes Filho, a socialist, began a lifetime of labor ministry service in 1934, two years after his father quit.[41] At any given time, however, most of the ministry's young lawyers were careerists such as Rego Monteiro, whose shallow ideological allegiances merely echoed, at any given moment, the political configurations that might affect their futures.[42]

Thus, the emerging legal terrain of this branch of law, marked by jostling ambitions as well as conflicting ideas, was subject to sudden transmutations in light of the period's kaleidoscopic shifts. Searching desperately for consistency, analysts have for too long focused on ideological, political, and doctrinal labels, derivations, and postulated systemic logics. Yet these cannot explain how the idea of a systematic and comprehensive labor law emerged in the 1930s or shed light on the dynamics of the law's elaboration and implantation. What united these lawyers qua government employees, however, was participation in what Pierre Bourdieu has called the juridical field, "organized around a body of internal protocols and assumptions, characteristic behaviors and self-sustaining values—what we might informally term a 'legal culture.' The key to understanding it is to accept that this internal organization, while it is surely not indifferent to the larger and grander social function of the law, has its own incomplete but quite settled autonomy."[43]

The individual Brazilian lawyers who contributed to labor law in the 1930s thus were shaped by a sedimented historical inheritance and common habitus as *bacharéis* (degree holders). The spectrum of political or parapolitical outlooks they shared can best be characterized as ranging from a conservative progressivism to a progressive conservativism.[44] Legally, their disparate voices were united in the field of social policy by their adherence to the juridical concept of legal *tutela* (tutelage or protection). Their sense of kinship is suggested by the fact that the "rightist" Oliveira Vianna's 1932 appointment as top legal adviser occurred at the suggestion of the "leftist" Moraes, one of Oliveira Vianna's former students.[45] The two men may not have been alike in their political alignments in 1932, but both were members of a generation of lawyers that set out in the 1930s to "correct Brazil" through law.[46]

two

The Scholarly Politics of Brazilian Labor Law

For Brazilian workers and employers alike, the most dramatic feature of the fifteen years that followed the Revolution of 1930 was the establishment of effective government intervention in employer-employee relations. Yet Brazil was not the only Latin American country that saw a proliferation of government social welfare initiatives and state sponsorship of labor organizations beginning in the 1930s. These developments spawned an intense debate, starting in the 1960s, about the dynamics of this "process of political incorporation of the lower class groups," which produced an array of different political party structures and systems of class alliances throughout the region.[1] Precisely for this reason, noted Christopher Abel and Colin Lewis, "the history and sociology of labour" emerged by the mid-1980s as "one of the growth points in Latin American scholarship" in all fields.[2] It was particularly challenging, Abel and Lewis noted, to understand the "significance of increased labour agitation" at midcentury and its relationship with this height-ened "state involvement" in industrial and labor relations.[3]

Whatever their source, these regionwide processes clearly had fundamen-tal "implications for our theoretical understanding of populism" and its deter-minants.[4] Indeed, the early 1970s saw heated political and academic contro-versies regarding Latin American populism, which was commonly viewed as an unequal multiclass alliance through which the industrial bourgeoisie di-rectly or indirectly dominated and controlled the urban working class. *Var-guista* populism, New Left theorist Theotonio dos Santos argued in 1978, "represented in reality the alliance of classes between the industrial bour-geoisie . . . and its principal mass support: the workers' movement."[5] Even a 1988 English-language survey of "Third World politics" continued to classify Latin American populism as a "temporary alliance between an industrial bourgeoisie dependent upon the state and a working-class newly mobilized through the state itself."[6]

Yet this debate about the significance and impact of populism and state intervention was marked, from the outset, by problems of miscategorization, faulty conceptualization, and imprecision. Most analysts were content to stress "the authoritarian structure of state-controlled trade unions in Brazil, Mexico and other countries where ministries of labour established the frame-work for working conditions and wage bargaining, fixed minimum wages and administered union funds." In this view, "state-sponsored unions" were in-struments for "labour management" that frustrated "genuine working-class aspirations."[7] In all of these discussions, the elaborate corporatist system of Brazilian labor relations became a key point of reference for wider compara-tive work.[8]

Both Vargas and the state-sponsored trade union movement had been politi-cally controversial at midcentury, but only in the last years of the Populist Republic (1945–64) did newly emerging scholarship began to address this dimension of the Brazilian polity.[9] Radicalized by the 1964 military coup, this generation of scholars identified strongly with sociologist Fernando Henrique Cardoso and his associates at the University of São Paulo, the country's top institution of higher education. Disillusioned with nationalism, populism, and *varguismo*, these youthful intellectuals broke successively with the shibboleths of postwar Brazilian politics.[10] "Only after the 'collapse of populism' in 1964," wrote Paulo Sérgio Pinheiro in 1975, could one see "the real limits and roots of the labor legislation" that Vargas had "imposed from the top down."[11] Luiz Jorge Werneck Vianna's influential *Liberalismo e Sindicato no Brasil* (*Liberal-*

ism and the Union in Brazil), first published in 1976, spoke of sweeping away the pre-1964 myths that had clouded understanding of the "real character of the *getulista* legislation—repressive and controlling of worker behavior."[12]

The emerging "corporatist consensus" was most closely identified with University of São Paulo sociologist Francisco Weffort, whose seminal early 1970s essays acquired "enormous theoretical importance" well beyond the intellectual milieu in São Paulo.[13] This developing New Left scholarship in the United States and Brazil tended to emphasize solely the antidemocratic drawbacks of the CLT system and the limitations of both the pre-1964 Left and what Weffort called "populist trade unionism."[14] This line of analysis viewed the labor legislation primarily as fulfilling capitalism's need to control the working class, whether economically, politically, or ideologically. Thus, the predominant interpretation of the juridicization of labor-management relations tended to collapse industrial employers and the "capitalist" state into one category while placing an overwhelming emphasis on the negative impact of state-sponsored unionism.

Having seen the military regime once again triumph after the 1968 student protests, these activist intellectuals tended to assume that the authoritarian intentions of the earlier Estado Novo dictatorship (1937–45), which had promulgated the CLT, had been achieved in practice.[15] These intellectuals and other contemporary observers thought that a combination of "strict and uncompromising paternalism" and "authoritarian tutelage" since 1930 had weakened "autonomous class organizations" and led to the deradicalization of Brazilian labor.[16] Furthermore, the state's absorption or containment of class conflict was seen as having resulted in the dilution of Brazilian workers' class consciousness.[17] The answer seemed clear: Vargas's "gift" of the social and labor laws involved the exchange of "concessions to the workers in return for [their] political quiescence"—a surrender of their "political independence as a class."[18]

In its place, a simultaneously repressive and co-optive Brazilian state was believed to have created a dependent working class, encapsulated within a domesticated, bureaucratized, and corrupted labor movement directly controlled by the state. In exchange for "the Institutes of Pensions and Retirements, the Vacation Law, job tenure, firing with indemnification," said Leôncio Basbaum, a Marxist, in 1962, the proletariat "lost its liberty, its class consciousness . . . and saw its trade unions, with their long tradition of struggle, transformed into passive organisms, instruments of Getúlio's policies."[19] As Kazumi Munakata argued in 1981, the pervasiveness and insidiousness of the system implanted by Vargas left the workers demobilized, with little possibility of controlling their destinies.[20] Indeed, U.S. political scientist Kenneth Erickson was not alone in his contention that Brazilian workers had paid a high price even in terms of their inability "to demand a greater share of the material output."[21] "The proletariat, especially after 1937, was a caged beast," Basbaum wrote, "but after 1945, it was already domesticated."[22]

This chapter details the trajectory and terminal crisis of the corporatist consensus that dominated the discussion of labor in Brazil from the 1960s until the early 1990s. This New Left approach dealt with legacies and, to a limited degree, precursors of the CLT but also unwittingly duplicated the Vargas regime's mythologies. More importantly, this approach failed to offer convincing arguments regarding the intellectual, political, and juridical origins of the legal activism of the interwar years that made the "social question" a pressing issue in Brazilian politics and statecraft. Since the Brazilian redemocratization of 1985, the earlier New Left scholarly paradigm—largely the work of social scientists—has become less convincing.[23] By the early 1990s, a new scholarly generation—this time of labor historians—came to repudiate the previous consensus as fundamentally misguided and marred by a weak evidentiary base, factual errors, and conceptual sloppiness.[24] Unlike those who followed in Weffort's wake, today's revisionists have been acutely aware of the complex and ambiguous grassroots impact of state intervention, although they have not yet fully focused on the specifically legal dimension of the origins of the state's labor relations activity.

Two Sides of the Same Coin: The *Outorga* and Its Negation

This review of the origins debate has shown the difficulty of ascribing univocal meanings, whether progressive or fascist, to the lawmaking process that culminated in the CLT. The discussion now turns toward another peculiarity of the Brazilian case: the notion of the gift (*dádiva*) or bestowal (*outorga*) of the labor legislation. Here too, surprisingly, there is a coincidence of views between the claims of the Vargas regime and of those who sought to radically debunk its populist mythologies. Both the critics and the apologists agree that the role of the state changed after 1930 in that the social question was no longer exclusively a matter for the police (*caso de polícia*). Both agree that the regime's initiatives in this arena bore a preemptive and antiradical thrust that was aimed at ending class struggle. Both also agree about the fundamental importance of the state's role, especially its control over labor organizations.

Vargas on the labor laws. The text of this poster from the Estado Novo period reads, "The social laws through which the current government, on its own initiative, has sought to assist the laboring classes should make Brazilians proud." (Courtesy Iconographia/ Cia. da Memória/Brazil)

"AS LEIS SOCIAIS COM QUE O ATUAL GOVERNO, POR INICIATIVA PRÓPRIA, TEM PROCURADO AMPARAR AS CLASSES TRABALHADORAS, DEVEM CONSTITUIR MOTIVO DE ORGULHO PARA OS BRASILEIROS"

And finally, both believe that the results include a relatively successful pacification of industrial relations with a lessening of radical and disruptive forms of class-conscious behavior by workers.

Yet nowhere is the mirror-image nature of the leftist antipopulist critique more clear—though unperceived—than in the case of the regime's central mythology of the *outorga*, the gift bestowed (a term derived from the verb *outorgar*, meaning to grant, confer, award, or bestow).[25] The architects and ideologists of the regime, such as Francisco José de Oliveira Vianna, insistently advanced the proposition that post-1930 social and labor legislation was "an initiative of the state, a generous *outorga* by political leaders—and not a conquest realized by our laboring masses."[26] Brazil could proudly claim to be a country, government propaganda emphasized, "where the workers conquered everything without a single act of violence [and] without going to the barricades," all as the result of a "spontaneous concession by the state."[27] "The *outorga* of the social laws," noted Adalberto Paranhos in his recent study, "was the dominant element" of *estadonovista* propaganda, "repeated ad nauseum" through "all of the paraphernalia of mass communication" at its service.[28]

The *outorga* thesis was also central to the Vargas regime's mythology of the *estado benefactor*, the paternalistic "benefactor state" that protects the inter-

Workers march in a government-organized celebration of ten years of Vargas's rule, 1940. The banner says, "The worker also has his place in the Estado Novo." (Courtesy Iconographia/Cia. da Memória/Brazil)

est of the masses. As articulated most forcefully by Getúlio Vargas and his speechwriters, the idea presented the state as a neutral organ that both embodied the collective national interest, standing above society, and was untainted by the clash of parochial lesser interests.[29] Nor were such views limited to paid government agents; observers sympathetic to Vargas in the 1930s and later also agreed that these labor laws were *outorgadas*, without a demand on the part of the workers.[30] Even landmark international assessments included variants on this theme. Citing the Brazilian example by name but without study, Harvard political scientist Samuel Huntington concluded in 1968 that these "early gains are often handed" to workers "on a silver platter" at "the initiative of the political elite" rather than resulting from pressure by the workers.[31]

The regime's self-congratulatory propaganda sounded a similar note, with its constant emphasis on the "miracle" through which Brazil had "solved" the problem of class struggle that afflicted other countries.[32] In highlighting its newly enlightened policies, the post-1930 government's self-interested and self-dramatizing rhetoric was a source of anger and frustration for Vargas's opponents. By emphasizing their total neglect of the social question, the *outorga* thesis condemned the antigetulist politicians and statesmen ousted by the Revolution of 1930.[33] Faced with the regime's talk about capitalist oppression and exploitation, even if in the past, Brazilian industrialists and anti-*getulista* politicians objected to the government's claims that there had ever been a labor problem that required remedy by the state.[34]

The Left's early criticism of the *outorga* thesis was different. In 1952, Evaristo de Moraes Filho was eloquent in his denunciation: "There was no *outorga* at all, like someone who gives alms to a mental weakling. The working masses struggled for three decades—and still fight . . . for the advent of laws to improve their conditions of life. There were strikes, fights, blood, desperation, imprisonments, deaths. How can you talk about them as poor devils, without leaders, ideas, or aspirations, who received everything that others wished to give them as spontaneous and unilateral favors?"[35] Later observers continued to reject the *outorga* thesis on the basis of its obvious elitism and idolatry of the state.[36] Yet those who have tried to make sense of state intervention in labor relations from 1930 to 1943 have not found Moraes Filho's vigorous affirmation of faith in the working class a sufficient basis for historical explanation. Indeed, no one, including Moraes Filho, has tried to make the case that the social and labor laws of the 1930s were simple working-class conquests forced on the state.[37] This book does not argue the case for such a conquest but instead contends that Brazilian labor relations developed in a singular manner and that even the prevailing views critical of the state-linked labor relations system are not, despite their claims, a rejection of the essence of the *outorga* thesis.

All alternative formulations of the state's role after 1930 agree that state initiative from above was the fundamental factor. The implantation of a new system of labor relations "from the top down" resulted, in the words of Brazilian labor judge Aluísio Rodrigues, in an "artificial model" imposed on the workers by the state.[38] As Kenneth Mericle succinctly stated in 1982, Brazil's "corporatist labor structure" is an "artificial creation of the state" and "there is nothing organic or spontaneous about its evolution."[39] The labor movement after 1930 had "lost the spontaneity and authenticity" of earlier labor organizations, if not their effectiveness.[40] In Basbaum's words, state intervention after 1930 "managed to smash, in the course of a few years, all that was most pure [and] spontaneous" in the Brazilian workers' movement.[41]

Yet the assertion of the artificiality of the labor relations system and trade union movement after 1930 simply reformulates a key feature of the *outorga* thesis: the characterization of state action as preemptive, based on the state's ability to maintain control by anticipating labor's demands.[42] "One of the great virtues of Getúlio was to perceive problems ahead of time," José de Segadas Vianna, one of the drafters of the CLT, emphasized: "the government forestalled what could have happened later," perhaps to "guarantee the tranquility of the bourgeoisie." Repeating an analogy used by Vargas's labor minister, Alexandre Marcondes Filho, Segadas Vianna said that Vargas was like a U.S. movie Indian who "put his ear on the ground to hear the clatter of hoofs that comes from afar. In this way, Getúlio felt the clattering of hoofs of the social problem and tried to find ways to solve it—perhaps out of a bourgeois tendency he had, to avoid more serious crises."[43]

"The 'social question' was no longer to be considered 'a matter for the police,'" wrote U.S. historian Thomas Skidmore in 1967. Instead, it was now to be resolved "by concessions from the new political elite before pressures from below might force more basic changes."[44] In 1976, Raimundo Faoro, a courageous opponent of the post-1964 military regime, suggested that the labor legislation was adopted "even before it became a pressing demand of the workers. In this way, the state, in knowing how to anticipate social demands, was able to exercise a greater political control over the workers than if it had promulgated that legislation under pressure."[45] Almost two decades later, Almir Pazzianotto Pinto, a former radical labor lawyer turned labor minister, would capture this Brazilian peculiarity by citing the words of former President Juscelino Kubitschek (1955–60). In other countries, Kubitschek declared in his 1956 presidential message to Congress, "the unity of workers in powerful organizations occurred spontaneously and preceded the conquest of norms of labor protection, [while] in Brazil the trade union was the effect of that legislation and not its cause."[46]

Moreover, another peculiar twist to the artificiality thesis is that it is by no means a totally original creation of recent decades. Indeed, conservative opponents of Vargas's legislation in the 1930s consistently criticized it as artificial, meaning that it was uncalled for and destructive in nature.[47] When Morvan Dias Figueredo was appointed minister of labor, industry, and commerce in 1946, the *paulista* industrialist told the British labor attaché that "Brazil finds itself with a social legislation which is too advanced for the reality of the present economic and financial structure of society."[48] Ten years later, E. G. Saad, a powerful and notorious antilabor specialist employed by *paulista* industrialists, made a similar point in an interview with Robert Alexander: "The government of Getúlio Vargas [after 1930], without there being any demand for it from the public, adopted an elaborate code of labor legislation, which created artificially the labor movement of today."[49]

Another line of critical commentary might be called the "stand on your own two feet" critique: workers did not deserve that for which they had allegedly not fought. For leftist economist Celso Furtado, a minister in the Goulart government ousted in 1964, the problem with populism was that "the working class ceases to gain its own achievements and [instead] small concessions are granted from above, regardless of the needs of society as a whole."[50] During the 1960s and early 1970s, at least some observers on the left embraced the artificiality thesis because of their uncertainty regarding the capacity of the Brazilian working class, which was invariably compared unfavorably to an unknown but idealized class-conscious or radical European proletariat. Again, the analogy to the *outorga* school of thought is clear: leftist artificiality advocates hail the "class-conscious" European example, and the proponents of the *outorga* fear precisely the same specter. In 1933, Vargas hailed the fact that in Brazil "the laboring classes do not possess the powerful associative structure or the combativeness of the proletariat of the industrialized nations. . . . Misunderstandings between capital and labor happily do not present a belligerent aspect."[51]

Moreover, the oft-remarked state-centeredness of Brazilian political and intellectual life clearly permeates the discussion of the issue of labor. Not surprisingly, this tendency was deepened by the experience of authoritarian military rule after 1964, when the labor question came to be seen as part of the larger debate about the relationship between the state and civil society.[52] Yet even in the 1970s, some Brazilian scholars were aware of the dangers of the state-centered perspective, which, as Fábio Wanderley Reis noted presciently, "distorts the problem being studied by formulating it in the form of a dichotomy or opposition between 'society' and the 'state,' treated as separate terms or principles. As a result, this fatally biases empirical work by increasing the researcher's attentiveness to certain aspects of reality and reducing it in other respects. Thus, anyone who posits the state will always find it in the data—insensitive to the realization that cases of greater or lesser state 'presence' or 'initiative' must necessarily be explained by reference to different *social* conditions."[53]

In summary, we can see areas of common agreement between the *outorga* and artificiality positions about the decisiveness and ultimately the success of state action in shaping working-class life and politics. Yet this raises a profound question: Why did the state take these initiatives, and in whose interests? Not surprisingly, we again find a broad area of agreement between the two interpretations. In his capacity as top legal adviser of the labor ministry, Oliveira Vianna argued that the regime's actions aided capitalist development by resolving social problems created by capitalism without destroying Brazil's traditional order or threatening individual property, private enterprise, or employer authority.[54] José Maria Bello, a supporter of the new order, argued in 1936 that the "union dominated and directed by the state" was fundamental to the operation of the new system.[55] In eliminating the workers' "anti-employer attitudes," resolutely suppressing harmful agitation, and creating a cooperative working-class elite, the Brazilian state safeguarded the capitalist social order by "taking the winds out of the sails of communism."[56]

Beyond claiming that state action ensured the survival of the capitalist system, Oliveira Vianna argued that these measures were carried out "with the approval of the employers themselves," however paradoxical that might seem. Although admitting that some initial complaints had occurred, he argued that employers had never shown "any significant reaction" against these government measures.[57] Subsequent observers would later claim that social and labor legislation was *outorgada* "to activate an alliance of aims between the laboring classes and the 'national' bourgeoisie."[58] In this way, preemptive and preventative state action laid the foundations for an effective and harmonious system of collaboration among workers, employers, and the state. Even the material benefits brought to the workers, as Vargas would argue, served capitalism by expanding the internal market for Brazilian manufactured goods.[59]

Radical critics of the regime's policies would have no problem in accepting all of these points but instead value negatively what the *outorga* school values positively. In his pioneering 1977 survey of Latin American labor, New Left historian Hobart Spalding presented Brazil's social and welfare legislation as "the second prong of the ruling class counteroffensive against labor." Vargas's legislation, Spalding argued provocatively, admirably achieved its purposes of deradicalizing the working class, suppressing progressive elements within labor, and establishing a system of state control and manipulation of workers. These steps guaranteed popular support for the system, and the result was an absence of significant unrest or visible discontent among workers prior to 1943.[60]

These accomplishments, in Spalding's view, were all the more remarkable since he claimed that the wages of Brazilian workers had "declined almost steadily after 1930." Only "strong state control," he went on, could impose such wage scales on workers, contain any subsequent protest, and thus increase the capitalists' profits.[61] In making his case, Spalding quite accurately summarized a thesis in the literature: state action after 1930 was intended to neutralize labor's capacity to intervene in the labor market. Thus, the demobilization and depoliticization of labor contributed to the primitive accumulation of capital at a decisive moment of industrial development.

Writing during the full flush of the "revolution" sparked by Weffort in 1971–73, Antônio Bernardo's pioneering 1974 thesis posited the labor laws as "instruments of control imposed by the reordering of international capitalism." Yet like Spalding, Bernardo was aware of the absence of direct evidence on this point and rested his case on the regime's "fundamental preoccupation" with "impeding the emergence of class struggle in the interior of the Brazilian social formation." The regime's unionization laws, he said, were an attempt "to hitch the union to the rear of the car of state" and thus imprint "on the union the discipline demanded by the logic of the capitalist economy."[62]

The corporatist consensus variant of the artificiality thesis thus overwhelmingly emphasized state interventions as a tool of the capitalist class or the industrial bourgeoisie. Spalding clearly states the chain of causality: state initiatives beginning in 1931 led "toward building a labor movement that would cooperate fully with the state and therefore capital." In an influential 1977 article, Brazilian economist Francisco de Oliveira even presented the regime's social and labor legislation as fundamental to a new stage in capital accumulation.[63] Others spoke about how the industrial bourgeoisie in the late 1920s and early 1930s elaborated a new project of domination based on accepting trade unions as controlling agencies in the labor market—as long as the unions themselves were controlled by the state. For British political scientist Peter Flynn, writing in 1978, labor initiatives going back to Lindolfo Collor provided "just the kind of controlled system the industrialists and employers required, and the process" simply speeded up after 1937.[64]

This asserted consensual relationship between Vargas's government and the industrial bourgeoisie is fundamental to the *outorga* and the corporatist consensus. Yet this proposition has been decisively disproven by the empirical research of the past twenty years.[65] Indeed, both before and after 1930, industrial employers consistently avoided or resisted attempts to establish effective state regulatory and social welfare policies. This argument does not presuppose that industrialists in São Paulo or elsewhere unequivocally and publicly opposed state intervention in labor relations.[66] Rather, industrialists were at best skeptical, if not critical, and the intensity of their opposition was directly related to the economic interest at stake in dealing with any particular labor law provision.[67] When unsuccessful in blocking such legislation, business leaders undermined enforcement or simply ignored the laws. And of all forms of state intervention in industrial relations, government support of any type of unionization proved the most unacceptable.[68]

The shallowness of existing debates about employer responses to Vargas's earliest labor initiatives can be seen from the 1932–33 fieldwork of U.S. scholar Dudley Maynard Phelps, who published the first study of foreign investment in Latin America. His *Migration of Industry to South America* (1936) was based on extensive interviews with managers of U.S. enterprises in Argentina, Brazil, Chile, and Uruguay. His account of the responses of U.S. company managers to Labor Minister Collor's policies offers fascinating insights into the modus operandi of employer–central government relations as it first emerged in the early 1930s. Before 1930, Phelps reported, "there was little legislation concerned with labor, and the laws in force were largely disregarded by business enterprises." The creation of the new labor ministry, however, initiated an ambitious new program, mostly "of questionable character, to improve conditions for workers." Summarizing his informants' views, Phelps commented on government mandates regarding employment of Brazilian nationals (the "two-thirds law") as well as new stipulations about holidays, hours, and pension payments. The government's promotion of "the unionization of all workers under government auspices" was viewed with particular suspicion as a government attempt "to organize the workers and then serve as an intermediary for arbitration between employers and labor groups."[69]

Yet Phelps also reported that this incipient labor legislation was not, on the whole, particularly severe or difficult to comply with. "Although the desirability of the 'two-thirds law' is open to question," he said, even those who failed to meet its provisions for the "nationalization of labor" encountered little difficulty "since the law was not being enforced." Moreover, its provisions had been modified, after protests by employers, through a series of amendments that gutted its nationalist content by counting as Brazilians all foreigners who were married to and had children with Brazilians as well as those with more than ten years of residence. Moreover, "various industries are exempted from the provisions of the law, among them farming, animal husbandry, and the extractive industries. If the employer can prove to the Ministry of Labor that Brazilian workers are not procurable, or that the work to be done is of a technical nature and demands unusual abilities and training, he may be exempted" as well.[70]

Thus, even with Collor as head of the MTIC, the central government was highly responsive to employer concerns, a phenomenon that led Phelps's informants, even when uneasy, to feel a certain confidence about measures on paper that were potentially unsound. "The law pertaining to retirement and pension funds," for example, was judged to be "dynamite," but only if the government were to "unwisely" yield "to illegitimate demands of workers." As for the "Means of Protection against Government Regulation," Phelps offered a detailed description of the individual and collective forms of defense that businesses used to "protect themselves against governmental action which is inimical to their interests." Methods in South America, he said, were "little different than those used elsewhere, but their application differs. Forceful objection, publicity, appeals to the courts, the aid of friends in positions of authority, and, perhaps, more direct and possibly less ethical means—all are used."[71]

Companies, Phelps advised, should on the whole "attempt to adhere as closely as possible to the laws," based on "the extent to which a regulatory measure affects branch plants." Where plants are unaffected, companies should comply strictly; if there is no "important right or principle at stake" or if the law is likely to change, "compliance without too much objection may be the course of wisdom." At the same time, Phelps emphasized that resistance was called for when laws were "so uneconomic and so prejudicial to effective operations that compliance would have been tantamount to relinquishing all control over factors vitally affecting company interests." Phelps concluded with a phrase that succinctly captures business strategies in relation to a wide array of government policies, including labor. Enterprises should take advantage, he said, of the "opportunity for lax compliance, possibly suggested by law enforcement or by government officials."[72] In other words, an inextricable link between lax compliance and lax enforcement had already emerged when legal protections for industrial workers first came into existence in Brazil.[73] If this statement is true, the confrontation of worker and employer interests in the workplace can offer only part of the explanation for the emergence of a government bureaucracy dealing with labor. What was at stake in these developments, however, remains none too clear.

A Benevolent *Outorga*? The Origins of Labor Law in the Early 1930s

As we have seen, the artificiality consensus, although based on different value judgments, is essentially a mirror image of the Vargas regime's mythology of the *outorga*. Although this similarity should not be overdrawn, it can be seen as further proof of the modern Brazilian state's power to frame even the questions asked in Brazilian history. Yet we would do well to pursue the very different path suggested by Emília Viotti da Costa's observation that some objective reality necessarily underlies the creation, acceptance, and even rejection of any successful historical mythology.[74]

Ironically, the ideologue of the Brazilian corporatist labor legislation, Oliveira Vianna, most clearly stated this objective reality on the same page where he authoritatively advanced the *outorga* thesis in 1939. The government's initiatives after 1930, he said, could not have been workers' conquests because the working class was weak and disunited. In the early 1930s, he observed, Brazilian workers were "disaggregated and disarticulated" and lacked even the unity that might flow from the presence of a dominant ideology. Moreover, the working class lacked the solidarity, regimentation, and organization that could have "imposed an orientation in its favor upon the state."[75] One of Oliveira Vianna's successors, Segadas Vianna, who would serve as labor minister in the early 1950s under Vargas, confidently asserted that "the truth is that the union gave nothing to the worker; it was the government that gave everything because the trade unions had no power."[76]

Taken as an empirical observation at one moment in time, Oliveira Vianna's statement can indeed be judged to be an essentially accurate assessment of the level of working-class consciousness, cohesion, and organization. For reasons of ideology, of course, Oliveira Vianna linked this truth to his false belief in the nonexistence of class struggle in Brazil.[77] To make sense of history, however, we must not substitute moralistic or wishful assessments of working-class strength for hardheaded empirical judgments. Indeed, any reasonable discussion of the early 1930s must begin with an objective assessment of the level and nature of workers' consciousness and the extent and class embeddedness of existing workers' organizations. At that time, labor strength varied greatly from region to region and was strongest in Rio de Janeiro and Rio Grande do Sul,[78] less strong in São Paulo, and even weaker in the northeast. Even in more industrialized regions, enormous variations occurred among occupations, with pockets of organized strength in certain crafts, and relatively effective organization existed in certain types of work in certain places (work on the docks, in the maritime industry, and on the railroads, though such was more the case in Rio than São Paulo).

The lack of penetration and representativeness of the labor movement—in geographic terms as well as in terms of the social ecology of incipient industrialization—weakened the fight for the most urgent and elementary needs of urban wage-earning workers. That workers recognized their essential weakness vis-à-vis their employers, especially in São Paulo, does not impute "blame" to the workers themselves (Weffort's "ideology of backwardness")[79] but rather points to the employers' enormous all-around strengths. This recognition also does not imply—as the *outorga* and artificiality theses assume—that the low level of power exercised by urban workers in 1930 was inherent to the class or to Brazilian social reality.

The fundamental truth of the early 1930s was that the least organized and the least powerful urban working-class group was the factory proletariat, which included the bulk of urban wage earners. Moreover, this fully proletarianized group working in large-scale industry most needed organization. Yet unlike certain artisanal or craft groups, the industrial working class had few advantages in skill or market position that would allow these employees to achieve organization and recognition of their demands based solely on their initiative. Thus, to fulfill their pressing class demands, the industrial working class and its activist minority in practice welcomed state action as a counterbalancing force from outside the private employer-employee nexus. This recognition of the importance of wider alliances was central to labor politics in the 1930s, which was increasingly influenced by the industrial proletariat.

To fully grasp the state-labor tie, we must recognize that state intervention did not originate with the industrial bourgeoisie even if this involvement often served bourgeois interests. In judging the state's new role in industrial relations, the crucial issue is whether such legislation and the political initiatives behind it created space for the strengthening of working-class power and organization. This is precisely what can be demonstrated for core industrialized regions, as in the case of the suburban ABC region of São Paulo, and was even more true for the struggles of working people in peripheral regions.[80]

The range and variation of regional, local, and sectoral realities and levels of power is central to the conformation of the distinctive local labor relations arenas into what will come to be called the CLT system. Similarly, the study of the geographic expansion of the CLT between and within states would help establish a clearer understanding of how its on-the-ground functioning reflected differing local histories of popular struggle as well as political configurations. An observation made by Charles Bergquist for the very different case of Argentina under Juan Perón is quite apropos here. Looking at the wider Latin American context, Bergquist argued that the greater strength and organization of Argentine labor when Perón emerged during World War II was responsible for the greater depth and substance of the corporativist labor policies followed by the Perón group once it reached power in 1946. The result, during the Peronist heyday through 1955, was a far more wide-ranging "scope of the concessions they were forced to make to workers" to maintain power.[81]

At the same time, the pressing nature of working-class needs provided an opportunity for those who had seized control of the central state apparatus during the Revolution of 1930 to offer an opening to urban labor. Far from a disinterested *outorga*, the labor initiatives of the early 1930s originated among those at the helm of a weak national state as they desperately tried to build a firm social base for their power. If workers needed and could use the state in the early 1930s, the same was true for important components of the regime, which was at best a shifting and divided coalition of conflicting social forces and class and regional factions that circled around the figure of Getúlio Vargas.[82]

Definitively and insistently formulated under the Estado Novo dictatorship, the *outorga* mythology cast the developments before 1937 in a false light as actions of a strong state. In reality, however, those who controlled a weak central state apparatus consciously fostered the organization and structuring of the urban working class in an effort to vanquish the government's powerful and by no means resigned or defeated enemies. Moreover, this intense conflict coincided with the regionalist and oligarchical rivalries that pitted the new regime and its federally appointed *interventors* against the interests of São Paulo's cohesive upper class of capitalist planters and industrialists and their solidly structured mass base within the state.

Thus, the regime's labor initiatives of 1930–33 were aimed, above all, at the *paulista* working class, although employer strength was sufficient to neutralize these early initiatives from Rio. Having aided working-class activists in gaining a toehold in the antilabor industrial heartland, the regime nonetheless found that labor and certain radical middle-class minorities in São Paulo were too weak to serve as a regional power base. As a result, the Vargas regime turned toward conciliation with the *paulista* oligarchy in 1933–34, followed by a classic double-cross in 1937 that robbed the *paulista* camp of the certain victory of its presidential candidate in 1938. After 1937, a powerful centralized state emerged for the first time. Relatively well financed and cohesive, the central government during the Estado Novo would build new and far more ambitious and all-encompassing institutions designed to enhance the state's capacity for effective action in shaping the nation.

Under the Estado Novo, the dictatorship's labor relations bureaucracy received a free hand to comprehensively organize and give coherence to the accumulation of decrees and amendments that had proliferated since 1930. Simultaneously, the labor ministry began to energetically create key institutions, such as the labor court, while establishing the mechanisms, such as the minimum wage, that were central to the functioning of what would become the CLT system. Henceforth, the labor ministry would no longer be—as it was called during the mid-1930s—"a deformed organism, with an enormous head [in Rio] and almost without a body" anywhere else in the country.[83] With the CLT and funding in hand, the MTIC's leaders set out to make real the ambitious institutional structure that lawyers had aspired to establish since the early 1930s. New opportunities were created that fitted a new period: the time for action was now—at least for lawyers.

The part of the CLT that protects the employee, understood as an isolated individual, is perfect, or almost so. The law anticipates, down to the smallest details, that which can and should happen here: nothing escapes it. Not a single strand is left loose. Everything a treat to the mind. With a law like that, who is going to find it attractive to analyze, interpret, and resolve the imperfect facts of work relations in the real life? For what? [Throw the] CLT at them, *pôxa*! —JÚLIO ALEJANDRO LOBOS, *Manual de Guerilla Trabalhista para Gerentes e Supervisores*

three

The CLT in Practice
A Generosity Akin to Fraud

Although described by its framers as merely an interim consolidation of existing law, the CLT has functioned since 1943 as Brazil's labor code and has thus contributed to the legal and institutional stability that has characterized the nation's system of industrial and labor relations.[1] In scope and ambition, the CLT is a truly kaleidoscopic body of law that provides guidance on almost all important aspects of the world of work, broadly considered. In addition to setting down fundamental principles and legal norms, the CLT addresses hundreds of secondary questions, large and small.

The CLT establishes, for example, the rules for the creation of class organizations by employees, employers, liberal professionals, and the self-employed.[2] In addition, the measure defines the prerogatives, jurisdiction, and internal procedures of the federal labor ministry and of the specialized tripartite labor court system that stands at the center of the structure. Another function of the CLT is to set standards regarding terms of employment and conditions of work as well as to establish procedures for the resolution of collective and individual disputes.

The matters covered include hours of work and the setting of wages and salaries (including minimum wages, overtime, and extraordinary pay);[3] discipline, hiring, firing, and quitting; working papers and pensions; employment of women, minors, and the foreign-born; industrial health and safety; and guaranteed job tenure based on seniority (*estabilidade*). The CLT also contains sections devoted to the peculiarities of fourteen specialized subcategories of working people, including railroad workers, stevedores, dock workers, professional musicians, journalists, and chemists.[4]

In addition to setting the procedures for factory inspections, the CLT establishes two basic mechanisms for dispute resolution. In the case of "individual disputes" (*dissídios individuais*), the labor courts hear individuals' or small groups' appeals of violations of the law or, more commonly, individual grievances regarding alleged instances of unjust treatment according to the law. The category of "collective disputes" (*dissídios coletivos*), by contrast, covers the legally mandated annual negotiations about wages that occur between employers and employees in a given industry, whether at the county, regional, or state level. This procedure for collective bargaining operates within a larger structure based on compulsory arbitration of such disputes by the labor courts.[5]

Translated into English in 1944 by a government proud of its handiwork, the CLT makes for remarkable reading. If read without preconceptions or prejudice (something that few people do), the CLT is an impressive document because of the care with which its framers strived to encompass all eventualities.[6] Indeed, the CLT was the culmination of thirteen years in which a sequence of outstanding legal minds set out to create an entire new arena of Brazilian law.[7] Yet the results of that "intensive legislative activity [in the 1930s] in the field of labor law," inspired by "multiple doctrinal orientations," had quickly reached "such a degree of complexity as to threaten its efficacy"; hence, the CLT consolidated and systematized the legislation.[8]

For a labor historian familiar with the United States, a first reading of the CLT produces a decidedly curious reaction. One is immediately struck by the extraordinary liberality with which the CLT accords rights and guarantees to urban working people and their organizations. If the universe of work did in fact operate according to the CLT, Brazil would be the world's best place to work. And if even half of the CLT was enforced, Brazil would be one of the more decent and reasonably humane places for those who work. Of course, it would be the height of naïveté to draw even the most tentative of conclusions merely from reading a legal text. Indeed, it takes little insight to foresee that the apparent content of the law could easily be eviscerated through nonenforcement and administrative and legal interpretation or misinterpretation. And when the world of work is examined, it quickly becomes clear that the CLT, despite its expansive and inclusive scope, was very unevenly applied in practice—it was enforced differently in rural and urban areas, in various regions, and within occupations and sectors in the urban areas on which it primarily focused.

If the CLT were to have real force, one would expect to find its impact felt most clearly in the core of modern industrial Brazil. Yet even the most cursory examination of the situation in São Paulo demonstrates that more than skepticism is required. The CLT system was thoroughly problematic in practice, and the difficulties were systematic and far-reaching. This realization is even more striking because the system's formal institutions were well implanted in the city and state of São Paulo, where thousands were employed in the vast bureaucratic empire that included the federal labor ministry, labor courts, and government-financed trade unions.

Yet even in the state of São Paulo the gap between appearance and reality was so large as to seem unbridgeable. Rights guaranteed categorically in law were systematically and routinely denied in daily practice in the expanding industrial sector. And large numbers of workers were employed under conditions and with pay that made a mockery of the CLT's marvelously humanistic legalisms about an adequate wage and safe and decent working conditions.[9] As for the legal recognition accorded the workers' class organizations, employers and the government systematically frustrated trade unionists' efforts to use those powers formally accorded them by law.

Disdainful Industrialists, Discontented Trade Unionists, and the CLT's "Swindles and Trickery"

It would be a mistake to suppose that employers supported the CLT system because it was thoroughly and routinely vitiated through nonenforcement. Far from being grateful, industrial employers were openly contemptuous of the CLT, which they saw as a symbol of the country's ridiculous and unreal approach to labor and industry. In fact, industry leaders routinely bemoaned the legal restrictions that the CLT placed on their freedom and authority as well as the costs that fulfillment of its unrealistic demands would entail.

Despite government restrictions on trade union autonomy, Brazilian industrialists were quick to blame politicians and bureaucrats for periodic problems with workers. These complaints are placed into perspective in a 1962 article by Claude McMillan based on his experience teaching business administration in São Paulo in 1956–60. "The Brazilian employer," he explained, "views labor as a more serious problem than does the American [employer in Brazil] partly because [the Brazilian] is not familiar with encroachment upon management's rule-making authority by really effective union leaderships." Unlike their U.S. industrialist counterparts, he went on, Brazilian employers had never experienced the "collective harassment by labor" and "competition for allegiance of the employee" that were the norm in the U.S. industrial sector, which had been unionized during the powerful labor and popular struggles of the New Deal era.[10]

Viewed from a U.S. employers' perspective, the Brazilian labor relations scene looked somewhat different. As McMillan put it, "The American manager in Brazil finds an environment in which the collective interests of labor are supposedly protected by government through legislation, but where actually unions are relatively weak." In particular, he noted with favor the absence of "shop stewards of the U.S. pattern in Brazilian industry."[11] Another U.S. specialist, John Shearer, interviewed managers at thirty-five U.S. companies in Brazil in 1958 and concurred that "labor relations were way down on the list of worries of the American businessmen." Shearer told Robert Alexander that despite "the existence of *sindicatos* [unions] everywhere, there were few cases if any of presentation of collective demands and relatively few cases presented to the labor courts."[12]

Organized labor's relative weakness made many U.S. managers in Brazil enthusiastic, McMillan noted, but this was tempered by a less positive feature of the country's industrial relations scene: "While unions do not interfere significantly with management's rule-making powers, government does," he said, offering specific criticism of the CLT's restrictions on "management's freedom to establish wage differentials and to discharge employees." Although such measures were ostensibly designed to guarantee job security and protect "workers from discriminatory and arbitrary treatment," McMillan was skeptical of such justifications for government interference in management prerogatives.[13] McMillan's and Shearer's observations about São Paulo's industrial relations scene in the late 1950s might suggest a relatively simple hypothesis. After all, it would not be surprising that labor's efforts to muster its collective strength might meet with difficulties in an industrializing capitalist society, even one blessed with the world's most advanced labor legislation.[14] Thus, the CLT might have represented a straightforward trade-off in which restrictions on trade union freedoms were exchanged for the observance of individual worker rights as enforced by the labor inspection system and labor courts.

Yet the gap between ideal and real was equally wide in the case of individual rights and grievances. "The extensive and advanced labor laws of Brazil," noted U.S. labor attaché Irving Salert in 1953, "are almost completely ignored at the factory level."[15] The inadequately staffed labor inspection services of São Paulo's regional labor delegacy (Delegacia Regional do Trabalho, or DRT) never came close to guaranteeing respect for workers' legally mandated rights. As the DRT noted in 1962, the state of São Paulo had experienced a decade of "vertiginous demographic and industrial growth." Although 1.1 million workers were employed in sixty thousand establishments in 1962, the number of DRT labor inspectors had fallen over the preceding ten years. Whereas in 1953 the DRT had employed 241 inspectors, 9 doctors, and 7 engineers, in 1961 those numbers had shrunk to 161, 7, and 6, respectively (out of a total of 1,155 employees).[16] By 1965, the DRT's industrial health and safety division complained that its staff of 3 doctors and 1 engineer faced the impossible task of handling eight thousand annual requests for expert opinions (*laudos perícias*).[17]

In 1951, São Paulo labor lawyer Alberto da Rocha Barros noted that "the principal weakness of this legal system lies in its enforcement, even in São Paulo, where inspection services have never attained the necessary effectiveness despite the existence of a complex apparatus dedicated to the problems of labor."[18] Yet the situation worsened because sparse coverage was combined with the routine bribery of labor inspectors and the tolerance of such practices by administrative higher-ups. In Salert's pungent words, "the Inspection Corps [*fiscalização*] is a small and provenly corrupt organization which has a reputation for accepting petty graft from factory owners."[19] When interviewed in 1956, the São Paulo DRT's director of inspections, Antônio Barreto, was quite open about the corruption among inspectors. To cope with the problem, he had instituted a new system in which inspectors were no longer assigned to a regular beat. The possibility that a reinspection might be carried out by a different individual, he hoped, would hang over an employer and thus make it "not as profitable to bribe an inspector as it might have been."[20]

The CLT's clear and forthright provisions regarding unsafe and unhealthy industrial working conditions provide a compelling example of the gap between the letter of the law and glaring shop floor realities.[21] Philadelpho Braz, secretary-general of ABC's metalworkers' union from 1956 to 1964, recalled that workers would often come into the union with their complaints: "There's acid where they're working. The boss doesn't give them safety glasses. . . . The factory doesn't give the pay differential required by law [for dangerous and unhealthy jobs]. There's dust. When it rains, water enters the factory, and the worker is obliged to work in it." In such matters, he said, the law was clear, but "you had to depend on the labor ministry to raise a question about unhealthy or dangerous working conditions." So the union would send off a request for a DRT inspection of a particular factory, and many months would pass before the visit was finally carried out. Even then, however, "there always existed a suspicion of corruption because the engineer, the inspector, those who come from the labor ministry, the first thing they do when they arrive is go into the office." The inspector is in there "with the boss, talking, laughing, and every-thing. So the worker already has lost confidence. The guy [comes out] and would glance around and sometimes, if he was really corrupt, he didn't even do that. So the man takes the records of the complaint and does a finding [*laudo*] favorable to the employer."[22]

Thus it is not surprising, as Salert noted, that "within the ranks of orga-nized labor, the word *fiscalização* is usually spoken with contempt."[23] Yet the story was only slightly more encouraging for those workers who in good faith brought their grievances to the labor courts for resolution. Administrative inefficiencies, overloaded dockets, and a bias toward "conciliation" routinely produced what can only be called justice at a discount. Even when his legal case was strong, for example, a Brazilian worker was usually forced to settle for far less than the value of his legal rights or entitlements (*direitos*).[24] Most workers learned from experience that "a bad conciliation settlement is worth more than a good case."[25] Yet even if the worker rejected the court's proposed conciliation proposal and won his case, he would still be forced to settle early and for less to avoid lengthy delays while the company engaged in legal maneuvers and appeals.[26] Such hollow victories would lead to a popular adage cited in recent memoir by a conservative Rio trade unionist. Discussing the labor ministry's deliberations, Romulo Pereira de Souza observed that "although everything was resolved on paper, money in the pocket, no one saw."[27] As was commonly recognized, most of the CLT would remain *letra morta* (dead letter), not only in the workplace but also in the labor courts.

From the outset, labor leaders consistently criticized the MTIC for its "swin-dles and trickery."[28] The conduct of labor court business itself was marked by a chronic pattern of excessive delay, a problem that judges and officials recognized, although they used it primarily to argue the need for additional judges and employees.[29] "The courts didn't get around to their cases in a reasonable amount of time," the TST's president, Delfim Moreira Junior, admitted in 1956.[30] The labor justice system had fallen so far "behind in its work" at one point in 1954 that it had "a backlog of about four thousand cases."[31] The impact was directly felt by trade unionists such as Marcos Andreotti, the president of the metalworkers' union of ABC (1932–37 and 1958–64), who recalled "a case here in the Laminação Nacional de Metais that took twelve years to resolve, and it involved older workers. When the case was finally settled, almost all had died, [and] only one managed to receive what was owed him [his *direitos*]." To make matters worse, Andreotti went on, the money the worker was awarded disappeared with the passage of time because the sum went uncorrected for inflation until 1965.[32] Even many non-workers complained about the endless delays. "The social laws here are not worth anything," a young company labor lawyer told Alexander in 1953. "The labor courts take an interminably long time to settle matters." In one case the lawyer had handled, the courts "took five years before a final decision was reached. This is good only for the lawyers."[33]

Tripartism, Justice, and Class Struggle

Andreotti was not alone in denouncing Brazilian labor law as a joke and a swindle (*tapeação*) perpetrated on the workers. "The law didn't resolve the problem," he often observed, since workers usually lost two to one in the tripartite labor courts "because the bosses and the government are always the same thing."[34] In theory, the participation in the labor courts of "class judges" (*juizes classistas*) drawn from the trade unions (as well as management) should have guaranteed workers a minimal level of voice in the legal decision-making process.[35] The rationale for worker participation was laid out clearly in 1972 by a São Paulo labor court judge, Wagner Giglio, who discussed the question in light of existing social hierarchies: "Career judges come, as a general rule, from the well-off classes" and are therefore "psychologically inclined, in light of their social, economic, and cultural formation, to better understand the point of view of the employers than that of the workers." Career judges thus tend "to dispense legality" because they lack the "realism that only direct experience can furnish." The worldly wisdom of the class judges, by contrast, tempers the court's tendency toward "excessive legalism" by dispensing justice in concrete cases on the basis of equity considerations.[36]

Yet not all those involved with the labor court system shared Giglio's idealization of tripartism as a philosophy. In 1956, for example, the president of the Regional Labor Court (Tribunal Regional do Trabalho, or TRT) in Minas Gerais, Herberto de Magalhães Drummond, argued that the main purpose of class representation was "a political one. It gives the decisions of the courts more standing in the eyes of both parties if they know that representatives of their group have sat in on the decisions taken. It makes it much easier to make the decisions of the court stick."[37] Yet even this more pragmatic justification failed in practice because most center-left trade unionists shared Andreotti's blunt opinion that the workers' alleged representatives in local labor courts could never be depended on since the labor ministry selected for the post only the most compliant and least militant minority of union leaders.[38] Moreover, even Giglio recognized that his idealized vision was false since he reported that class judges almost always deferred to the career judge.[39] In fact, Drummond defended nonlawyers' participation in the labor courts precisely because the individuals in question acted as judges rather than as "representatives of a class while sitting on the court" and often voted against members of their own class.[40]

These realities clearly undermined the notion that tripartism necessarily contributed to the political legitimacy of the labor court system and its decisions. Yet even if a TRT president were to mistakenly select an individual who did not support the government's economic and labor policies, the results would likely have been the same, as Kenneth S. Mericle has suggested. Under the rules of the labor court, the career judge's decision prevailed over any individual dissent; the career judge could be overruled only if both the employer and the worker judge voted against him, an extremely unlikely circumstance. Thus, the vast majority of those appointed as *juizes classistas*, especially from the labor unions, treated this system as a route for social mobility based on never making waves. Class judges from the working class consequently did not play, in Mericle's words, the "role of militant articulator of class interests" but were swayed instead by the powerful pull of bureaucratic careerism and patron-client ties in a high-prestige occupation that paid good salaries.[41]

Thus it is all the more striking that the government's labor laws, regulations, and legal procedures were the object of vigorous criticism by even the accommodationist trade union leaders most likely to be named *juizes classistas*, men who bitterly opposed communists such as Andreotti. This was especially true during the late 1940s and early 1950s, when the labor courts, health and safety inspectors, and labor ministry officials had fallen fully under the sway of the employers. The resulting blatant abuses tried the patience of even rightist PTB union leader Henrique Poletto, president of the textile workers in Santo André. Interviewed after an April 1951 lobbying trip to Rio de Janeiro that included an audience with President Getúlio Vargas, Poletto attacked the labor courts for having established, "under the ideological pressure of inhumane and reaction-ary employers," what was known as the total attendance clause (*assiduidade integral*) in collective *dissídios*. Created by the labor courts in 1948, this provi-sion required that individual workers maintain perfect attendance for a whole month to enjoy even legally mandated wage increases. To win even "this 'generous' crumb," Poletto concluded sarcastically, the worker was "reduced to a slave through the celebrated *assiduidade integral* clause. A small delay in arriving at work, of five, two, or even one minute [results] in the total loss of the readjustment for the month," which could amount to 50 percent of his total wage.[42]

Poletto's devastating criticisms—which were identical to those offered by the communists—came from a *trabalhista* union leader who was on the front lines in the fight against the communists; indeed, Poletto had no qualms as union president about calling on the police to disperse a 1946 Andreotti-led protest at a union assembly.[43] Poletto and Andreotti would have also found common ground in their complaints about the system of *carteiras de trabalho* (individual working papers) instituted by the labor laws of the early 1930s.[44] Each worker's employment history was supposed to be recorded on the *car-teira*, thus guaranteeing the individual, among other *direitos*, the paid vaca-tion set forth in the laws. Unfortunately, as Andreotti noted, some employers failed to annotate the *carteira* although the law obliged them to do so within forty-eight hours of hiring an individual. Others took advantage of the law's three-month trial period, holding on to a worker's *carteira* and then firing him "after three months or before the trial period was over. . . . This caused great losses to the worker affected because it filled up his *carteira*. So he would work two months in one firm, two months in another, and the *carteira* would be full, and a new boss, just looking at the annotations in the *carteira*, some-times wouldn't hire him. Because [the boss would think,] 'If this one worked only two months, it's because he's no good for work,' so the worker would live at the factory gate," begging for a job.[45] This type of capricious action was legal because the CLT never touched on such "trial employment" regulations, which were judged to be a matter of internal employer policy.

The Role of the Labor Courts

Even in politically more favorable times, such as the late 1950s, the perverseness of some labor court rulings could be startling, as Luiz Roberto Puech demonstrated in 1960. Based on his experience as state attorney (*procurador*) in the São Paulo labor courts, Puech discussed employers who demanded labor from minors or women at times or under conditions from which the CLT barred them. Having done the work demanded, he went on, workers often, even "habitually," encountered employers who, "taking advantage of the legal prohibition, refused to pay the corresponding salaries." When these workers turned to the legal system for relief, the local, regional, and national labor courts were unanimous in denying their petitions on the grounds that the situation involved "illicit work, from which the courts should maintain themselves apart [*alheia*]." Beyond this manifest misunderstanding of the CLT's concept of prohibited labor, Puech also criticized the courts for being blind to the legal principle of "*unjustified enrichment* and the social reality of *economic dependency*."[46]

Such *esperteza* (cunning or astuteness) by employers was not, however, confined to fly-by-night, small-scale enterprises or to nonindustrial employment in São Paulo. In 1966, Joseph Springer, a U.S. graduate student, was surprised to find such practices in a São Paulo metalworking factory with five hundred employees. Confidential discussions with company management revealed that "employees are often hired but not officially recorded or reported so that the employer might evade paying" the minimum wage, SENAI payroll tax, and other government-mandated fringe benefits. The injustice was compounded, Springer reported, because such infractions, if discovered, led automatically to the dismissal of the workers whose *direitos* had been defrauded (*sonegados*).[47] Although such actions were subject to fines, Carlos Grandi, the regional labor delegate for São Paulo, noted plaintively in 1959 that it was difficult to collect the "active debts of [labor law] violators . . . because the parties in default felt impunity in ignoring the authority of the DRT." In his laconic words, "the effectiveness of this delegacy, unfortunately, has not been of the best" in guaranteeing "compliance with the labor code."[48]

Moreover, the laxity of the labor court system in defending workers' inter-

Underage child at work at a cobbler's bench, ca. 1941–42. Vargas's photo hangs on the wall. (Photograph by Genevieve Naylor/Courtesy Reznikoff Artistic Partnership)

ests also extended to enforcing court decisions regarding wages in *dissídios coletivos*. Throughout the Populist Republic and into the mid-1960s, many companies simply refused to pay the legally obligated wage increases. Even labor leaders allied with the government routinely denounced employers for their refusal to meet the terms of the *dissídios coletivos* despite having formally signed them. In 1951, for example, the conservative leaders of the railroad workers' and rubber workers' unions in the ABC region complained that their powerful and wealthy employers still refused, to pay for the weekly rest periods provided for in otherwise inadequate *dissídios* from 1949.[49] And in March 1950, the Justifício Maria Luisa jute factory in Santo André had not complied with the inadequate raise ordered in the 1948 textile *dissídio*.[50] This widespread flouting of the law was not limited to the conservative government of President Eurico Dutra during the late 1940s, when *paulista* indus-

A group of adolescent boys in São Paulo on strike against the Irmãos Gasparotti factory at a meeting on 5 March 1964 at the headquarters of the Santo André Metalworkers' Union, headed by Marcos Andreotti and Philadelpho Braz. (Courtesy of the author)

trialist Morvan Dias Figueredo headed the labor ministry, but persisted in some industrial enterprises into the 1960s.

Fernando Lopes de Almeida provides a striking example of another type of carefully prepared legal trick or swindle (*armadilha*) in his discussion of the annual wage negotiations conducted under the aegis of São Paulo's TRT in the 1960s and 1970s. While awaiting a final national TST judgment, employers were exempt from complying with the wage increases awarded by the TRT. And even if the TST ultimately ruled against the employers, the process might have dragged on for more than a year—unions sometimes faced their next year's annual wage negotiation without knowing the final outcome of the previous year's labor court decision. To add to the aggravation, even the celebration of a labor victory at the level of the TST could be spoiled because it did not enter into legal effect until it was published, a process that could take months.[51] In some instances, union leaders had to expend considerable time, influence, and even money to overcome even this petty bureaucratic hurdle.

Even more significant, however, was the federal TST's propensity to overrule TRT decisions that were favorable to workers.[52] The most infamous case occurred after a massive October 1957 generalized strike in São Paulo that had ended when the TRT awarded strikers a 25 percent wage increase with no ceilings. When the TST reduced the wage increase to 18 percent with ceilings, trade union leaders responded violently, although they were unable to carry through on a threatened general protest strike.[53] In this case, the TST's action was not only outrageous but gratuitous, since many employers, especially large and more profitable ones, continued to pay the original 25 percent wage increase. Beyond lowering the wages of some unlucky workers, the TST's reversal of a carefully negotiated settlement was meant to humiliate militant union leaderships, even at the cost of discrediting the labor court system as a whole. As a union manifesto put it, "The workers felt deceived and despoiled of their rights by the decision of the TST. They were the victims of maneuvers, including of [sic] the prosecuting attorney general of Labor Justice, who had already assured them he was in favor of the original 25 percent decision."[54]

On the whole, the federal labor ministry and the labor court system proved either unwilling or unable to impose the rules in any decided or predictable way; indeed, these government entities even failed to effectively handle the outright nonpayment of wages, which was by no means uncommon in industrial Brazil. The CLT's guarantee of an adequate minimum wage,[55] or the oft-discussed family wage, was inevitably undermined by the high rates of inflation that rapidly destroyed every much-heralded increase that the government awarded to workers. Furthermore, the government did not pay its legally mandated share of retirement funds owed to workers, thus leaving government-created pension funds perpetually on the brink of insolvency.[56] Adding to the workers' sense of injustice, even relatively large employers dishonestly economized for considerable periods at the expense of workers' future pensions through *sonegação* (fraud). In 1951, for example, Santo André's large Moinho Santista, Lanifício Kowarick, and Sociedade Productos Agrícolas e Industriais textile plants had been deducting the legally mandated percentage from the workers' paychecks but had failed to turn the entire sum over to the Industrial Employees' Pension and Retirement Institute (Instituto de Aposentadorias e Pensoes dos Industriários, or IAPI), pocketing the difference.[57] As Achim Fuerstenthal, a Brazilian management consultant for foreign firms, told Alexander in 1956, "Brazilian companies cheat a great deal, listing a worker's pay, for instance, at less than it really is, so that in case of severance pay, social security payments, etc., the company will be forced to pay less."[58]

The IAPI was so notorious for its manifest abuses and maladministration that even the most progovernment top union functionaries privately commented bitterly on the situation. The corrupt leader of the National Confederation of Workers in Industry (CNTI), Deocleciano Holanda de Cavalcanti, for example, told Robert Alexander in 1956 that IAPI's medical and retirement programs worked "very badly. There is a very great delay in paying the workers the subsidies which they are supposed to get when they are sick, and it is not unusual for the widow of a worker who has died of illness to get a notice from the instituto some months later saying that after [a] thorough examination of her husband, they now find him fit to go back to work. Furthermore, the medical service is poor, the hospital service is not adequate. The main trouble with the institutos is that they are very badly administered, and they are fraught with politics. They are used to reward the politicians' friends and are staffed in many cases with people who know nothing about what they are doing and are totally incompetent."[59] From the outset, however, the funds accumulated by an array of government-sponsored retirement institutes were used for a different and truly sacred trust: the wide-scale enrichment of directors and their friends and patrons through insider schemes involving the sale and purchase of real estate or simply outright theft.[60]

Brazil offers a rich language for the multitude of stratagems and *armadilhas* carried out by the powerful, well-connected (*pistolão*), and *esperto* (cunning). Employers are commonly referred to as having set out to *sonegar os direitos* of their workers, and "legal features of undeniably immediate interest for workers were often *burlados* [cheated on] by their employers."[61] Even the word *direitos* itself has a far more complicated meaning in Portuguese than does "rights" in English. *Direitos* can mean rights, privileges, or entitlements, and a legal dictionary further develops the broader meanings that escape the world of state-made law: "all that is correct, according to morality, reason, customs, and the law; the faculty, or privilege, or power inherent in one person and falling upon another."[62] The quest to understand labor and law in Brazil requires that we both grasp how employers dodge payment of that which they owe their employees (*sonegando os seus direitos*) and understand that the term *sonegação* contains a strong overlay of disapproval of what is seen as an unlawful withholding from or secret defrauding of what is due. Similarly, to *burlar os direitos* means to trick, cheat, dupe, or swindle those who work, while communicating the victims' powerful sense of disappointment, frustration, and being mocked.[63]

A half century ago, in Switzerland, a group
of jurists gathered in an international congress
chose the Brazilian [labor] legislation as one of
the most advanced in the world. . . . That which
the Europeans hadn't even thought of at that
time, the Brazilians had already put in the
law. . . . The illustrious judges didn't know,
however, that none of these laws were
enforced. Details.

The optimists say that the situation has
changed in recent years. In fact, the Brazilian
labor law no longer figures as among the most
advanced in the world. That's what has changed.
Only that. The rest continues the same.
—JÚLIO ALEJANDRO LOBOS, *Manual de
Guerilla Trabalhista para Gerentes e Supervisores*

four

For the English to See?

The CLT in Foreign and Domestic Perspective

The glaring and almost schizophrenic contrast between law and reality, the-ory and practice, and words and deeds is of course a classic problem much discussed in labor relations and historical literature. It is by no means rare to encounter a situation where things exist on paper but not in reality, where law, justice, and rights exist in name only, formally, and without consequence. The problem of the CLT, from a North Atlantic perspective, lay precisely in the general Latin American penchant for "statutory regulation of working condi-tions." In the words of a 1961 ILO article, this disposition stands in sharp contrast to the more "pragmatic" Anglo-American approach to labor, with its emphasis on collective bargaining. While the latter tradition "usually speaks of 'labor relations' or 'labor management relations,' thus emphasizing the wider nature of the relationship between men at work," Latin Americans tend to "think in terms of *derecho de trabajo* or *derecho social* (labor law), thus stressing the legal aspects of the relation which, in their view, is primarily a set of legal rights and obligations."[1]

As a result, labor law in Latin America, the ILO authors argued, has tended "to codify all conceivable matters relating to labor and social questions into one comprehensive statute book," and this strong "desire for legal perfection leads to a situation where the [labor] law is in advance of the real economic and social situation." As an example, the article cites the region's tendency to legally define working conditions not in terms of "minimum standards but rather [in terms of] the most favorable conditions," a generous disposition not unconnected to the fact "that the function of the written law in some of the Latin American countries is more educational than normative in character," which seems "somewhat alien to national traditions" in the United States and Canada.[2]

This comparative perspective permits a better understanding of the type of lawmaking process exemplified by the CLT. In a social and legal system that minimizes the gap between law and reality, it is possible to imagine a hypothetical law that promises a 20 percent improvement and fulfills 80 percent of that which is pledged. In a system such as that in Brazil, by contrast, where the law-reality gap is maximized, a law like the CLT may promise an 80 percent improvement yet deliver only 20 percent of that.[3] Even if the net outcome were the same, these two different approaches to lawmaking would decisively influence not only how people perceived the law (their "legal consciousness") but how they shaped their actions in response to the law.

Even knowledgeable Brazilians involved with the CLT system often expressed similar concerns about the unrealistic nature of Brazilian labor law. Writing for a U.S. audience in 1951, J. V. Freitas Marcondes noted with some pride that "our social legislation is advanced in comparison with that of other civilized countries." Yet even this member of the Institute of Social Law in São Paulo, writing eight years after the CLT's establishment, expressed concern about "the avalanche of new laws" and suggested that Brazil might be experiencing "a period of 'inflation' in regard to labor law." He also recognized the valid concerns of those who criticized "the abundance of labor laws in Brazil, many of which lack any a priori plan [and have] no relation to social reality; instead, they are enactments made exclusively for the codes, divorced from the people and from the institutions."[4]

This general criticism of the excessively advanced nature of Latin American labor law would remain a constant in much later scholarly discussion. Writing about Latin America as a whole in 1972, Louis Goodman argued that the most "subtle means of undermining union strength" in Latin America was through promulgating "a body of welfare legislation which is in advance of what their economies could support if fully enforced." Such labor laws, he went on, slowed down economic growth and "effectively subverted the logical basis" for union organization. Rather than creating a situation in which unions had fought for benefits, "traditional Latin paternalism was merely transformed into welfare state paternalism with the government acting as [a] 'patron,'" awarding benefits arbitrarily.[5]

In fact, the issues raised in discussing the CLT are central to the larger debate about state intervention and corporatism in Latin America, a region where state action has played a far larger and more visible role in establishing systems of industrial and labor relations than has been the case in Europe and the United States. Indeed, the consolidation of Latin American labor movements occurred, for the most part, in tandem with a proliferation of government social welfare and labor initiatives after 1930 that included, in Brazil and elsewhere, actual state sponsorship of and support for trade union organization. Within this wider Latin American spectrum, Brazil under Getúlio Vargas stands out as the most extreme case of state interventionism.[6] "In no other Latin American country," argued Victor Alba, a Spanish anticommunist journalist, in 1968, "does the state control the unions so completely as in Brazil."[7] Thus, Brazil's elaborate system has long served as the benchmark for studying corporatist systems in which, to quote Kenneth Mericle, "the state plays a major role in structuring, supporting, and regulating interest groups with the object of controlling their internal affairs and the relations between them."[8]

Corporatism: The Culturalist and Marxian Variants

Until the 1990s, the attempt to make sense of the Brazilian state's role in labor relations had given rise to two successive lines of interpretation, both of which shared the notion of corporatism. The earlier culturalist variant, which has had little influence in labor history, found the origin of the Brazilian penchant for statism, formalism, and legalism in the country's patrimonial culture and politics. In vogue among many mainstream U.S. observers (and some Brazilians) in the 1950s and 1960s, this culturalist explanation can be identified with Richard Morse, Kalman Silvert, and Howard Wiarda.[9] For example, political scientist Silvert proudly affirmed in 1974 that his argument "boils down to the view that there is something in the quality of the Latin American man in his culture which has made it difficult for him to become truly modern. Of course that is the case. If country X in Central America, say, were emptied of its inhabitants, and a similar number of Swedes substituted for them, there can be no doubt that in a very short time country X would be fundamentally changed—and obviously in the direction of greater modernization."[10]

Profoundly idealist and often ethnocentric, this group of predominantly foreign observers interpreted modern Brazilian political and trade union developments in light of a postulated Iberian, Mediterranean, and/or Catholic cultural inheritance.[11] In 1974, for example, Wiarda, a U.S. political scientist, offered the Brazilian labor relations system as a central proof of the "culturalist" argument. Latin America, he suggested, was characterized by a pervasive "corporative framework" for representation, with its characteristic emphasis on the state as arbiter, that was "carried over by Spain and Portugal to the New World."[12] Yet this idea did not appear convincing to such specialists in the history of modern Spain as Colin M. Winston, who studied such rightwing ideological movements. Winston denied Wiarda's claim that corporatism was "a, if not the, typical form of Ibero-Hispanic social organization [or one] particularly congenital to the institutions of the Hispanic world." Rather, Winston argued that "corporatism was only one of many competing ideologies in Spain, and it is difficult to prove that it was more widespread there than in other countries at comparable levels of development. It was neither an exotic import nor a peculiar Hispanic mutant but a local variant of a pan-European phenomenon."[13]

For culturalist analysts, the result of this patrimonial heritage is "a particularly tutelary and paternalistic form" of political participation that can be seen in state-sanctioned trade unions and interest group organization based on "the paternalistic hegemony of the state."[14] Naturally, these commentators offered a radically different reading of the meaning of "advanced" labor laws like the CLT. While a Latin American might see them as evidence of at least an aspiration for modernity, even if foolhardy, many U.S. observers interpreted the CLT as a prime example of Latin American cultural pathology. "When labor disputes arise in most Latin countries," Silvert argued, "it is an automatic procedure to avoid the face-to-face collective bargaining process and, as a matter of normal practice, to have recourse to government for their settlement." Silvert saw this tendency as the realization of the region's cultural pattern, with its "neat order and love for hierarchy and organization, which also serve to contain class conflict and to prevent individuals from attaining a social level in accord with their abilities."[15]

Putting aside its ethnocentrism, the culturalist approach can be easily criticized for treating "tradition" and "culture" as univocal, positing discursive formations as the key to historical explanation, and assuming that the past ruled over the present as cause to effect. Not surprisingly, the culturalist interpretation of the Brazilian and Latin American propensity for corporatism and statism did not appeal to most Latin American or U.S. scholars of labor.[16]

In many ways, the politicization of discussions of labor in Brazil in the 1960s and 1970s defined the second and more influential line of analysis, which I have called the "corporatist consensus." This approach placed an inordinate emphasis on the negative impact of corporatist state intervention on the self-organization and struggle of the working class and on its consciousness.[17] In this view, Brazilian workers unfortunately came to be structured, in the words of Maria Helena Moreira Alves, in "corporative organizations by a labor code copied from Mussolini's legislation for control of unions." The Brazilian state is thus said to have installed a labor-repressive system based on a corporativist-fascist model.[18]

Not surprisingly, this Marxian variant of a corporatist explanation could be read as supporting the larger culturalist interpretation. From Wiarda's point of view, the influence of Mussolini and the corporatist Italian labor legislation of the 1920s on the CLT could be seen as further proof of a shared cultural universe. Leftist scholars, by contrast, would tend to interpret such Italian influence in light of notions of fascism drawn from the Marxist tradition. In retrospect, both lines of analysis had difficulty coming to terms with the peculiarity of the Brazilian case precisely because of the primarily foreign referents with which they tried to interpret the CLT.

Another drawback to the corporatist consensus was that it tended to see through the law to its "essence," which was interpreted not as a cultural construct but as a direct reflection of intentional action by the "bourgeois" state. These observers saw the CLT as a capitalist imposition on the workers. Highly deterministic, this model treated the CLT as a tool of either capitalism as a social system or the capitalists as a class; some variants saw the CLT as a structural imperative of capital accumulation, and others viewed the law as an elaborate ideological apparatus or ploy by the capitalists and their lackeys.[19] Yet both approaches shared the sense that the CLT and its political aura (populism) were merely or primarily a pretense, a successful false front that was simultaneously an act of concealment and a form of deceitful self-promotion designed to bamboozle the workers. On the whole, the experience of the CLT seemed an extreme case of hypocrisy as it was so ably defined by the Duc de La Rochefoucauld: "Hypocrisy is the tribute that vice pays to virtue."[20] In this view, facile discourse and empty talk had a more sinister purpose: to divert attention away from the underlying violence and inequalities of Brazil as a class society. The aim was to cloud the workers' eyes with imaginary rights while fastening the chains of state control on those weapons, such as trade unionism, that might help free the workers.

The Brazilian Workers' ABC dissented radically from the bourgeois fraud interpretation of the state interventionism symbolized by the CLT. The book argued that the industrial bourgeoisie did not impose the CLT on the working class and demonstrated that state action often had unanticipated and even paradoxical results at the grassroots level. The CLT was indeed aimed against autonomous working-class organization, but it also was not in essence or inherently antilabor. Instead, the meaning of corporatist state intervention, which responded to contradictory impulses, varied systematically according to the balance of power among classes, regions, and factions at each level of the power structure. And state action—against the wishes of its designers—in fact contributed to the creation of space that could be and was used for working-class self-organization and mobilization.

More importantly, *The Brazilian Workers' ABC* reinterprets the culturalist point that a specific type of formal dispute resolution characterized the corporatist model of labor relations. In a stimulating article comparing the U.S. contractualist and Brazilian corporatist labor law systems, Tamara Lothian noted that the latter tended to downplay "the voluntary determination of wage and work conditions. The corporatist labor regime permits collective bargaining, but only within a framework that invites frequent and pervasive governmental influence. A broad range of working conditions, job security terms, and even wage differentials is determined by law. Even in the area where collective bargaining takes place, the government is involved. Thus, collective bargaining relations must be brokered and/or ratified by the labor courts, a specialized branch of the judiciary—injecting a full panoply of rules, standards, and principles into the employment relation."[21]

Yet Lothian's discussion of these contrasting labor relations systems also pointed to the unintended consequences of the corporatist model that prevailed in Brazil. Although the system was designed to produce quiescence, it has in practice contributed to a "politicized militancy" by Brazilian labor, which is quite different from the thrust of "the contractualist or voluntarist model of labor relations [in the United States, which] encourages a moderate, economistic style of militancy."[22] The centrality of the state in Brazilian labor relations, Lothian suggests, has produced a vigorous, independent, and politicized labor movement, in striking contrast to the privatization and isolation of worker mobilizations within the North American contractualist system.

In addition to discussing industrial and labor relations, *The Brazilian Workers' ABC* examined the political-electoral field to suggest the falsity of the bourgeois fraud image by studying these governmental initiatives' effects on workers' behavior. Workers' massive and positive response to the promulgator of the CLT, Getúlio Vargas, after the end of his dictatorship in 1945 suggests a fundamental weakness of the corporatist consensus.[23] The CLT was linked not to the destruction of trade unions and the demobilization of the working class but to the reverse. Indeed, the political moment of 1943–47, of which the CLT forms an integral part, featured democratizing and participatory trends in both electoral and industrial relations arenas; that is, CLT-type initiatives were inseparable from the birth of Brazilian and Latin American populism, which cannot be explained, as has been common, solely on the basis of propaganda and demagoguery.

Bacharelismo and "Out of Place Ideas"

While the lack of an "adequate" fit between law and society may strike North Americans simply as backward or dysfunctional, the paradox suggested by the CLT points to an important aspect of Brazilian political and legal culture going back to the country's formation as an independent nation in 1822. Nineteenth-century Brazil, as captured so well by Emília Viotti da Costa, was a patriarchal slave-owning society whose ruling elites embraced the ideologies of European liberalism while reshaping them to suit Brazilian interests and emptying those ideas of any potentially radical or democratic content.[24]

Economically dependent on traditional forms of production based on agricultural exports, these profoundly conservative elites were culturally and politically oriented toward Europe. In part at least, the CLT too was promulgated for show, for external display, *para Inglés ver* (for the English to see), to cite a favorite Brazilian expression that originated in the first half of the nineteenth century.[25] Under British pressure, slaveholding Brazil's newly independent monarchy agreed to a formal 1830 treaty that solemnly outlawed the slave trade, although the traffic continued unabated, the law unenforced. The empire's rhetoric about the horrors of slave trafficking and official plans for its suppression were all meant "for the Englishmen to see," it was said. Indeed, the slave trade did not end until 1850, when the British blockaded Brazilian ports (and slavery would last another thirty-eight years).[26]

One of the most striking characteristics of the Brazilian empire and the 1889–1930 republic that followed was a precocious attachment to a highly refined legalism and formalism. Immediately after independence, the elites of monarchical Brazil established medical and law schools, the earliest institutions of higher learning in a country whose first modern university was not established until the 1930s. For the next century, Brazilian politics would be marked by the ubiquitous discursive construct of *bacharelismo*, in which the actual conduct of politics and policy making was identified as a peculiarly disconnected and bookish enterprise of the "lettered" (*letrados*), those who held bachelor's degrees (*bacharéis*), especially lawyers.[27]

In 1968, U.S. political scientist Philippe Schmitter noted the intense Brazilian preoccupation "with legal phraseology, precision of expression and rigidly designed, exhaustively contrived and minutely detailed provisions and rules." Schmitter also noted how the CLT "regulates with exhaustive formality."[28] At the same time, Brazil's culture, politics, and mythologies were formed around the realities of patronage and clientelism. Thus, Brazilian policy makers and the general populace were and are more realistic than North Americans in acknowledging the role of the *jeito* (knack or maneuver) and *pistolão* (good words, connections, and pull) in determining life outcomes.[29] While embracing equality before the law as part of a critique of patronage, Brazilians have always maintained a greater degree of what U.S. citizens might call cynicism about the law.[30] While not resigned to it, Brazilians freely and frankly recognize that there is, in practice, one law for the powerful and another for the weak, one for the well-connected and another for those without friends. Another Brazilian saying about the law is as accurate as it is deliciously malicious: one aims for justice for friends and the law for enemies.

Like all societies, Brazil is riven by such contrasts between the ideal and the real, cracks that are papered over by formalism, legalism, and empty words. For example, Brazil's 1824 constitution outlawed torture, but this prohibition never reached the slave quarters.[31] And even today, although capital punishment does not exist in Brazil, heavily armed police routinely execute hundreds of persons a year for "resisting arrest."[32] Similarly, abortion is illegal, yet the government makes no serious attempts to enforce the ban, and hundreds of thousands of abortions are performed every year.[33]

So perhaps the CLT is, as many Brazilian observers believed, simply another example of liberal *bacharelismo* and "out-of-place ideas" (*ideas fora do lugar*) in a country where liberalism has always been a great misunderstanding.[34] In this view, the post-1930 labor legislation was a product of the excessively theoretical and European-fixated *bacharéis*. In 1939, *paulista* industrialist Roberto Simonsen linked the proliferation of unrealistic labor laws to the *bacharel's* slavish imitation of inappropriate foreign models and his complete lack of practical knowledge of economics.[35] Speaking from the opposite camp, communist trade union leader Roberto Morena offered in 1946 a similar explanation for the origin of Brazil's "first really serious laws concerning labor": "Most of these laws were products of the brain of the labor minister and had little connection with things as they were, and [the laws] certainly were passed without consulting the worker and without any public discussion: then, as now, there was much legislation but little enforcement."[36]

If such cheap shots by government critics are predictable, it is more surprising to hear a similar explanation advanced in 1956 by José de Segadas Vianna, one of the four labor ministry lawyers who drafted the CLT during the Estado Novo.[37] In a private conversation with visiting U.S. scholar Robert Alexander, the former PTB labor minister (1951–53) explained that Vargas "had real sympathy for workers" and that his demagoguery in the early 1930s was much influenced by Labor Minister Lindolfo Collor, who was well acquainted with labor in Europe and sought to apply "with Getúlio's backing, many European things which did not really have applicability here. In fact, Brazilian labor and social legislation in general has been written more with an eye on Europe than on the reality of the Brazilian situation."[38] Segadas Vianna's frank criticism of Collor, father of the labor laws, is striking.[39] Rather than hailing the CLT system that he helped to design, Segadas Vianna openly admits its "demagogic" origin while casting doubts on the appropriateness of its European "inspiration" for Brazilian realities. Even more surprisingly, Segadas Vianna went on to estimate that 80 percent of Brazilian labor law was not applied.

Such statements cannot be explained solely by Segadas Vianna's bitter dispute with his PTB rivals during the mid-1950s.[40] Indeed, other important party leaders from the same period shared similar opinions regarding the CLT. In 1956, for example, national PTB leader Paulo de Campos Moura told Alexander that the Brazilian labor law, although "one of the most extensive and complete in the world, . . . is the result of demagoguery from the time of the Estado Novo down to the present. It was not developed in view of the needs of the country, or of the workers, but rather for demagogic purposes."[41] And even Segadas Vianna's foremost rival, Jango Goulart, who replaced Segadas Vianna as labor minister, admitted in 1972 that Brazil's "very extensive body of labor law" was not being enforced when he came to power in 1953.[42]

What are we to make of such common agreement and admirable frankness among members of the PTB, the party of Vargas and the CLT? Such observations by the formulators, administrators, and beneficiaries of the CLT certainly gives the lie to the Vargas regime's public claim that the laws were an *outorga* from an enlightened elite to workers, an image central to *getulista* propaganda.[43] These statements also undermine any temptation to present the laws as a conquest of the Brazilian working class, a product of a deeply rooted battle for political power and/or working-class citizenship, as in the case of the Mexican federal labor law of 1931.[44] Professional *trabalhistas'* self-conscious cynicism suggests that the CLT was far from an idealistic effort to implant a comprehensive moral standard of justice in the workplace, a drive that succeeded only in part because of reasons beyond the control of its farsighted creators (a laudatory self-image central to Brazilian legal culture).

Many Brazilians formulate the "problem" with Brazilian law as a dysfunction caused by a "gap between the formal and the applied law." Scholars who adopt this stance, anthropologist James Holston rightly suggests, are merely echoing Brazilian legal culture more generally: "law students are taught that formal law in Brazil is based on the transcendent values of a liberal legal culture corrupted by real-world, class-ridden, and statist interests. . . . I do not doubt that utopian principles may exist in law or indeed that they are desirable. What I doubt is that the law's dystopias are external to its construction" in Brazil.[45] In 1985, João José Sady, a Marxist labor lawyer in São Paulo, ended a discussion of the "highly contradictory character" of the Brazilian labor law with a wry, if sexist analogy: "Reality is complex because the law is like a daughter who leaves home: the father no longer has control over her destiny, and she could turn into a saint or a prostitute [*mundana*]. The same is true for the law."[46]

The emergence of labor law as a new branch of the Brazilian legal system is best seen, in other words, not as something deeply thought through or planned but rather as a sustained improvisation by a small group of *bacharéis* who were discontented, if not with the socioeconomic order at least with their individual roles in society. When the *paulista* establishment was ousted from national power in 1930, the advent of a new leadership from the more socially diverse and politically pluralistic state of Rio Grande do Sul offered these individuals the opportunity to create careers for themselves through an expansion of the newly strengthened centralizing state.[47]

Rather than overlooking such mundane and self-interested motives, it makes sense to consider whether the CLT might in fact have more to do with jobs, contracts, and the perquisites of government and judicial office than with resolving the social question.[48] This analysis strengthens the hypothesis first advanced by Maria Hermínia Tavares de Almeida in 1978, when she denied that these labor relations innovations were a function of capitalist development. Instead, she suggested that the labor law originated in the "specific gravitation of segments of the state bureaucracy in the political game and the decision-making process" of the 1930s.[49] As has been wryly observed, during the 1930s and 1940s, the MTIC's *Bulletin* published many more articles justifying labor law as a new branch of juridical science than discussing prospects for its enforcement.[50]

If legal improvisation marked the elaboration of the labor laws in the 1930s, those who drafted the CLT in 1943, like Segadas Vianna, stood at the apogee of centralized power before the Estado Novo dictatorship had entered into frank decline. These policy makers acted at a time when illusions about the independence and solidity of the state apparatus were rife and when social actors, especially workers, were publicly quiescent. They seized the opportunity offered by opportunistic, short-term, political maneuvering by sectors of the Vargas regime to establish a more ambitious version of their legal labor empire during the political transition of 1943–45.[51]

At the same time, these labor ministry officials could not have foreseen the impact of placing "the government, the entrepreneurs, and the workers in a constant, detailed, varied and unequal confrontation about the shaping of the public space being opened by the legal regulation of capital-labor relations."[52] These government bureaucrats also could not have known that their carefully constructed *"trabalhista empire"* would come crashing down during the 1945–47 popular insurgency that would decisively influence the subsequent trajectory of the CLT system.[53]

Oliveira Vianna in 1945: The Authoritarian Reformer as Lonely Moralist

Addressing a Catholic rally in Niterói in late 1945, famous sociologist Francisco José de Oliveira Vianna (1883–1951) spoke in a tone of shock and disappointment at the collapse of the dreams he had entertained as a top legal adviser to the labor minister beginning in 1932. Having drafted a great deal of the labor legislation that was systematized in the CLT, Oliveira Vianna was horrified in 1945 by the advances of atheistic communism in Brazil, a dangerous and anti-Christian ideology that, he admitted, had begun to agitate "our laboring masses." As the preeminent ideologue of the Estado Novo's corporatist labor system, Oliveira Vianna was deeply committed to his vision of a conflict-free labor relations system achieved through the "incorporation of the worker into the state." Not surprisingly, he could not help but view the first signs of the postwar explosion of industrial militancy and working-class radicalism as a deturpation of his carefully conceived and crafted solution to the social question. Concluding that "the truth is with the [Catholic] Church" and its doctrines, Oliveira Vianna demanded "intensive and systematic action against this dangerous communist ideology" in both its evolutionary socialist form and its revolutionary communist form.[54]

Oliveira Vianna's 1945 call for state action against leftism clearly anticipated the 1947 crackdown on communism and labor militancy by Brazil's newly elected president, Eurico Dutra, the Estado Novo's former military strongman. In advocating such repression, Oliveira Vianna faced no moral crisis of conscience since this original and deeply authoritarian thinker had never embraced liberal chimeras such as trade union autonomy or even electoral democracy. Yet Oliveira Vianna's disappointments after World War II were more general and his disillusionment more profound than might be expected. In his eyes, workers were not the only group responsible for the failure of Brazil's carefully constructed corporatist labor system, which he still believed had the potential to end the class struggle. Indeed, Oliveira Vianna apportioned a large share of the blame for the popular eruption already visible in 1945 to the selfish Brazilian employer class. The industrialists, he complained, had not only failed to embrace the "new mentality" preached by the Vargas regime but had persisted in their earlier antialtruistic attitudes toward workers.[55]

Although no longer a labor policy maker in 1945, Oliveira Vianna's worldview was consistent with the themes he had enunciated so forcefully as a juridical consultant to the labor ministry. Despite his best efforts, he had failed at that time to achieve any significant degree of control over Brazilian industrialists, whose class organizations—like those of their workers—were to have been fully incorporated into the system of state-sponsored *sindicatos*. Having been thus deprived of the possibility of achieving a salutary symmetry between employers and employees vis-à-vis the state, Oliveira Vianna was forced to content himself with inculcating new cooperative mentalities among those who led the union organizations of the weaker of the two sides of the conflict—the urban working class. Drawing on the experience of the early 1930s, Oliveira Vianna had foreseen in 1939 the creation of a new working-class elite that would, by its leadership of the trade unions, eliminate the workers' "anti-employer spirit." As responsible collaborators with the employers and the state, this labor elite would also facilitate the social advancement of capable workers, who would rise to positions of prominence through education and the raising of their cultural level (a U.S.-style dream that Silvert deemed antithetical to Brazil's fundamental cultural values).[56]

Coherent in his views, Oliveira Vianna had taken seriously the proposition that the Vargas regime's corporatist labor legislation was designed to do more than just combat communism and class struggle, as important as that was. Before his forced departure, Oliveira Vianna had also believed that the state was truly committed to changing the mentality of the industrialists by lessening the social distances between the rich and the laboring classes. In a 1939 article, the highly moralistic Oliveira Vianna had written that none of "the captains of industry, occupied with the accumulation and counting of their millions and the enjoyment of their riches, . . . were preoccupied with the living conditions of their workers," thus creating the "flagrant and violent contrast between the superworld of the rich and the subworld of the poor." As he would put it at the Niterói rally, "Either the Brazilian employers [*patronato*] will" adopt a new altruistic attitude, "or they will continue to insist on their old previous attitude—and then no one can know what may come, but it is certain that . . . it will be terrible and destructive."[57]

Single-minded and otherworldly in his vision, Oliveira Vianna was not to be reduced to a plaything of the rich industrialists of whom he disapproved, nor was he content to be merely a publicist for a government that they corrupted in opposition to his dreams of an ideal state.[58] In a 1943 book, *Problemas do Direito Sindical* (*Problems of Trade Union Law*), he censured "this prejudice against the state, this attitude opposed to the protection of the state, this preoccupation with staying distant from the state, which is absolutely unjust [among us]. Especially so when it departs not from a theorist of the academy or a doctrinaire publicist but from our captains of industry. We all know that, for them, the state has been a generous father that gives to them with open hands [*de mãos largas*] as in no other part of the world. Call on these chiefs of prosperous enterprises, from one end of Brazil to another, and you will find them all, without exception, sheltered under an enormous umbrella, and this umbrella that sustains them in its mighty hands is . . . the state."[59]

These resentments reflected Oliveira Vianna's stubborn refusal to bend with the winds at the end of his career in the labor ministry. Imbued with a sense of higher mission, Oliveira Vianna in office refused to be realistic and simply resign himself to the wishes of the powerful, in this case the industrialists of São Paulo. Unlike many other *bacharéis*, he fought a series of unsuccessful juridical and bureaucratic battles regarding employer unionization and the minimum wage. When the August 1940 minimum wage degree was finally issued, its text demonstrated "the degree to which the Estado Novo was responsive to the interests of the industrialists." In an unpublished private memorandum, Oliveira Vianna railed against the decree, which he called "the most authentic piece of juridical roguery which this ministry has given birth to in its ten years of existence. This is taking up a position contrary to the whole spirit which has presided over and inspires the social legislation."[60]

In the end, the labor legislation drawn up by Oliveira Vianna, which took on new life as part of the CLT, did not match his hopes. The paradox of utopias, as Vanda Ribeiro Costa notes, "is that fragments of the dreams" they contain end up in "a different place, where they are realized in a perverse way. The dream of the thirties was to correct Brazil," with Oliveira Vianna in the vanguard. "His utopia was to believe in the law as an instrument of this corrective project" and as "a moral force of social change."[61] As João Quartim de Moraes notes, "The perception of the *paulista* employer class that the Ministry of Labor was creating class struggle" was in essence correct because such a "struggle is only possible through an equilibrium of the opposing forces. The corporativism proposed by the MTIC aimed [in theory] for this symmetry. The refusal of the employer elite to recognize the legitimacy of a program that sought to organize workers, giving them a voice and a say, is the origin of the perversion of the utopia of Oliveira Vianna."[62]

The Death of Illusions: The CLT System under President Eurico Dutra

The CLT system survived its postwar baptism of fire, with its mass strikes and highly visible communist political activism, but was profoundly influenced by the repressive period of conservative reaction under President Dutra (1946–50). During the late 1940s, the government eschewed *trabalhista* (laborite) demagoguery and openly shared the employers' conviction that the govern-

Rally celebrating Adhemar de Barros's election, with communist support, as governor of the state of São Paulo, São Paulo, 11 March 1947. The hammer and sickle were highly visible after World War II. (Courtesy Iconographia-Pesquisa de Texto, Imagem, e Som S/C Ltda)

ment labor apparatus was useful only to control the working class. The Dutra government, recalled a high labor ministry functionary José Gomes Talarico, was "harsh, powerful, [and] authoritarian; it trampled on the workers' freedoms, union rights, [and] the right of free association and strangled everyone. Although it was constitutionalist, it was really an extremely harsh government, implacable in police persecution."[63] Dutra's closest collaborators always stressed his military emphasis on "order, discipline, and unity," as Daniel de Carvalho did in 1954. This led Dutra's government, Carvalho said admiringly, to suffocate "in the womb strikes and similar caprices of class struggle" while avoiding "a dangerous elevation of the minimum wage."[64]

For staffers in the government's labor apparatus, this dynamic guaranteed that those who thrived, especially at the top levels, were calculating, cynical, ambitious men who, unlike Oliveira Vianna, knew and accepted that the system was not intended to work for workers. Prudent "men of confidence" like Segadas Vianna, who lacked illusions, would play a vital role in managing the labor relations system in the interests of the powerful (although not necessarily at their direct behest in every instance). Moreover, these men already possessed a highly developed understanding, inherited from earlier generations of *bacharéis*, that allowed them to feel comfortable with the yawning chasm between the law and reality. Brazilian Supreme Court Justice Oswaldo Trigueiro de Albuquerque Mello captured this realistic but not entirely resigned sentiment at the end of the 1960s under the military regime: "In countries at a stage of political development equivalent to Brazil, there is always a hiatus between the legal country and the real country."[65]

The subordinate position occupied by legal and constitutional reasoning has always frustrated Brazilian lawyers and judges, a point well illustrated in a 1956 interview with Pedro de Albuquerque Montenegro, a TRT judge in Recife, Pernambuco: "The question of strikes has been handled here in a very Brazilian manner," he pointed out resignedly.

> The constitution of the fascist Estado Novo forbade strikes as subversive. But while that constitution was still in effect, a decree was issued, in 1945 or 1946 [Decree Law 9,070], which provided that strikes were legal in industries which were not basic. That, of course, was unconstitutional under the existing constitution [of 1937]. Then the [new democratic] constitution of 1946 provided that strikes were legal and should be regulated by law. However, now, ten years after the adoption of that constitution, the law regulating them has not been passed. Instead, the [labor] courts have interpreted the former decree, providing for strikes in industries not considered basic, as having precedence. This decree was thus unconstitutional under the former constitution and is unconstitutional under the present one.[66]

As with the liberal *bacharéis* of nineteenth-century slaveholding Brazil, to cite Sérgio Adorno, these juridical elites always had to temper their exaggerated legal liberalism (*liberalismo jurídico*) with a high degree of "political prudence."[67] The reflexive antiradicalism that characterized the behavior of the *bacharéis* was essential to avoid the threat to the social order that could occur if a significant number refused to accept the law-reality gap.[68] A little-known proletarian novel by Amando Fontes, a *sergipano* author who received a law degree in 1928, captures this war between the *bacharel*'s attraction to "advanced" thought and his ingrained disposition to political prudence. Fontes's 1933 novel about working-class life in the northeastern state of Sergipe includes a convincing portrait of Celestino, a young and progressive-minded *bacharel* who is appointed to the plum position of police chief in Aracaju, the state capital. When a strike occurs that serves the electoral needs of the governor, the *delegado* commits himself enthusiastically to a public role as champion of the oppressed.[69]

When the interests of his patron shift, Celestino is called to the governor's palace and ordered to put a clear and decisive end to the strike. Disconcerted, he tries to dissuade the governor from punishing "these poor men" whose defense of their rights, Celestino says, had received our full support. Angered, the governor responds by attacking the strikers: "They have committed true crimes that neither you nor I authorized, that's for sure. And punishment is the fate of those who offend the law!" In his moment of indecision, the young lawyer weights his solemn promises to the strikers against the energy required to bravely break with the governor. If Celestino persists in demanding that the strikers not be punished, he realizes, he'll risk his career and his future, which certainly will not "improve the workers' situation one bit." If he continues as police *delegado*, however, he "might prove even more useful" to the movement: "he could lessen the assaults, deflect persecutions." Holding tightly to that evasion, Celestino says that he is not a man who deserts his post in the heat of political battle. Calming down, the governor offers some paternal advice, showing his understanding of Celestino's "delicate position" by arranging for the *delegado*'s subordinate to carry out the dirty work. Celestino needs only to point out the leaders, nine of whom are deported the next morning by boat to destinations unknown.[70]

Dependent on the patronage of the dominant class, the worldview of this narrow stratum of juridical elites was also profoundly shaped by the peculiarities of bourgeois ideology in Brazil, where the ideology's liberal variant was not dominant. Instead, Brazilian society was characterized, in the words of Gisálio Cerqueira Filho, by a conservative paternalism ("authoritarianism plus the system of favors") that handled the objective of masking class antagonism through social integration in a different way: this "paternalistic content . . . bestow[ed] on bourgeois discourse [in Brazil] the special character of an authoritarian thought that is kindhearted (*bonachão*) and benevolent, paternal."[71] When confronted with social inequality and conflict, Adorno observes, the *bacharéis* worldview suggested a prudent policy: to unquestionably reject radicalism but at the same time to give without the popular strata having to fight; to broaden without having to abdicate control; and to distribute power without having to share it.[72] In other words, it was advanced and progressive to change the laws as long as the realities of power remained untouched.

After surveying the prolific rhetoric about "advanced" labor laws in the 1930s, Cerqueira Filho observed with bitter irony, "Thus, the grand comedy of the dominant political discourse about the 'social question' in Brazil is mounted, a discourse that combines social integration and paternalism (the favor plus authoritarianism). A bourgeois discourse is not discarded; it is reinterpreted. But it is precisely here that it loses its footing and slides toward the grotesque, toward comedy, but pathetic comedy. For every social legislation created there corresponds a *jeito* [knack, maneuver], a *'jeitinho'* [little knack] (see the favor appear once again) destined to protect its nonfulfillment. The ambiguity of paternalism will enhance that which in vain the legislation seeks to curb: oppression, disrespect, the ongoing disposition to violence, venality."[73]

The labor relations arena governed by the CLT was characterized precisely by the politics of the *"jeitinho* (a knack or way of getting around a bureaucratically or legally difficult problem) as this extralegal process is called."[74] The "paradoxical characteristic of the Brazilian legal ordering of labor relations," noted a *paulista* labor lawyer, José Francisco Siqueira Neto, in 1996, "is that Brazilian labor law before the [1988] constitution, even though extensive, was not enforced, just as it is not today." Brazil's highly detailed regulatory labor law system, he went on ironically, could be characterized "as a system that is intrinsically flexibilized and unregulated," a reality that not even the powerful labor and democratic struggles that swept Brazil after 1978 had fundamentally changed.[75]

At midcentury, the *paulista* industrialists understood how to play the game. They had no need, after the 1930s, to frontally oppose the idea of labor laws per se as long as they could be sure that antilabor provisions were enforced and that proworker features could be avoided, delayed, or minimized through appropriate "interpretation" and nonenforcement by the government and courts.[76] In dealing with issues of great interest to employers, recalled Segadas Vianna in 1987, there was always an alternative to the "strict application of the law." After all, he went on, the function of legal interpretation is to find a formula that, when needed, makes possible "a reasonable interpretation that partially attends to the interests of the industrialists of São Paulo."[77]

In his superb 1991 study of urban land law in São Paulo, Holston has aptly described this feature of the Brazilian legal system as the process whereby "illegal practices produce law [and] extralegal solutions are incorporated into the juridical process." In this way, law ensures "the maintenance of privilege among those who posses extralegal power to manage politics, bureaucracy, and the historical record itself. In this sense," he concludes, it "is an effective, though perverse, means of rule."[78] Thus, "the deliberate use of particular stratagems to influence an easily manipulated bureaucracy" is fundamental to the Brazilian legal system. But he rightly cautions that "as a construction of law, the system is too inoperative, contradictory, and confusing on its own terms to attribute these characteristics to corruption, incompetence, or individual manipulation. Rather, its predictable dysfunction indicates a more systematic mode of irresolution. It suggests that the legal system skillfully embodies intentions to perpetuate judicial irresolution through legal complication. For that very reason, the law facilitates stratagem and fraud."[79]

A 1987 interview with one of the CLT's authors, Segadas Vianna, revealed the cynicism that characterized the political culture of the legal elites linked to the dominant class, even during the populist heyday under Vargas. Factory owners never really feared the labor laws, Segadas Vianna explained, "because the bourgeoisie didn't believe that they would be put into practice. They thought that it was more a question of us showing off to people abroad—which it was in part." In addition, the CLT was a matter of self-promotion, "saying that we were doing something." Segadas Vianna also offered an unflattering analogy between the CLT and the labor code of the Dominican Republic, which was adopted thirty years after the CLT. The Dominican measure was very advanced, but it contained a provision at the end "saying that the government would enforce it when it deemed it appropriate to do so." Brazilians, he went on, also "had a very advanced social legislation, and the real truth is that up to 1940, when [the labor ministry] was instituted, we had no enforcement of the social legislation . . . because the negative reaction from businessmen was very strong. [What] was done in terms of social security in Brazil is all a great farce, [and] our trade unionism was not active, it was a trade union facade. First of all because union membership was extremely low, as it still is in Brazil. Trade unionism in Brazil is a utopia. It is a farce, isn't it? In those days it was even more so."[80]

In 1986, São Paulo management consultant Júlio Lobos offered readers a cynical and humorous commentary that plays with the themes of this chapter: "The law exists to be enforced. In Sweden, perhaps. But in Brazil, things are a little different. Nothing pejorative or critical about this finding. Just a question of concepts. For us, the law is an orientation, a trail, a light (sometimes rather dim) that illuminates the path. It is there to be interpreted, not obeyed blindly, [and] according to the viewpoint of each one, of course. After all, no one is necessarily obligated to follow all trails, and if a light is too bright, you disconnect the electricity and you're through with it. The Greeks called this praxis."[81]

five

The Enigma of Brazilian Labor Law

Vargas and the Government's Bureaucratic *Trabalhista* Empire, 1950–1954

For many, the fatal flaw of the Brazilian labor law system has been the chasm between what was proclaimed on paper and the reality of what was practiced in the workplace and accepted in the labor courts. If we assume, however, that the architects of the labor laws were not acting in good faith, this gap can instead be seen as the key to the CLT's survival and the source of its enduring success. If the CLT had been vigorously enforced, profound conflict would have ensued between the government bureaucracy and powerful private interests. By inconsistently enforcing the law, however, government and judicial officials gained at least the tolerance of these groups by acting on their behalf, even if the system was not established at their behest.

Such a hypothesis speaks directly to a crucial issue clearly formulated by Maria Célia Paoli. To grasp how the new "legal guarantees were actually incorporated in[to] workers' daily lives," she suggested in 1988, it is necessary to understand "the extent of political confidence they could actually have in the State."[1] This chapter examines to what extent, if any, workers could have confidence in Getúlio Vargas in the early 1950s. This is a vital question in light of the work of some recent scholars, who have credited Vargas with good intentions and a substantive reformist project of *trabalhismo*. Are such claims convincing, or do they largely reflect Vargas's rhetoric, which generally exceeded what can legitimately be claimed on behalf of his deeds?[2] The answer can best be found, this chapter suggests, in Vargas's labor relations record between his return to the presidency in the 1950 elections and his suicide in office on 24 August 1954.

Trabalhismo: On the Campaign Trail and in Office

During the 1950 election campaign, the sixty-seven-year-old Vargas visited seventy-seven cities in twenty states in his drive for vindication through a return to the presidency, this time by the popular vote rather than a coup d'état. In the complicated lead-up to the four-way election, Vargas emerged as the joint candidate of the PTB, which had been founded in 1945 by MTIC officials, and the Partido Social Progresista (Social Progressive Party), a regional party controlled by São Paulo's governor, Adhemar de Barros). While campaigning, Vargas renewed his image as the patron of the labor laws and proclaimed the continuity of his efforts to protect working people. Those "who construct the nation's prosperity in the factories" and other workplaces, he said, had for too long been disinherited, "unarmed and defenseless victims of the greed of some and the oppression of others." Even his opponents, he declared, "cannot deny the reality of the labor legislation of my government," and the Ministry of Labor, created in 1930, had always acted decidedly, directly, and promptly.[3]

Vargas dismissed his political opponents as partisans of the "old parties under new labels," intransigent defenders of "political democracy, based on laws that assure their enjoyment of the privilege of oppressing and exploiting the labor of others." Brazilian *trabalhismo*, by contrast, fought against those who would sacrifice social equality "in the name of political freedom." As in the Estado Novo's propaganda, Vargas cited the abundance of legal guarantees, rights, and regulations he had bestowed on the *povo*. Yet he also hailed, as befitted the new electoral environment, the workers' status as "free citizens" whose support would help him to achieve the reforms needed for national development. "In its best ideological meaning," he went on, *trabalhismo* stands for "a social democracy, a harmonious conciliation of individualism with socialism, through the surpassing of both in an original, fruitful, and typically Brazilian solution."[4]

Visiting Brazil's manufacturing heartland in São Paulo, Vargas hailed the "impetuous force of industrial development," which had not only made the state unique in South America but had "produced the largest proletarian concentration in the country." He also criticized the perversion of the CLT system at the hands of President Eurico Dutra, the Estado Novo military strongman who had helped oust Vargas from power. Expressing frank sympathy for wage earners, he asked why the minimum wage had not increased in the five years since he had left office. And why did workers every day lose the legal benefits to which they were entitled solely because they arrived a few minutes late to their jobs (*assiduidade integral*)? And had not the labor ministry become an obstacle when unionized workers sought to elect their own leaders? Under Dutra, when workers voted for a union president who did not "please the government," it intervened. Indeed, why were unions "violently gagged whenever they demanded their most sacred rights?"[5]

Having passed his years out of power on his ranch in Rio Grande do Sul, Vargas also spoke movingly about the "precarious situation of rural workers." The men and women of the countryside, he said, lacked the protective laws and material benefits of their urban counterparts. Agricultural laborers also needed minimum wages, job tenure, medical care, insurance, and pensions. Only "reactionary spirits" imbued with semifeudal concepts, he declared, would resist such "profoundly just and humane measures."[6] In his memoirs, Vargas's vice presidential running mate, João Café Filho, who had never been close to Vargas, noted the radical nature of such statements. At the end of one speech in Londrina, Café Filho recounted, Vargas even improvised words "of a socializing tenor, with threats against capitalists and landowners."[7]

Despite Vargas's big heart and splendid speechwriters, he could do little, in immediate and concrete terms, to resolve Brazil's enormous problems of rural misery and backwardness. He did, however, face a number of practical issues regarding trade unions and urban workers that could be addressed when he returned to the presidential palace. Labor had, after all, been given rhetorical prominence during a presidential campaign in which Vargas, the man above political parties, dreamed only of the future of the nation and its people. On this most pressing front, in January 1951 Vargas appointed national PTB president Danton Coelho as minister of labor, industry, and commerce.

A *gaúcho* like Vargas, Coelho had been a revolutionary in 1930, became São Paulo's chief of police in 1932, and held a series of foreign economic and

diplomatic positions between 1940 and 1947. During the political articula-
tions leading up to 1950, Coelho was one of Vargas's key political emissaries,
serving as a "courier pigeon" between the ex-president and the armed forces.
The "right friend in uncertain times" (*amigo certo das horas incertas*), with
close personal ties to Vargas, Coelho was in a strong position to assume the
leadership of the MTIC, although he was forced out of office after only nine
months because of PTB factionalism. In the words of a ministry insider José
Gomes Talarico, Coelho was an "eminently political man, a loyal and proper
man, but one without any experience in social, in union life, without any
strong attachment to the labor question. He was above all a political man,"
not a *trabalhista* or unionist; as such, he was ill-suited to serve as minister of
labor.[8]

As labor minister, Coelho's top priority was to increase the PTB's share of
MTIC jobs and influence, which had been in the hands of Vargas's *dutrista*
enemies. Thus, Coelho's first moves responded to both the political impera-
tives of the moment and Vargas's long-standing hostility to political parties.[9]
Whether as dictator or as democratically elected president, Vargas had always
preferred organized interest groups organically linked to the state, which
could be said—at least theoretically—to operate beyond the realm of petty
party politics (*politicagem*). His postwar experience with a sharply divided and
fractious PTB only reinforced his personalist stance above parties, leading him,
as in 1943–45, to once again visualize the mobilization of workers through
state-recognized unions. Rather than linking workers to the PTB, the objective
would be to increase the number of unionized workers and to channel their
energies into the labor ministry and its associated trade unions, labor courts,
retirement funds, and social welfare agencies, whose jobs and resources were
to be controlled by the PTB.[10]

The popular dimension of Vargas's strategy would stand or fall in terms of
the relationship between workers and the state through the government's
bureaucratic *trabalhista* empire. Success on the government side of this project was imaginable, if difficult. Politically connected *empreguismo* was already widespread within the MTIC during the Dutra administration, and jobs
and money were a powerful and recognized currency in Brazilian politics.
Thousands of jobs were at stake, including exalted positions held by well-paid
bacharéis, a vast array of *funcionários públicos* (secretaries, file clerks, and so
on), and an assortment of drivers and general flunkies (in addition to the
common *servidores* who filled janitorial and other low-level jobs). Hundreds
of MTIC appointees could and would be fired in 1951 as part of Coelho's quest

to root out Dutra loyalists as well as those who had failed to do all they should on behalf of Vargas's campaign.[11] Yet the government's complex bureaucratic, juridical, and labor union empire continued to be marked by an anarchic free-for-all that involved unconditional *ministerialistas* (those who automatically and shamelessly sought the favor of whoever was in power in the ministry), newly appointed friends of top MTIC officials or PTB politicians (as likely to be enemies as allies of each other), and an array of professionals, including lawyers and judges, who survived by playing the same game. The MTIC's internal dynamic was governed by an exacting if well-established Brazilian etiquette of patron-client relations, including backbiting yes-men and shameless "carpet divers" practiced at the rituals of submission to superiors.[12]

Coelho's most immediate goal was to remedy a humiliating concession that had been made to São Paulo's industrialists and politicians after the end of the Estado Novo. In 1946, the Dutra administration had agreed to delegate the MTIC's labor relations responsibilities in the state of São Paulo to an agency of the state government, the Departamento Estadual do Trabalho (DET). Available to no other state, this agreement meant that the ministry lacked authority over or voice in a manufacturing region responsible for more than half of the country's industrial production and employment. Moreover, this aberrant situation was unconstitutional under paragraph 2 of article 36 of the 1946 constitution, which granted exclusive jurisdiction to the central government. As Henry S. Hammond, the U.S. labor attaché, noted, "The record of the State Labor Department in the past has been substantially anti-labor," with its leaders having "frequently been chosen from among the ranks of industrialists, apparently for political reasons." The result was not surprising: the DET "has not always shown the impartiality expected of it in enforcing the labor laws, at least insofar as employer infractions are concerned."[13]

While *paulista* union leaders hailed the move to establish a DRT, few doubted that Coelho's fundamental objectives were driven by calculations of politics and *empreguismo*. As labor minister and PTB president, Coelho's revocation of the agreement would enhance his and his party's political capital. In returning responsibilities to the MTIC, the DET jobs would no longer be distributed solely at the discretion of the governor of São Paulo, a matter of some delicacy given Adhemar's role in Vargas's election. Yet the opportunity to control 1,422 government jobs in one of Brazil's richest and most populous states was too good to pass up.[14] Although it took some time, the transfer was finally legalized in September 1952; the labor ministry representative for São Paulo since 1950, Enio Lepage, become the new DRT.[15]

If the São Paulo raid was an MTIC success, the government's desired outcome on the workers' side faced far more formidable obstacles. After gaining strength during 1945–47, the trade unions had been radically repressed under Dutra, and their legitimacy and mass ties with rank-and-file workers were fragile at best in 1950. The labor movement's capacity for even a controlled mobilization was virtually nonexistent, and the reestablishment of government credibility would have to start with lower-level union leaders. It would take time before the MTIC could even begin to think about mobilizing the workers whose interests had been trampled. Despite high inflation in the late 1940s, for example, no minimum wage increases had occurred during Dutra's four-year administration.

Dutra's MTIC had also intervened in almost all the major unions in 1947 and had refused to authorize elections that might threaten the control of the government's appointed juntas (whose members often practiced gross corruption). When union elections did start to be held in 1950, they were conducted in an irregular fashion to prevent the election of unsound elements, which included communists as well as the more pressing problem of ambitious individuals without radical political commitments who might threaten the famous *pelegos*, with their good-paying jobs in union federations and confederations and plum appointments as class judges. To maintain tight control, the Dutra government had reestablished an Estado Novo–era requirement that candidates for union office had to present an *atestado de ideologia* (certificate of ideology) issued by the Social and Political Order Department (Departamento de Ordem Política Social, or DOPS).

The working-class targets of the *atestado de ideologia* were individuals who were *fichados* (whose names appeared in DOPS files as subversives). Some were publicly known communists (*queimados*), whereas a few were noncommunist leftists. Another group consisted of independent-minded *trabalhistas* or even Catholics who had clashed with a labor ministry official or the police. Some workers ended up as *fichados* because their employers had sent denunciations to the DOPS (a routine occurrence); others had made trouble in union meetings.[16] All in all, the Brazilian labor scene was a McCarthyite world of *policialismo* (repression), stratagems, *jeitos*, and *pistolão*. The arbitrariness was compounded by the multitude of decentralized and competing schemes of surveillance and informing (*dedo-durismo*) run by various branches of the police, government ministries, factory owners, and even industry-supported agencies such as the Social Service of Industry (Serviço Social da Indústria, or SESI).[17]

Vargas meets with José Gonçalves, president of the Port Service Workers' Union in Santos, 1952. (Courtesy of the Centro de Memoria Sindical e Arquivos de Santos)

To begin to remedy the situation, Coelho had to restore a semblance of internal electoral legitimacy within the official unions. The decision to hold union elections was followed by a May 1951 announcement that candidates no longer needed to present *atestados de ideologia* from the DOPS. (The law to this effect was issued in September 1952.)[18] This vital liberalizing measure can be directly traced to Vargas's hand. Unlike most of what we know about his views on labor, which is based on published speeches, this specific shift in labor ministry policy can be directly tied to a handwritten *bilhete* (note) from Vargas to his speechwriter, Lourival Fontes. Thus, Vargas's words and guidance can be compared to the final written text of his 1952 May Day address.

This May Day speech, only Vargas's second since his election, occurred four months before the final *atestado de ideologia* decree. His words clearly sanctioned the forthcoming shift in policy, influenced in part by the fact that the enemy persecuted under Dutra was just as likely to have been *getulista* as communist (although Vargas took the suppression of communists for granted). While Vargas viewed electoral democracy as dubious at best, his words recognized that an elemental democratic principle was needed to guarantee representative leadership within unions.[19] At the same time, abolishing the *atestado* requirement did not directly cost the government or employers any money, at least in an immediate sense, so the likely political gain clearly outweighed any

TABLE 2: Comparison of Preparatory *Bilhete* and the Final
Text of Getúlio Vargas's 1952 May Day Speech

Vargas's Preparatory Bilhete *to Speechwriter Lourival Fontes*	*Final Text of Vargas's 1952 May Day Address*
When I talk about leaders of the workers, I am not referring to political representatives but to representatives of the interests, aspirations, and needs of the classes—wages, housing, assistance, the well-being of the classes. These must be represented by their unions.	When I talk about leaders of the workers, I am not referring to political representatives but to those who defend real interests, aspirations, and needs of the classes, demanding wages, housing, assistance, well-being. Worker organizations should be represented by their unions.
Union elections need to be free and freely and effectively undertaken and freely recognized. These aspirations should be attended to through the labor ministry.	I have decided, for that reason, on the most complete freedom of union elections, which should be freely undertaken and freely recognized.
I know that your efforts are often paralyzed by the bureaucratic machinery. Ministers of Labor themselves frequently approve of the obstacles created for your organizations.	I know that your efforts have been paralyzed many times by the bureaucratic machine.
True leaders of the working classes, dedicated and full of abnegation, are at times unjustly accused of being communists to remove them from electoral competitions in the unions.	True leaders of the working classes, dedicated and full of abnegation, were often unjustly accused of being communists so that they could be removed from electoral competitions in the unions.
I receive your complaints, and I recognize that these accusations are unjust.	I have received your complaints, and today I understand that many of these accusations are unfounded. The fault lies, in these cases, with the Ministry of Labor itself, which, on more than a few occasions, has made unionization difficult [and] removed sincere leaders to render important those who serve as its instruments but who have never represented the opinion of the class. This will be corrected.
I have confidence in the workers and they should have confidence in me.	Just as I have confidence in the workers, they can have confidence in me.

Sources: L. Fontes and Carneiro, *Face Final*, 99–100; Getúlio Vargas, "Comemoração do Dia do Trabalho: Discurso do Presidente," 5 May 1952, attachment to U.S. Embassy, M1487, roll 7, Department of State Records.

disadvantages. Moreover, the *atestado* decree was itself not as liberal as it seemed on the surface.[20] The fine print still banned those who professed "ideologies incompatible with the institutions or interests of the nation," but candidates for union office now needed only to file a notarized statement that they did not hold such ideas.[21] The responsibility for policing the anticommunist ban had been shifted to the MTIC's anticommunist specialists and away from external bodies, the many state-level DOPS, each of which had its own political agenda.

Vargas also used his May Day 1952 speech to formally present Labor Minister José de Segadas Vianna, who had been appointed the previous September and would serve until June 1952. Segadas was praised by name as a capable and intelligent man with deep knowledge of labor legislation. As the president said, Segadas Vianna possessed vast experience, having helped to draft the CLT and having served as head of the MTIC's National Labor Department. A key PTB founder in 1945, Segadas Vianna was a powerful political figure within the national party, a federal deputy, and the boss of the fractious PTB section in Rio de Janeiro in the late 1940s.

As a well-connected ministry veteran, Segadas Vianna's appointment brought greater legal and bureaucratic professionalism to the MTIC's operation.[22] As minister of labor, he sought to restore *getulista* political unity to the state labor apparatus, its various satellites, and the unions. Segadas Vianna sought to build a powerful and relatively independent position for himself, although he arrived, in Talarico's words, with the "musty smell of the [Estado Novo] dictatorship" at its heyday.[23] Segadas Vianna's well-known authoritarian disposition gave a cynical aura to Vargas's May Day pledge that the government and the minister would "definitively guarantee union liberty."[24]

At the end of his first business meeting with Vargas, the new labor minister issued a statement that called, among other things, for a common front against all "ideologies contrary to the Brazilian traditions of social peace."[25] Although boilerplate *getulista* and Cold War rhetoric, Segadas Vianna's statement offered a clear reminder that the MTIC was not about to embark on an indiscriminate liberalization, much less an opening to the Left. Like Vargas, Segadas Vianna did not intend to allow leftist enemies in the labor movement to gain strength just because the government was searching for immediate political advantage. Indeed, his administration became famous for using the resources of the well-funded Technical Commission for Union Orientation not only to control unions but also to mount a secret service operation in each DRT.[26] Segadas Vianna described the commission's role "as a kind of SNI," a reference to the post-1964 military regime's much-feared National Intelligence Service. He also recalled with humor the routine harassment carried out by one administrator in the ministry's Division for Union Organization. Whenever he received a report from a union whose leader was somewhat leftist, he would cause trouble. In the final instance, the administrator would reject the paperwork, saying, "The comma is turned to the right instead of to the left. Come back later for more information."[27]

In truth, during the first two and a half years of his term, President Vargas and his labor ministers did little on behalf of workers or their unions. Within the MTIC, this scenario of neglect was firmly anchored in the authoritarian top-down methods of the Estado Novo era. Looked at more broadly, this stand-pat approach was part of Vargas's overarching goal of achieving political stability and conciliation with his conservative opponents, even at the expense of any ideals of social reform.[28] Once in office, Vargas even failed to fulfill his modest pledges to reform what had become antilabor MTIC bureaucracies in industrial states including São Paulo. While a policy of neglect was viable at the end of a period of popular defeat and quiescence, the political calculus shifted decisively as a result of the dramatic events of March 1953 in the city of São Paulo. Although Vargas had received overwhelming support there in 1950, a little-known state deputy, Jânio Quadros, swept the election for mayor (*prefeito*) with 67 percent of the vote, defeating the candidate backed by both Vargas and São Paulo's governor, Lucas Nogueira Garcez. On the heels of this memorable campaign, which launched the populist Quadros on his path to the presidency, a mass strike wave unfolded in the metropolitan region, eventually encompassing between 250,000 and 300,000 workers. As observers, including Segadas Vianna, would later admit, only at that point did Vargas finally offer labor something more than mere words.[29]

As the 1953 labor crisis unfolded in São Paulo, Vargas had two April meetings with Segadas Vianna in which the labor minister presented the president with two confidential reports that offered a dismal portrait of the government's labor relations system in São Paulo. These richly detailed memorandums were written by Talarico, a well-connected PTB journalist who served as the labor ministry's chief press officer.[30] Talarico's forcefully stated opinions were based on interviews with noncommunist trade unionists, politicians, and government officials during a recent trip to São Paulo.[31]

Although U.S. labor attaché Irving Salert judged Talarico "an active and well informed anti-communist," Talarico's reports to Segadas Vianna and Vargas accorded communist agitation a relatively minor role among the factors that had led to the strikes. First and foremost, Talarico wrote, the strikes stemmed from the workers' obvious economic difficulties, which were compounded by the fact that workers and labor leaders felt deceived by a discredited labor justice system.[32] Talarico placed a significant share of the blame for this state of affairs on the shoulders of Lepage, who had served as the MTIC's representative for São Paulo since the start of the Vargas administration.[33] Talarico portrayed the São Paulo DRT as a morass of corruption, conscious trickery, and administrative inefficiency. Although it was a federal agency, he said, it paid little if any attention to enforcing the labor laws or to supporting the trade unions. In addition, Talarico strongly criticized the DRT's close ties with the DOPS as well as Lepage's generally abusive and high-handed behavior toward labor leaders.[34]

The indictment of the São Paulo DRT by Talarico's informants was wide ranging, detailed, and passionate, particularly because many *paulista* unionists had invested great hopes in the transfer of authority from the DET to the DRT. Instead, the DRT operated "more as an organ of police repression than an organ that is zealous in its execution of the labor laws." In addition to failing to appear for scheduled negotiating sessions, Talarico reported, Lepage had ignored hundreds of petitions, complaints, and requests from labor unions. As a result, according to textile leader Nelson Rusticci, a noncommunist, the DRT had become "an unpopular organ, even one hated by the workers, since it places itself on the employers' side and not in an impartial position equidistant from the two sides."[35]

In summarizing the report, Salert went further than Talarico, suggesting that Lepage might be "in the secret employ of the São Paulo Federation of Industry." Salert also suggested that Lepage had specifically consented to the Siderúrgica Alberti metalworking firm's "complete disregard for the labor and safety laws."[36] Yet the most telling details offered by Talarico dramatized the sense of humiliation felt by the elected leaders of tens of thousands of workers as a result of treatment by the DRT, the police, and the industrialists. The employers, union officials complained, had mocked them during negotiating sessions at the DRT during the March Strike of the 300,000: "Weren't you the ones who elected this government?" "Why don't you stop moaning at us and go complain to President Vargas?" "Why don't you go to the Catete [presidential palace] and let the head of state resolve your problems?"[37]

Segadas Vianna approved of the São Paulo DRT's repressive posture in declaring the strikes illegal and defended Lepage from what the minister said was exaggerated criticism.[38] Such behavior, after all, was very much in line with Segadas Vianna's emphasis on anticommunist intelligence and his long-standing belief in dealing firmly with the trade unions. Segadas Vianna's response was to plan a national campaign to remove "all known communist agents from the labor unions of Brazil,"[39] by which he meant a purge of any labor leaders who were at all daring or independent. (At that time, only a handful of communists had made their way into top leadership positions, although more would do so a few years later.) With new labor crises looming, Segadas Vianna was unimaginative, possessing only excuses and no alternatives other than more of the same: *metendo pau* (applying the stick) without the carrot.

During his April meetings with Vargas, Segadas Vianna ignored Talarico's concrete suggestions about changes in the São Paulo DRT. Rather, the labor minister told the president that rising popular discontent required a rooting out of "notorious communists" and the detention of communist agents whenever they appeared during strikes. Segadas Vianna also shared his plans to make an example of the Rio garment workers' union: "If this legal process I have instituted is not interfered with by the PTB, I will then know that I have a free hand in dealing with the communists in the trade unions and other social entities of Brazil."[40] In interviews conducted during the 1980s, Segadas Vianna vigorously defended his repressive stance toward the 1953 strikes, using highly cynical language: "I have a certain fetishism for the law," he insisted with no apparent irony, and, when confronted with illegal strikes, "a man of the law" had no choice but to propose that the draconian National Security Law be used against the workers.[41] As he remarked frankly in 1987, "Police repression against labor movements is a tradition in Brazil. [There are] more violent times and more discreet periods," but when the unions are "in the hands of the communists, we beat them up." The event that sealed his fall from power in mid-1953 was his proposal to draft striking maritime workers into the military, an idea Vargas rejected after PTB President João Goulart deemed it impolitic.[42]

As his discontent with Vargas grew, Segadas Vianna complained to Salert about both the president and Segadas Vianna's enemies within the PTB. In April 1953, the labor minister reported that "the President kept dozing off into short cat naps. He is old and tired and cannot possibly believe that he is losing ground among the Brazilian working class." Segadas Vianna also skewered his rival, Goulart, a favorite of Vargas, for "deliberately giving the President misinformation" about his popularity while providing "secret and substantial encouragement to the small but effective communist leaderships."[43]

The Power and Limits of Rhetoric and Style

Vargas's willingness to tolerate labor ministers who countenanced such abysmal labor relations conditions demands that we sharpen our judgments about Vargas, *trabalhismo*, and populism. At the very least, it demonstrates that sensitivity to the interests of workers and trade unionists ranked low in terms of Vargas's policy priorities, at least after his return to power. It also strongly suggests that historians should be wary of treating Vargas as if he were primarily a consistent and coherent social reformer. Such naïveté could only lead to the false conclusion that populists such as Vargas were prolabor in an active, intentional sense rather than that they were forced to act in a prolabor fashion in certain political conjunctures by a combination of self-interest and pressure from below.[44]

Mass action at the ballot box and in the streets in 1953 led Vargas to replace Segadas Vianna with a wealthy thirty-five-year-old rancher, João "Jango" Goulart, who was the son of Vargas's neighbor and ally in Rio Grande do Sul. As Maria Celina Soares D'Araújo notes, the inexperienced Goulart rose to national prominence in the PTB precisely because he was "an inexpressive member of parliament," an unknown in national politics who owed his political career to his neighbor, Vargas. When Vargas chose Goulart to head the PTB, he was overwhelmingly elected because he was so weak that the warring party factions did not perceive him as threatening. At the time of his appointment, it was commonly recognized that Goulart knew "precious little about the labor movement," although most observers granted that he was "a very ambitious man" with an engaging personality.[45]

The 1953 ministerial shake-up that replaced Segadas Vianna with Goulart has always been central to overall interpretations of Vargas's second presidency. The reorganization has been depicted in radically different ways by both contemporary observers and later scholars. "During his second government, in 1954," wrote Maria Emília A. T. Lima, "Vargas became increasingly progressive and even revolutionary."[46] Armando Boito Jr. spoke of the state bureaucracy as having opted "for a strategy of radicalizing populist politics" in 1954.[47] This leftist weakness for a mythic vision of the populist era is well illustrated by historian Joel Wolfe. After quoting stirring words from Vargas and referring to Goulart's appointment, Wolfe wrote that "Brazil's workers finally had a voice in the cabinet. Although the new minister was Vargas's protégé and not from the labor movement, he did in fact represent workers' issues within the federal bureaucracy." Going even further, Wolfe claimed that "the Ministry of Labor finally functioned as an advocate for workers."[48]

Such fulsome praise for Goulart (as well as for the labor ministry) must be carefully qualified to avoid exaggerating the nature of Goulart's contribution between 15 June 1953 and 22 February 1954. Goulart's actions during his short tenure were more favorable to workers than were the actions of his predecessors (although Morvan Dias de Figueiredo, Coelho, and Segadas Vianna had not set a particularly high standard in this regard). And more importantly, Goulart did champion the doubling of the legal minimum wage, a measure that directly and materially met an important working-class demand. Yet the ferocity of the antigetulist attacks on these actions, which led to Goulart's ouster, should not lead us to credit him with far stronger actions and deeper commitments than he actually held (even putting aside the temporary and largely symbolic nature of the wage increase as a result of high inflation and the deterioration in the value of the minimum wage since the previous increase in 1951). It would be an error, in other words, if Goulart were presented as if the PTB were a European social democratic party (or even a pale imitation of one).[49]

In her analysis, D'Araújo properly criticizes those who present the 1953 cabinet shuffle as a decisive shift to the left by Vargas, an interpretation favored by many contemporaries and later leftist and rightist scholars.[50] Lucília Delgado admits that the 1953 shift was not a "reorientation to the left" but nonetheless argues that Goulart's appointment and his style of action as minister represented "not just an alteration in the style of government–working class relations" but a "return to and deepening of a populist strategy."[51] In this context, Goulart as labor minister did demonstrate a more prolabor disposition, especially in terms of his accessibility, informal style of interaction, and openness in his meetings with union leaders. Goulart's discursive posture also differed from that of Segadas Vianna, although this more likely reflects Goulart's lack of bureaucratic experience relative to Segadas Vianna, a lower-middle-class man who made his entire career as an operator (*um homen esperto*) and had maneuvered his way upward within the web of patron-client ties that characterized the 1930s and 1940s.

Moreover, Goulart's expansive personal style also reflected the independence of judgment and buoyant self-confidence derived from his status as a wealthy rancher, a rural man of power, a born patron. In particular, Goulart's discourse was marked by an openly paternalistic posture.[52] As Aurélio de Limeira Tejo, a journalist from Rio Grande do Sul, remarked in 1957, "Jango's

O DEMAGOGO «JANGO» DESFILA.

A 1953 communist cartoon expresses skepticism about Vargas's new labor minister, João "Jango" Goulart. The caption reads, "The Demagogue 'Jango' Parades," while the drum is labeled "The Labor Ministry" (*Notícias de Hoje* [São Paulo], 20 August 1953).

laborism [*trabalhismo*] is at bottom sentimental. He was already concerned with the problems and needs of the common people [*povo*] around him, even before he became a populist leader. He simply transferred his concerns about the effects of economic inequality in São Borja [site of his ranch and that of Vargas] to the nation as a whole, at first romantically—wishing that the state would perform the same patriarchal role that he did in his small world on the southern border."[53]

In a July 1953 speech, for example, Goulart attacked his opponents as advocates of military coups who sought to keep workers under "the yoke of economic oppression. . . . They don't understand," he went on, how a labor minister "could speak with spontaneity [with workers] and establish ties of affection with creatures of a humble condition." Or, as Goulart put it in a 1972 interview, he had tried "to give the workers real class consciousness and self-respect," a statement that would never have figured in Segadas Vianna's more authoritarian, "realistic" rhetoric.[54] Yet these rhetorical differences between

Goulart and Segadas Vianna should not be overemphasized: both men admitted the reality of nonenforcement of the labor laws and both claimed to stand for the enforcement of such measures.

Even a cursory examination of Goulart's brief interlude in the ministry also demonstrates that there were clear limits to how far he was willing to take his paternalistic prolabor discourse. Goulart was appointed on the eve of a ten-day national strike by one hundred thousand maritime workers demanding employer compliance with laws that benefited them. Paralyzing port operations and three hundred Brazilian merchant ships, the June 1953 stoppage was headed by a dynamic new leadership with strong leftist leanings and mass legitimacy. Vargas's appointment of Goulart just prior to the strike revealed the president's intention to mediate the conflict in an effort to rebuild support for the PTB among working people. Goulart involved himself directly with the strike negotiations and offered personal recognition to the new militant leadership. Goulart's aim, notes Dennis Barsted, was to increase "the political base of the getulista faction of the government by organizing the support of the working class, but without permitting strong autonomous nuclei of power" to gain excessive strength.[55]

In the aftermath of the strike, Goulart and his allies in the MTIC worked closely with losing factions among the maritime workers while seeking to divide and undermine the militants. The opportunity to establish the limits of the acceptable came in October 1953, when the militants called a second national strike out of frustration at the nonfulfillment of Goulart's June accord. While the labor minister took a convenient leave from his ministerial duties to travel to the Northeast, his substitute oversaw a vigorous repression that smashed the strike by seizing the unions, arresting the leaders, and breaking up mass marches. In the aftermath, the strike's key leader, Emílio Bonfante, criticized the naïveté that led them to act as if they lived in a democratic environment with rights: "We looked upon the law and the constitution as sacred things, just like religious people view the Bible or the Koran."[56]

Salert, the U.S. labor attaché, recounted a fall 1953 incident in which Goulart signed a letter, drafted by his subordinates, that invited the unions to collaborate with the government in the enforcement of the labor laws.[57] Within twenty-four hours of the first employer criticism, however, Goulart rescinded the letter, leaving his subordinates, Salert reported, disappointed by his "lack of courage."[58] At a minimum, this incident suggests that any vision of Goulart in 1953 as being strongly prolabor must be tempered. Moreover, Salert's 1953 memo about the rescinded letter also recounted a story that repeats a common theme in Brazilian political and juridical culture. Without comment, Salert reported that despite rescinding his letter, Goulart had nonetheless agreed to publish under his own name an article drafted by the same individuals responsible for the ill-fated letter to trade unionists. The article in question celebrated the fact that thirty years earlier, Brazil had been the first country to formally adopt an ILO recommendation that countries enforce their labor laws.[59] As his predecessor, Sagadas Vianna, observed, "The ILO always had enormous importance in Brazil even though we never fulfilled [the organization's labor] treaties and conventions."[60] Goulart's discourse was thus in line with the broader pattern of elite statecraft in Brazil: paternalistic talk of gifts, advanced rhetoric not linked to consistent action, and an ongoing disposition to substitute symbolism and speeches for concrete actions and benefits (especially "for the Englishmen to see," as in the case of the ILO). The CLT system so closely identified with Vargas, Goulart, and the PTB ultimately reproduced, in yet another arena, the enduring "dichotomy between the Brazil of the law [*Brasil legal*] and the real Brazil [*Brasil real*]" that characterized a lawless society permeated by a surfeit of juridical discourse.[61]

"The Myth Takes the Place of the Man": Vargas's Suicide and the Labor Law in Popular Song and Poetry

The leftist interpretations of *trabalhismo* are largely driven by the political implications of Goulart's subsequent trajectory as vice president in the late 1950s and then briefly as a reformist president whom the military ousted in 1964. The personalistic mystique that was thus built up around his name owed more—as contemporary observers suggested—to the attacks of his opponents than to his political capacity and talents. "The laborite [*trabalhista*] chief is not at all the conspirator, as he is painted by his adversaries," observed *gaúcho* journalist Limo Tejo in 1957. "It is the circumstances that conspire in his favor," not the reverse.[62] Yet Goulart's rise and fall as labor minister under Vargas in 1953–54 continues to be seen as a preview of Goulart's later fate, and his credentials as standard-bearer of the Left in 1964 are thus read backward onto the Vargas presidency of the early 1950s. Doing so, however, underplays the "strongly conservative component of the *getulista* project" at that time.[63] And this brings us back to the question of the meaning, depth, and limits of Vargas's discourse during his second presidency.

Confronted with the chasm between Vargas's words and his deeds, one might assume, as do many leftist proponents of the *trabalhista* interpretation, that the progressive Goulart, Vargas's heir apparent, spoke for him while serving as minister of labor. It may be unconvincing to cite the denial of this equation by Vargas's longtime associate and speechwriter, Lourival Fontes, but the evidence of Vargas's *bilhetes* is also clear. Goulart's openness toward labor leaders who encouraged "agitation" irritated Vargas, who, like Segadas Vianna, placed such individuals automatically into the communist category. Indeed, Vargas directly rebuked Goulart in January 1954 and ordered him to "discontinue working with the communists, to cease encouraging mass demonstrations, and to stop helping communists to make substantial gains" in the unions. To contain a threatening militancy, Vargas promulgated a new national security law in January 1954 to punish those who "called or carried out a rally or open-air public meeting" without police authorization. And Goulart's top aides were publicly warning labor leaders in February that the MTIC would "no longer tolerate communists" or their fellow travelers in the labor movement. In a private *bilhete*, Vargas expressed disgust at a strike agitation among doctors, "something unheard of," instigated by communists and "incited by a slanted press." (He asked his aide to tell the publisher of a pro-government newspaper to stop covering the issue.)[64]

As a man of balance and equilibrium, Vargas was put off by the political daring shown by Goulart in championing a 100 percent increase in the minimum wage. In one *bilhete* on the subject, Vargas asked an aide to tell Goulart to "reduce the demands, which were a little much, to their proper dimension." The president felt most comfortable calling on workers to trust him personally while eschewing direct institutional responsibility for the outcome of their struggles. Thus, one *bilhete* emphasized the message that the president understood the need to do something about the high cost of living but that "there is no reason for strikes and disturbances." Workers would "always find me, their eternal friend, ready to assist them in their just struggles. Don't let yourselves be swept up by agitators and disturbers of order." While prepared to indirectly assist in vital cases, President Vargas preferred to avoid direct and public commitments in dealing with striking workers and labor leaders. Leaving himself room to maneuver, his *bilhetes* emphasized that the outcome of worker demands depended on the labor courts, which were independent of the executive branch as a result of the 1946 constitution, a state of affairs he had opposed.[65]

Vargas's election in 1950 helped to guarantee the consolidation of the Populist Republic that would survive until the 1964 military coup. But political analysts of Vargas's second presidency have seldom focused on the lessons learned by the generation of labor activists who lived through this period. How much trust could they have in Vargas, the "father of the poor" and supporter of the humble? The evidence is clear: workers and labor unions most needed Vargas's help at the start of his second presidency in 1951, as they tried to recoup their losses from the Dutra era. Yet they got little if anything from the newly elected president. Workers gained something more, however limited, only during the Goulart interlude, but these gains were prompted by and won as a result of the votes of workers and their mobilizations as they were refracted through the political calculations of populist politicians such as Goulart.

If these conclusions have not been clear to many analysts, the explanation lies in the direct links among the 1953 Strike of the 300,000 in São Paulo, the rise and fall of Goulart, and Vargas's death by his own hand on 24 August 1954. Having returned to power "in the arms of the people" as a result of their votes, Vargas's second government was marked by an accumulation of unmet promises, bourgeoning scandals ("a sea of mud," as it was called), and the botched attempt to assassinate a political enemy that was organized by the chief of Vargas's personal guard. Increasingly isolated in parliamentary, military, and even popular circles, Vargas received an ultimatum from top military officers, who demanded his immediate resignation. His initial response was deceptively subdued, but the denouement was unexpected, and his defiant gesture shocked the nation whose politics he had dominated for twenty-four years. The mass grief and popular anger that appeared in the streets was further intensified by the release of his sentimental and incendiary posthumous message to the Brazilian common people (*povo*).

"After decades of domination and plunder by international economic and financial groups," Vargas wrote in his *carta testamento*, "I made myself chief of an unconquerable revolution" and "instituted a regime of social liberty." But facing "a subterranean campaign of international groups joined with national interests revolting against the regime of workers' guarantees . . . I have fought month after month, day after day, hour after hour, resisting constant, incessant pressures, unceasingly bearing all in silence, forgetting everything and giving of myself in order to defend the people that now fall abandoned. I cannot give you more than my blood." These "birds of prey," he went on, "wish to continue to suck the blood of the Brazilian people," so he had decided to offer up his life: "I choose this means to be with you always. When they humiliate you, you will feel my soul suffering at your side. When hunger knocks at your door, you will feel within you the energy to fight for yourselves and for your children. When you are scorned, my memory will give you the strength to react. My sacrifice will keep you united and my name will be your battle standard."[66]

"To hatred, I reply with forgiveness," begin the memorable final lines of Vargas's *carta testamento*. "And to those who think that they have defeated me, I reply with my victory. I was a slave of the people and today I am freeing myself for eternal life. But this people whose slave I was will no longer be a slave to anyone. My sacrifice will remain forever in your souls and my blood will be the price of your ransom. I fought against the looting of Brazil. I fought against the looting of the people. I have fought bare-chested. The hatred, infamy, and calumny did not defeat my spirit. I have given you my life. Now I offer you my death. Nothing remains. Serenely I take my first step on the road to eternity and I leave life to enter history."[67]

Three and a half hours after the news of Vargas's death was released, the Undersecretary of Labor, João Oliveira Santos, briefed U.S. labor attaché Irving Salert about the grave situation in the country. Vargas's message was "extremely bad," Santos said, although he had stopped its transmission over the Labor Ministry's radio station despite protests by Radio Mauá's pro-Goulart director, Doutel Andrade. The pendulum, Santos concluded, had now swung back in favor of Vargas, especially because "no one wanted his death, not even his most antagonistic foes." With rioting raging in Rio, Santos spoke of his work with the police and military, who were rounding up "communist agitators and pro-Jango elements of the labor movement," while the DRTs appointed by Goulart had been called to Rio to be kept under observation. As Segadas Vianna recalled in 1987, the twenty-four hours leading up to Vargas's burial "was undoubtedly the most emotional spectacle that I have ever seen. Something really hallucinatory, with the common people [povo] crying, . . . really indescribable."[68]

Vargas's grandiose gesture upended the plans of his powerful civilian and military enemies, and his government's recent past was quickly reconfigured by supporters into a post-facto narrative of progress versus reaction, the nation against internal and international enemies. Under these charged conditions, his administration's highly conservative and antipopular policies toward workers were quickly forgotten or passed over, both then and later. Instead, people hailed Goulart as the inheritor of Vargas's *trabalhista* mantle and interpreted Goulart's 1953 resignation as labor minister, forced out because of a military officer's manifesto, in light of the martyrdom of his political patron and *gaúcho* neighbor. Clear political benefits were now to be

Observance of Vargas's death on 24 August 1954 at the headquarters of the Port Service Workers' Union in Santos. The banner reads, "Getúlio Vargas continues alive in the heart of the Brazilian worker." (Courtesy of the Centro de Memoria Sindical e Arquivos de Santos)

reaped from the progressive rhetoric and gestures of Goulart and Vargas, and little was to be gained through critical attention to their far more ambiguous record in terms of labor policy and practice. As historian Cliff Welch has noted, "Vargas's legacy [now] belonged to those who could make the most of it."[69]

A martyr in a Catholic country, Vargas was lionized for his saintliness while his death was rendered an unspeakable crime committed by the enemies of his beloved common people. Whether in chants in the streets, in popular song, or in interviews, the *povo* decried the death of Vargas at the hands of the rich, the powerful, and the foreign. In the words of popular poet Francisco Chagas, Vargas had "won in the revolution, worked for the good of the poor [*pobres*], was hated by the nobles [*nobres*], and came to die for the nation." Another poet, Rodolfo Cavalcanti, declared, "Did Vargas kill himself? No readers, not that! They killed Dr. Getúlio with the arms of betrayal." He had been murdered, the poet went on, by politicians without honor, by the greedy, the vilely ambitious, and the jealous—traitors all.[70] In the renderings offered both by Vargas and by voices from the popular classes, the poor and the workers—the *povo*—had been loyal to Vargas, although this perspective required suppressing the record of the *povo*'s actual silence until after his death during the 1954 crisis.[71] Vargas had been killed not by the little people but rather by the educated (*doutores*), the big shots (*medalhões*), and his many erstwhile friends, men with false hearts who had taken benefits from Vargas and then betrayed their patron.[72]

Yet this flattery of and praise for an ideal, even imaginary, Vargas was by no means new in the discourse of Brazilian urban and rural folk. Indeed, it constituted the sentimental core of the popular *getulismo* that had grown immeasurably during Vargas's years in power. In a 1950s poem by a black shantytown dweller from Minas Gerais, Carolina Maria de Jesus, Vargas "was the pride of our people [*gente*]." Jesus, who would become a world-famous diarist of São Paulo favela life in the 1960s, hailed Vargas as "heroic and potent, a great national soul." Indeed, she declared that Vargas "should have been president since the time of Cabral," who discovered Brazil in 1500. Before Vargas, she went on, "we were an inhibited *povo*, apathetic and without action," but he provided a push. "He took the timidness out of the worker [*operário*], gave him support and protection, and invited him to collaborate in the progress of the nation." Four years after Vargas's death, Jesus recorded in her diary of favela life a conversation with Sérgio, "a one hundred percent black [*preto*]," who had been fired by a bus company before he could finish a second year's employment. Although offered some sort of indemnification as provided by the labor law, he complained "that now the bosses don't want to permit their employees to complete years and years in house" (thus avoiding still larger indemnities). "I told him," Jesus said, "that in Getúlio's time, there weren't such messes [*marmelada*]. He agreed that Getúlio's absence is already being felt by the worker."[73]

Orígenes Lessa has noted that rural nordestino folk poets also praised Vargas for "his love for the little ones, for those without help." The labor legislation and "its continued affirmation and development," Lessa emphasized, served as the symbolic core for both praise before and lamentations after Vargas's death. It was "the tyranny and boss rule [*mandonismo*] of those who are 'noble' that Getúlio combated with his labor legislation," Lessa went on, citing examples of *cordel* poems that were published, likely with funds provided by Vargas's political supporters. A 29 August 1950 poem, "The Candidacy of Getúlio Vargas," written and published by Delarme Monteiro da Silva of Juazeiro, Ceará, uncritically echoed all of the most exaggerated propaganda from the Estado Novo period: "Today the man who works to serve his boss knows that he has vacations, good pay and, when disabled by age, receives his pension." The contrast, however, was made clear: before Vargas, the worker "received only kicks and beatings as vacation."[74]

This type of fawning flattery (*bajulação*) of powerful men is ubiquitous within the discourses that circulated among the less powerful, even when these works were not paid for. Thus, the DOPS surveillance files for the state of São Paulo included a December 1948 handout distributed among chemical workers in São Miguel Paulista, in greater São Paulo. (Each reader was encouraged to "make five copies to send to your most patriotic friends.") Modeled after the "Our Father" prayer, the "Prayer of a Getulista" began, "I believe in Getúlio Vargas, all powerful, creator of the LABOR LAWS. I believe in Rio Grande do Sul, in their son, our patron. He was born of a saintly mother" and will "judge General Dutra and his ministers. I believe in his return to the Catete Palace" as president. "Amen."[75]

In recent years, increasing attention has been paid to these types of source materials, especially the thousands of letters that supplicants sent to Vargas while he was president. Some observers have seen the mindless praise and simpleminded affirmations that fill such documents as expressions of an authentic political culture or outlook of the working and popular classes, even if these traits embarrass intellectuals. Along these lines, these scholars tend to emphasize Vargas's legitimacy as a popular leader while rejecting criticism as the work of arrogant elites, whether communists, leftists, or merely intellectuals. Jorge Ferreira uses this posture to right a perceived imbalance in the vision of the Vargas era that originated during the days of the New Left, the corporatist consensus, and Francisco Weffort.[76] However, Ferreira's analysis of this discourse seems at times to unwittingly lead the reader toward a reproduction of older dichotomous visions that Ferreira rejects: the authentically and enthusiastically *getulista povo* versus the deluded and brainwashed *povo* that parroted regime propaganda.

Evidence drawn from Lessa's study of *cordel*, however, suggests that caution is needed before equating discursive tactics such as *bajulação* with the political imaginary of popular actors, especially in a society based on patron-client relations. After all, Carolina Maria de Jesus also wrote a poem praising *paulista* Washington Luis, the president whom Vargas overthrew. In particular, Lessa cites another poem by Delarme Monteiro da Silva, "Getúlio Vargas, Pride of Brazil," that praises a "family bonus" promised by Vargas's regime although the bonus was never effectively implemented. As Lessa suggests, popular responses to "all of the labor legislation, with its failures, especially given the impossibility of controlling its implementation throughout a vast country," are captured in Monteiro da Silva's phrase, "it is little, but it helps [*alivia*]."[77]

A critical perspective is essential to place fawning flattery into the broader repertoire of stances, tactics, and gestures that constitute mass popular discourse about both Vargas and the labor law. Because Monteiro da Silva knew the family bonus was inoperative, his praise that "it helps" could be seen as either ignorance or a studied misinterpretation. In the same way, his original 1950 campaign song/poem could be seen as *getulista* lies—even in São Paulo, most workers did not receive holidays, good pay, or a pension when they retired. Such exaggerated and misleading claims would surely meet with a smile from those who paid the songwriter, of course, although these statements stand totally at variance with the reality of workers, even the minority of the poor northeastern workers who did have a *carteira assinada*. In that situation, the critical phrase comes at the end, when the poet smuggles in a simple truth: workers who demand respect for their rights are met with "kicks and blows." At this point, the poem calls on powerful men like Vargas, as well as the law they created, to stand with those who are being trampled.

The same cunning artfulness can be found in a poem recorded by Jozé Norberto Macedo during his late 1940s fieldwork in the semiarid region (*sertão*) close to the São Francisco River. In Petrolina, Pernambuco, he found a backlands poet (*poeta sertanejo*) who "forged through his verses an astonishing understanding of the unjust inequality between the worker of the cities, assisted by laws, and the rural worker, without any rights." The poem begins, "After the labor laws gave two free days, a free day for everyone, the Brazilian government forgot the cowboys who are also sons of God." The government "gave to the workers of the city security, freedom, and payment according to the law. For the rough men of the woods without ties or shoes, no advantage came." As Macedo noted, the rural folk thus began "to understand that a government exists and that laws and decrees should be distributed with equity."[78] Through such words, the subaltern forged an indirect and nonaccusatory appeal for redress from the powers that be that had failed to deliver on their much vaunted promises. Getúlio Vargas the (imperfect) man may have died, but Getúlio (the ideal) remained more alive than ever.

six

Labor Law through the Prism of Subjectivity

Legal Consciousness, Grievances, and Class Mobilization

Although often a facade, the CLT nonetheless came to form, as Maria Célia Paoli has observed, "the basis of class struggles where culture and politics met everyday life," because the law recognized, however ambiguously, "the broad cultural demands of justice and fairness in labor conditions."[1] The conquest, if any, lay in the "institutionalization of the idea that labor relations should be regulated, in some fashion, by publicly defined parameters."[2] Yet this normative ideal could become real only in the context of action from below by a new and growing social class of urban workers.

The precedent was set, even as the Estado Novo came to an end, when a tiny minority of workers, many of them active in the legally sanctioned but powerless unions of the period, were quick to use "the new 'legality' in labor relations [in an attempt] to breach the factory walls. The linking of the labor laws and efforts to organize workers in the shop marked the emergence of a new labor strategy made possible by the existence of a credible, if flawed, state enforcement apparatus. . . . By concentrating their agitation around the employers' violation of the law, they sought to co-opt the state as an ally, in order to shield their own efforts to organize. . . . The ability to anchor working class rights in law . . . produced the enduring synthesis of direct and indirect action that would characterize shop floor organizing in the future, whether such labor initiatives were connected to or independent of the legal unions."[3]

Faced with doubtful friends and powerful enemies, these activist workers would have failed if they had naively believed in the CLT, its promulgators, or its enforcers. Yet these activists were acutely aware of their weakness, which made it impossible for them to do without the often fictitious "protection" of the labor law. The written law was central to the humorous parable from the early 1930s recalled by a communist worker, Eloy Martins. As told by Mário Couto, a *gaúcho* party leader, the story featured a devious poker player who had printed his own rule book to cheat his opponents. One way or another, he could always find some legal fine print that guaranteed him victory.[4] Designed to discredit the labor laws in a particular political conjuncture, the story can also be used to suggest a larger insight that is directly relevant to the role of law in the class struggle in Brazil. If the swindler's poker manual is made available to all players (as with the CLT), then even those not involved with drafting the fixed rule book may be able to turn the rules to their own advantage, at least some of the time.

Skepticism and Hostility

Worker activists maintained a complicated—indeed, fundamentally con- flicted—relationship with the CLT that was characterized by two central, counterbalancing themes: a rejection of the law and its idealization. One side of this doubled discourse is well illustrated by a Pernambucan worker named Joaquim who was interviewed in the 1980s by anthropologist José Sérgio Leite Lopes: "All my life, I thought that if the law of the nation [*lei da nação*] was fulfilled, the worker in Brazil would live much better. Because by the law of the nation, all are free men [*libertos*], even if they are suffering hunger, *né*! But there is hunger, because the nation's law is not being carried out, but if it were [complied with properly], I think the worker would not suffer so much. . . . The problem here is that [the employers] never liked laws."[5] The discourse of this former textile worker, an assistant in the stamping section of the Fábrica Aurora, illustrates the law as an ideal and a hope. The contrasting view of the law as fraud is demonstrated in an observation by Marcos Andreotti, a communist who served as president of the ABC metalworkers' union (1932–37, 1958–64): In Brazil, "there is no justice. Capitalism always tries to tip the scales [of justice] toward its side to the detriment of the common people [*povo*] and the working class. That is the capitalist regime, and [under it] there will never be justice in favor of the people."[6]

In a sensitive analysis, Leite Lopes suggests that Joaquim's discourse aptly reflects the position of Brazilian workers as a social class that is "as subordinated to the law as it is verbally tied to it [*atrelado à lei*] for its class action." Yet Joaquim uses this ambivalent evaluation of the law (as false beacon or true hope) to produce a discourse for working-class collective action: "If the nation gave us that right, why doesn't the boss want to obey it? Then let's go on strike! Let's impose ourselves! Let's go to court!" In doing so, Joaquim shows himself to be a realist who uses the law, "which is historically weak in the face of employer power," but without illusions.[7]

In fact, such skepticism about the law and open hostility toward the government and its labor court system was widespread among trade union leaders and rank-and-file workers during the Populist Republic. Three-quarters of the São Paulo and Rio metalworker delegates interviewed during their 1959 national conference, for example, expressed the belief that the labor court system and the government favored employers' interests.[8] And when a questionnaire was given to a nonrandom group of 154 populist voters in São Paulo in 1962, 55 percent of the supporters of Adhemar de Barros and 61 percent of the supporters of Jânio Quadros disagreed with the statement "that the labor legislation protects the worker and is against the employer" (10 percent had no answer, and only 34 and 27 percent of each group respectively answered yes).[9]

It is not surprising that such doubts were fully shared by the seventy-eight São Paulo union presidents who responded to a 1963 questionnaire. Asked if the labor courts "resolved cases in the best manner possible," 54 percent responded negatively, and only 35 percent answered favorably, although even some of these positive responses were lukewarm (one-fifth of those who answered affirmatively, for example, explained that going to court "satisfied those who appealed to it"). Only one in ten of these respondents agreed that the courts resolved cases rapidly (one of the biggest complaints), and nine of ten answered affirmatively when asked whether the labor court system should be modified.[10]

To better understand the Brazilian working class in formation at midcentury, it is necessary to probe more deeply into this elusive aspect of the labor law phenomenon: the interface between the objective and subjective dimensions that defines the intersection of class conflict and the law.[11] In other words, what impact did labor law have on the individual and collective consciousness and behavior of both rank-and-file workers and union leaders? In her study of working-class North Americans, legal anthropologist Sally Merry observes that "the law consists of a complex repertoire of meanings and categories understood differently by people depending on their experience with and knowledge of the law. The law looks different, for example, to law professors, tax evaders, welfare recipients, blue-collar homeowners, and burglars. The ways people understand and use law I term their *legal consciousness*."[12] Using Merry's language, how are we to understand the complexities of the legal consciousness of Brazilian workers, the ways in which they understood law, and how those understandings changed through their encounters with the law? In particular, we will need to highlight the role and impact of the *dissídio individual* mechanism, through which perceived injustices could be contested by individuals and small groups (with many such complaints transformed into charges of legal violations in the labor courts).

The Labor Court and Grievance Patterns

This individualistic dimension of the labor law system, which has long been neglected in the literature,[13] is especially important in Brazil because the field of labor law is not simply or even primarily a collective experience. Indeed, one of the peculiarities of Brazilian labor law lies precisely in the absence of formal in-plant mechanisms for grievance resolution, such as shop stewards or arbitration systems. As a TRT judge in Recife, Pedro de Albuquerque Montenegro, noted in 1956, there was "no very well established method or procedure for resolving grievances [in Brazil]. Instead, most matters come before the labor tribunals, and they must decide all the things which, in other countries, would be determined by negotiations between workers and employers directly."[14]

Even today, the most routine disputes about workplace grievances are handled through individual legal action within the labor court system. Indeed, the functioning of the industrial and labor relations system is strongly shaped by the CLT's protectionist stance and discouragement of direct negotiations, which guarantee a prominent role for the labor courts. As Kenneth Mericle points out, worker rights in Brazil are grounded in the individual labor contract, but it "is not equivalent to the 'free' labor contract of Nineteenth Century laissez-faire

FIGURE 1. Typical Procedure for a Grievance Solved by a Formal Court Hearing, 1972

```
┌─────────────────────────────────────────────────────────────────────────┐
│  ┌──────────────┐      ┌──────────────┐         ┌──────────────┐          │
│  │ Union legal  │      │ Verbal       │         │ Private law  │          │
│  │ department   │      │ grievance    │         │ firm         │          │
│  └──────────────┘      │ at court     │         └──────────────┘          │
│                        └──────────────┘                                   │
│                                                  Grievance                │
│  Initiation           ┌──────────────┐           reduced to               │
│  of process           │ Labor court  │           writing                  │
│                       │ distributor  │                                    │
│                       └──────────────┘                                    │
│                                                                           │
│                       ┌────────────────────┐                              │
│                       │ Secretary of labor │                              │
│                       │ court              │                              │
│                       │ Employer notified  │                              │
│                       │ Hearing date set   │                              │
│                       └────────────────────┘                              │
│                       Average delay three months                          │
│                                                                           │
│                       ┌────────────────────────┐                          │
│                       │ FIRST HEARING:         │                          │
│                       │ Presentation of        │         Parties          │
│  Presentation         │ grievance              │         must             │
│  of proofs            │ Employer's defense     │         appear           │
│                       │ and evidence           │         or lose          │
│                       │ Conciliation proposal  │         grievance        │
│                       └────────────────────────┘                          │
│                       Average delay six months                            │
│                                                                           │
│                       ┌────────────────────────┐                          │
│                       │ SECOND HEARING:        │                          │
│                       │ Presentation of proofs │                          │
│                       │ Testimony of parties   │                          │
│                       │ Questioning of parties │                          │
│                       └────────────────────────┘                          │
│                                        Often                              │
│                       Delay            combined                           │
│                                                                           │
│                       ┌────────────────────────┐                          │
│                       │ THIRD HEARING:         │                          │
│                       │ Testimony of witnesses │                          │
│                       │ Questioning of witnesses│                         │
│                       │ Final statements       │                          │
│                       │ Conciliation proposal  │                          │
│                       └────────────────────────┘                          │
│                       Delay                                               │
│                                                                           │
│                       ┌──────────────┐                                    │
│  Judgment             │ Judgment     │                                    │
│          ┌──────────┐ └──────────────┘ ┌──────────────┐                   │
│          │ Execution│                  │ Appeal of    │                   │
│          │ of       │                  │ judgment to  │                   │
│          │ judgment │                  │ TRT          │                   │
│          └──────────┘                  └──────────────┘                   │
└─────────────────────────────────────────────────────────────────────────┘
```

Source: Mericle, "Conflict Resolution," 168.

liberalism since the parties are not completely free to establish the terms [because] the state plays a major intervening role by guaranteeing the minimum provisions of the individual contract in a vast body of labor law."[15]

The enduring significance of the labor courts is suggested by the gross statistics for Brazil's industrial heartland, the state of São Paulo. In 1939, there had been no complaints (*reclamações*) filed in the state, given the absence of functioning labor courts (unlike Rio de Janeiro, Minas Gerais, and Rio Grande do Sul).[16] Between 1944 and 1976, the state's share of all complaints filed in Brazil varied from a low of 27 percent to a high of 55 percent.[17] Although little is known about the reliability of this statistical series, the state accounted for an average of roughly two-fifths of all cases, which is less than São Paulo's 50 percent share of Brazil's manufacturing workforce in the 1960 industrial census.[18] Yet whatever the judgment about *paulista* underrepresentation, there is no denying the impressive increase in the absolute number of labor court filings in the state, which grew from 9,823 in 1944 to a high of 166,762 in 1969.

The number of legal cases filed with the labor courts in the country as a whole grew rapidly over the following decades. "Between the years 1980 and 1994, for example, the average annual increase in labor cases filed was around one hundred thousand a year. During the 1960s [by contrast], the average increase was of less than five thousand a year, which is to say that . . . the quantity of labor cases increased twenty times more" after the militant "New Unionism" that swept the nation during the 1980s.[19] This vast increase might appear surprising to some observers because the New Unionism discourse ostentatiously disdained the labor court system in favor of direct action, such as strikes. In truth, this trend speaks strongly against the proposition—popular in 1970s literature—that the recourse to the labor courts was demobilizing.[20] Contrary to widespread perception, in other words, an increasing resort to indirect action such as legal filings is more likely to parallel rather than have an inverse relationship to direct action.[21] This argument is also strengthened, in table 3, by the increase in labor court filings in São Paulo for earlier periods of heightened labor mobilization, such as 1944–46, 1952–53, and 1960–64. Moreover, Sonia Avelar's study of the textile workers' union of São Jose dos Campos, in the interior of São Paulo, further confirms the direct linkage between an increasingly mobilizational trade union practice and union-assisted individual labor court filings. While 88 percent of the 487 filings by local textile workers between 1947 and 1964 were individual, she found a clear association—at both the level of the union and for particular factories—between the number of labor court filings and enhanced militancy on the part of workers and the union (with a modest rise in the share of such filings focusing on collective issues).[22] A deeper irony is also apparent because the labor court system's creators conceived and defended it as a replacement rather than another arena for class struggle.

Another crucial aspect of the *dissídio individual* process is that it is used

TABLE 3: *Dissídios Individuais* Filed in the State of São Paulo as a
Percentage of the National Total, 1944–1976

Year	# of Labor Court Filings	% of National Labor Court Filings
1944	9,823	27
1945	18,221	40
1946	20,620	33
1947	22,146	37
1948	17,279	34
1949	23,925	35
1950	21,530	33
1951	24,749	32
1952	34,603	41
1953	68,909	55
1954	37,530	40
1955	50,398	45
1956	45,400	41
1957	60,099	46
1958	53,555	47
1959	54,564	39
1960	59,486	44
1961	68,452	44
1962	87,787	46
1963	119,019	44
1964	114,656	43
1965	130,286	42
1966	140,770	44
1967	141,700	39
1968	133,126	32
1969	166,762	36
1970	160,039	34
1972	102,380	34
1974	149,405	36
1976	157,628	36

Source: Drawn from summary statistics for the "Movimento Geral Número de
Reclamações Recebidas, Solucionadas, Adiados" by the Juntas de Conciliação e
Julgamento in the state of São Paulo and nationwide (Instituto Brasileiro de
Geografia e Estatística, *Annuário Estatístico*, 1947–77).

overwhelmingly by those workers and employees who have been laid off or fired. This was clearly demonstrated in Mericle's sample of labor court cases in 1964 and 1968, which found that three-quarters of the filings involved "grieving from a *defensive position*"—that is, after having been discharged— and that more than half of that group were advancing "*deferred demands* for rights that the worker was deprived of while still employed." The logic of this surprising result was well stated in a 1994 article by economists José Márcio Camargo, Edward J. Amadeo, and Gustavo Gonzaga, who noted that the worker, once off the job, "has no costs if he sues the employer for unlawful practices during the [employment] contract, except the cost of attend[ing] the hearings. This means that whenever a worker is fired, he has a strong incentive to sue the employer." As a result, "workers tend not to complain about unlawful practices during the employment period in fear of being fired, but are very active in the Labor Courts after they are fired for any reason." Echoing employer complaints, Camargo, Amadeo, and Gonzaga argued that the result was "an extremely congested Labor Justice [system], with millions of demands per year" as well as a multitude of appeals by employers, who "perceive the system as one that favors workers." Yet these economists, de- spite their disdain for such labor market rigidities, were honest enough to admit that Brazil was nonetheless characterized by "very flexible real wages and employment relations" (although they ventured no explanation as to why this might be so).[23]

The extent and range of these deferred grievances, as Mericle noted two decades earlier, "indicates a widespread evasion of the provisions of the labor law by employers and widespread fear of reprisals among workers."[24] Draw- ing implicitly on a U.S. comparative perspective, Mericle suggested that these deferred grievances could be interpreted as "a measure of suppressed conflict —i.e., situations where a dispute exists, but conflict behavior is restrained because of the costs involved."[25] At the same time, the sustained and growing level of participation in the *dissídios individuais* in São Paulo clearly demon- strates that the labor courts do, in fact, impose some restrictions, however small, on industrialists' freedom of action.

In fact, the growth in the number of labor court filings in São Paulo suggests that the results of the legal process were not entirely fictitious—that is, disad- vantageous for individual workers. The outcome had to be satisfactory in a large enough minority of cases to give the legal process the credibility neces- sary to attract working people's continued participation. Andreotti captured this dynamic when asked whether individual workers ever prevailed in the labor courts. They won, he explained, "since there was no fulfillment of the law on the part of employers, who sometimes did very arbitrary things that prejudiced the government. So [the courts] were forced to cede ground and recognize that the workers had to win this or that case, because what the employer had done to the worker was very unjust. At that point, when it was clear that this was an [employer] action that was much outside of the law, they had to conform to the law, which was also done to gain trust for the labor courts and the government itself."[26]

In the end, the labor courts can be said to provide workers with at least a "right to present grievances and hope to receive just consideration." As a result, as Neuma Figueiredo de Aguiar Walker noted in 1969, the courts were "never regarded by employers as entirely legitimate," even though the courts offered an abundance of legal loopholes.[27] This minimalist judgment is also suggested by the fact that trade union leaders in São Paulo, despite their criticisms, were committed to the preservation of the labor court system (only 17 percent favored its extinction in a 1963 survey of union presidents, for example, while Mericle's 1972 survey of union leaders found "a general acceptance of the institution, but a strong desire that it be improved").[28]

The 1961 Diary of Philadelpho Braz

The labor courts and the social process that leads workers to them consequently provide an especially useful fulcrum for examining the complicated dialectic between the individual and the collective, the particular and the general, within the working class. Sources encountered in my research on the metalworkers of the industrial ABC region of greater São Paulo after 1950 illustrate the central role that trade union leaders played as go-betweens in the process by which working-class people filed grievances. In particular, a diary kept by Philadelpho Braz, the union's secretary-general, for ten months in 1961 allows us to better understand the first steps in this process. The diary is almost entirely nonnarrative, with little first-person description by Braz of his activities. Instead, it takes the form of a numbered set of daily entries, written in telegraphic form, in which he listed the names of workers who came to consult with him, along with their employers, whether the workers were union members, some suggestion of the problem or issue raised, and some indication of the orientation he provided them.

In this, his fifth year as secretary-general, the thirty-five-year-old Braz was involved with 1,445 documented consultations initiated by 902 workers from ninety different factories.[29] Some general sense of the source can be reached by highlighting the preliminary results of certain summary questions asked of each of the consultations. (The questions are not exclusive of each other.)[30] Overall, 67 percent of consultations referred to a subject that is mentioned or discussed in the CLT, and 35 percent referred to some government institution. The labor courts are mentioned directly in 16 percent of all records, and other government institutions appear in 19 percent of the cases. The link between Braz and the workers' employment experience is made even more clear by the subject of consultation: 1,512 subjects are raised, of which 73 percent are linked to the employer, 21 percent are not linked to the employer (linkage is unknown in the remaining 6 percent of cases). In this regard, it is also helpful to note that 42 percent of all consultations involved an actual or imminent dispute between worker(s) and employer(s).

The most intriguing realization, however, came from the recognition that the words and phrases Braz used to capture the subjects of consultation were legal constructions or categorizations of the workers' problems. In other words, the CLT and its categories were located inside Braz's head as he translated or, better put, operationalized the workers' problems to record them. When Braz summarizes a given worker's problem as "equal pay for equal work" (*equiparação salarial*), he has transformed one worker's particular complaint into a generalizable abstract category by using the legal terminology of the CLT. This is yet another example of how, in Paoli's words, "the labor legislation de-privatized factory space" by injecting "generic but public rights" into the labor-management relationship.[31] After the government has bestowed such social and labor legislation on the workers, as Francisco Weffort has pointed out, it is transformed into a legal right so that when a worker demands that it be met, "the original relationship of 'donation' [*outorga*] (and thus of dependency) disappears. What counts now is that the citizen is demanding fulfillment of the law, that he demands 'his rights' as a free man."[32]

In the words of Pierre Bourdieu, the relationship between Braz, the union leader, and the workers who consulted with him illustrates the importance of the "collective labor of 'categorization' that tends to transform a perceived or even unperceived grievance into an explicitly attributable harm and thus convert a simple dispute into a lawsuit. Nothing is less 'natural' than the 'need for law' or, to put it differently, than the impression of an injustice which leads someone to appeal to the services of a professional. . . . The conversion of an unperceived harm into one that is perceived, named, and specifically attributed presupposes a labor of construction of social reality [through] redefining problems expressed in ordinary language as legal problems, translating them into the language of the law and proposing a prospective evaluation of the chances for success of different strategies."[33]

The finding that Braz had so thoroughly internalized the CLT was not entirely surprising in retrospect. During the ten years prior to his union election, Braz had developed a reputation at Fichet Schwartz-Hautmont, where he mounted metallic structures, as the man for workers with problems to see. When approached by a fellow worker, Braz would pull out a well-worn copy of the CLT, which he kept in his locker, and "look up the answer."[34] Similar stories are told about union vice-president Miguel Guilhen, and interviews, newspaper reports, and secondary accounts demonstrate that the use of the law in this way was common among working-class activists. While acknowledging the exaggeration, a U.S. labor attaché reported in 1953, for example, that "it is said that every working man in São Paulo carries a copy of the labor laws in his pocket."[35]

João de Almeida, a longtime member of Braz's union, suggests the outlook of many rank-and-file workers. Almeida recalls being recruited to the union by his friend, Guilhen, at that time a member of the Communist Party, who convinced Almeida to join so that he could know his legal rights. Indeed, he proudly claimed that Guilhen "knew more about the CLT than most lawyers."[36] Braz also took pride in his legal expertise, especially because he had little formal education: "I acquired so much experience, listening all day to complaints," that "through practice, I became an adviser to the lawyer. Because he has the juridical theory, study, but he doesn't know [the world of industry]. He's never entered a factory. He doesn't know that rigor, that discipline, those hard foremen [*capatazes*]. I had much more practical experience, and he had theory, study."[37]

The impact of the CLT, as well as its power of attraction, was demonstrated when Almeida explained his move from commerce to industry during the early Estado Novo. His prior employer, he said, had refused to register him, so he moved to industry, because there you had a "right to the [labor] laws" (*direito às leis* [*trabalhistas*]).[38] The legal basis for the distinction between employment covered by the CLT and that which is not (the informal sector) generates its own terminology. Discussing the translation of labor court concepts into English, Brazilian accountant Danilo Nogueira notes that "to have a *carteira assinada* means to be registered as an employee and the certainty of certain *direitos* (rights, entitlements)." Furthermore, he observes that the statement "*Quero os meus direitos* [literally, I want my rights] often is jargon

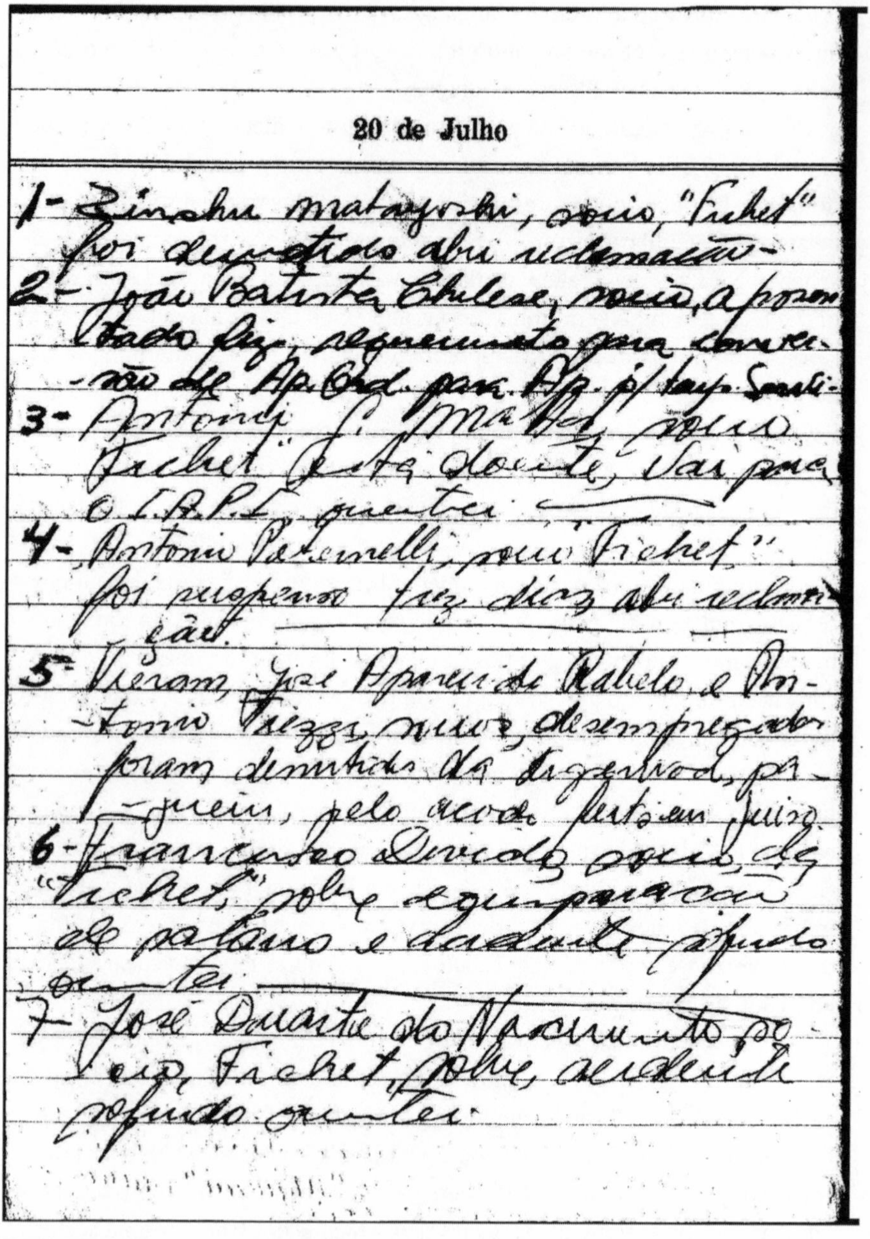
20 de Julho

1- Zinshu Matayoshi, socio, "Fichet" foi demitido abri reclamação-
2- João Batista Chilese, socio, aposentado fiz requerimento para conversão de Ap. Ord. para Ap. p/ temp. Servi-
3- Antonio [illegible] Maffei, socio "Fichet" Esta doente, vai para o I.A.P.I. quinta
4- Antonio Patarnelli, socio "Fichet" foi suspenso trez dias abri reclama-ção.
5- Vieram, José Aparecido Rabelo e An-tonio Trezzi, socios, desempregados foram demitidos da [illegible], pa-[illegible], pelo acordo feito em Juizo
6- Francisco Durcolo socio da "Fichet", sobre equiparação de salario e acidente [illegible] quinta
7- José Duarte do Nascimento so-cio, Fichet, sobre acidente [illegible] quinta

Philadelpho Braz's diary entries for 20–21 July 1961, illustrating the range of his activities as secretary-general of the Metalworkers' Union of Santo André. The numbered items on this page involve individual consultations about accidents, equal pay for equal work, firings, suspensions, illness, and retirement benefits. The next page includes references to a factory visit, a meeting at the DRT regarding unhealthy working conditions, and plans for a workers' assembly linked to a strike against the Pirelli factory in Santo André. (Courtesy of the author)

HOJE AS ½ *monte grève* *sua*

Prelli S/A. **21 de Julho**

1- Fomos logo cedo as firmas "Pierre Saby" e Alubrasil tratar de problemas de antecipação salarial

2- Fomos a I.R.T. tratar de assuntos relacionados com o problema salarial da "Prelli S/A" nada feito.

3- Fiz requerimento de Diversos Kiauriuis, seu "Masseur es St.º André" solicitando mesas, o.k. —

4

grande assembleia dos trabalhadores da Prelli pararam as 1000 hs. (22.00) grève

Philadelpho Braz as a trade union leader assisting workers in the early 1960s. (Courtesy of the author)

Philadelpho Braz as a trade union bureaucrat in the early 1960s. (Courtesy of the author)

for 'if you are not satisfied then fire me—and give me my termination pay.' To which the employer may retort *vá procurar os seus direitos* [literally, go look for your rights] meaning 'I am firing you for good cause and if you want your termination [pay] you will have to file a grievance—and win.' "[39]

Legal and Class Consciousness

The acquisition of legal rights, however uncertain, by the individual worker who moves into legally covered urban employment is one of the key specificities to the process of working-class formation in Brazil. *Paulista* labor scholar Azis Simão offered an important insight into the impact of this phenomenon when he referred in 1962 to the existence of a "juridical consciousness of class," a "consciousness resulting from [the existence] of legal labor rights [*direitos trabalhistas*]."[40] During the Populist Republic, the key question for labor activists and union leaders was how to transform this "juridical consciousness of class" into a "consciousness of class" linked to a broader collective project of organizing workers.[41] Discounting the reliability of the government and the courts, the dominant left-center trade unionists of Braz's generation believed that direct pressure on employers was the only secure means of winning working-class demands. Although these activists did not abandon legal action (especially for individual grievances), half of the metalworkers' delegates interviewed in 1959 judged strikes to be "the worker's best weapon."[42]

Yet the strike was not a standing option to be used at will, because metalworkers in ABC and elsewhere were still only semiorganized in the early 1960s. The majority were not disposed to the type of disciplined and militant collective action advocated by their leaders, largely because so many still believed in company paternalism and followed individualistic paths for the resolution of their problems. These generalizations were confirmed in one of the earliest studies of the industrial proletariat in São Paulo. In 1963, sociologist Leôncio Martins Rodrigues administered questionnaires to the autoworkers at the new Willys-Overland plant in São Bernardo do Campo, located within the ABC region.[43] His results demonstrated that only 21 percent of the unskilled workers and 39 percent of the skilled workers belonged to the union.[44] Moreover, a sizable number of workers saw no advantages to union membership, and some perceived real drawbacks in terms of employer disapproval.[45] In more general terms, Martins Rodrigues found that workers saw little need for labor organization, in part because they still believed that their personal efforts were the best means of advancing their interests.[46]

Metalworkers gather outside union headquarters during a strike at the Pirelli factory in Santo André, July 1961. (Courtesy of the author)

Yet in Andreotti's experience, even the most recalcitrant workers could eventually be convinced of the need for organization because all workers possessed some degree of "consciousness" (*consciência*), however small, as a result of their shared experience as wage earners in industry. Yet the president of ABC's metalworkers' union also knew that such sentiment and shared class interests were not easily converted into a capacity for collective action. With few exceptions, most factory workers lacked any clearly established traditions of joint action in defense of their interests (a finding that Juarez Rubens Brandão Lopes also reported for a São Paulo metalworking factory studied in 1957),[47] even apart from the union.

As a longtime organizer, Andreotti knew, however, that even workers who were unorganized in a union sense were not necessarily disorganized. The factory workforce, as Brandão Lopes documented, was characterized by informal organization based on small circles of friends, relatives, and coworkers.[48] These small groups of workers, Brandão Lopes reported, shared an awareness, however diffuse, of their common position of subordination. In spite of

Communist labor leader Marcos Andreotti, 1982. Andreotti was the most important leader of the ABC's metalworkers prior to Luis Inácio "Lula" da Silva, a 1970s labor leader who was elected president of Brazil in 2002. (Courtesy of the author)

the much-noted "lack of unity" among the plant's metalworkers, Brandão Lopes also observed that a "type of solidarity" existed based on workers' "latent and vague [sense of] conflict with the 'bosses.'"[49]

Andreotti saw this gut-level "us versus them" feeling as the *consciência* from which all collective action sprang. Echoing Andreotti's judgment, Brandão Lopes wrote that "the solidarity of the factory's workers could be reduced, in the final analysis, to the lowest common denominator of all solidarity—the feeling of belonging to one group that is pitted against another." This "vague and unformed" solidarity was demonstrated, he said, by the workers' response to specific management actions against individual workers. "In the case of a disagreement between a worker and the firm," he reported, the aggrieved individual would find that his "*companheiros*, workers of an equivalent skill level, were on his side." Yet such incidents did not for the most part produce organized action by the complainant's fellow workers. Although many were aware that they had rights, most did not know how to fight the employer, and many did not even think of turning to the union.[50]

Conflict between the individual and the company created an opening for class action, for altering consciousness to move workers toward organized struggle. Thus, organizers like Andreotti and Braz were acutely attuned to the importance of individual grievances, however insignificant in terms of metal-workers as a whole (the *categoria*). The most common source of grievances, Andreotti reported, was unjust suspensions and firings of workers for mis-behavior, often by unreasonable supervisors who acted without the knowl-edge of higher management.[51] Andreotti's statement is confirmed by Martins Rodrigues's finding that São Bernardo metalworkers (at least 68 percent of all subgroups) listed "just and honest supervisors" as the single most important aspect of a job.[52]

Motivated by the most immediate personal interest, workers who took their grievances to the union viewed doing so as a test; such workers expected, if not victory, at least a serious effort to resolve their complaints. Thus, a trade union that failed to champion these smallest and least collective of its constit-uents' problems created cynical and even actively antiunion workers who held back future growth. Brandão Lopes recorded a complaint to this effect by a São Paulo metalworker who had earlier quit the Santo André metalworkers' union because when he needed help, he got none: "They said, 'Come tomor-row,' and then I went on the next day and the lawyer wasn't there." He finally got help from SESI," an industrialist-sponsored group. This incident, which occurred between 1947 and 1956, when the Santo André union was in the hands of a government-appointed *interventor*, typified the cavalier attitude of the time and damaged the union.[53]

When Andreotti, Braz, and other such union leaders came to power after 1956, they made a point of intervening, whenever and however possible, in the handling of individual workers' complaints. In some cases, the union would try to get an action annulled or to convince the firm to pay the worker during a suspension; if attempts at annulment failed, union leaders would urge the employer to pay the worker at least some of the indemnification due by law for years of service.[54] The impact of even a partial success was felt far beyond the individuals involved, Andreotti recalled, since each victory spread the word (*aquelle zum zum*) of the union among the affected worker's friends and acquaintances.[55] As Brandão Lopes noted, an aggrieved individual's fel-low workers always followed the course of his conflict with the employer "with interest, expressing satisfaction when the worker got the better" of the boss and trying not to hurt the worker's case by making accusations against him to the supervisor or testifying against the worker in court.[56] Any successes earned with union help or even an earnest yet unsuccessful attempt to help could lead the worker to join the union and lay the basis for his long-term loyalty. In this way, even what Martins Rodrigues and Brandão Lopes called

Adelço de Almeida (at right), leader of the Chemical Workers' Union of São Paulo, congratulates a worker who won a case in the labor courts before 1964. (Courtesy Biblioteca Adelço de Almeida of the Chemical, Plastic, and Pharmaceutical Workers Union of São Paulo)

the worker's individualism (Andreotti preferred the term *imediatismo*)[57] could strengthen the union.

Thus, any actions taken by trade union leaders in response to individual factory complaints were, as Andreotti put it, "rallying cries to the workers to join" and taught them that the union's true purpose was to defend workers.[58] Moreover, Andreotti was aware that no aspect of a worker's consciousness was static or unchanging. After workers joined, he said, they "always enter into contact with union workers, with directors, [and] the individuals who are tight with the union, and from this they gain consciousness of the benefits that the union can bring them in the case of a break between them and their employer."[59] Thus for Andreotti, the worker's decision to join the union was the first step in a larger process of consciousness-raising (*conscientização*).

Worker Grievances and Class Mobilization

Braz recognized that in most instances, unions lacked the power to favorably resolve worker grievances in the face of employer opposition, especially when important issues were at stake. Thus, the resort to legal means of contesting actions by foremen and employers was unavoidable. In this regard, the logic of the praxis of Braz or Andreotti paralleled that of the worker Joaquim, from Pernambuco, who showed how to convert a discourse about the law into a weapon against employers: "If the nation gave us that right, why doesn't the boss want to obey it?" At the same time, Braz's tactics reflect the same pragmatic adaptation to discouraging realities revealed in Joaquim's subsequent words about possible actions to be taken: "Then let's go on strike! Let's impose ourselves! Let's go to court!"[60] Braz's and Joaquim's preference for the first option is clear, as is their willingness to settle for the law, if they have no choice, even if they don't respect it. In many ways, this attitude reflects the pragmatic calculus of the weak. It is always best for any social group to have both the law and power on its side. If only one of the two is possible, power is clearly preferable. If power is unavailable, however, the law is unquestionably better than nothing.

Yet Braz faced another dilemma when he spoke to workers about possible legal resolutions to problems. If he were to tell the truth—that the law and the legal process were a fraud and favorable results unlikely—he would be reinforcing the workers' passivity. As a 1960s study of workers in the *município* of Araraquara, in the interior of São Paulo, revealed, "The fear of being persecuted by employers, the fear of unemployment, and the conviction that the [labor] law was frequently cheated on [*fraudada*] to the benefit of employers contributed to weaken the degree of demand-making [*reivindicação*] of the employees and to discourage their recourse to the labor justice [system]."[61] Thus, Braz played along with the workers' illusions about law (illusions that he may have helped to create) to move things forward. At such moments, the law in its majesty was fundamental to union leaders. The CLT grounded workers' complaints in a supraprivate realm whose sanction—even if only apparent—helped overcome workers' fears and motivated them to act against their employers, even if the only concrete, immediate step was the modest one of opening a labor court case.[62]

Yet the complexity of Braz's position in this process does not end here. If Braz were to speak as if the CLT would resolve everything, as if it were in fact dependable or real, the results would be disastrous for his larger project of winning workers' loyalty for the trade union. If a case turned out badly and the labor courts failed to resolve the grievance, the worker would inevitably be alienated from the union. Thus, the key for Braz was to enter into a relationship with individual workers in which he could help shape their evolving legal consciousness as it changed, step by step, through involvement with the labor court system. Legal consciousness, Merry has argued, is never fixed or static but "develops through individual experience" and changes on the basis of those experiences. "In general," she concludes, "people have the possibility of creativity and resistance, of changing their consciousness as they test it against the experiences of everyday life. And legal consciousness can itself generate contradictions."[63]

For left and left-center leaders such as Andreotti and Braz, the trade union's most fundamental task was to raise the workers' consciousness by participating, at their side, in the daily struggles that often led to and through the legal system. Both Andreotti and a Pernambucan textile worker interviewed by Jacob Carlos Lima called the outcome of this engagement *conscientização*. Interviewed in Recife in 1990, the textile worker explained that "the guys [from the union] have made many conquests through strikes, but they're not managing to impose our rights. They always end up making agreements [*acordos*], because, unfortunately, the legal system that we have is a capitalist one. We cannot place our trust in that [legal] system. A deal is made that says we have job security for so many months, [but the employers] don't respect it. In one or two weeks, it's all over, suddenly the fellow comes to work and is fired. But the most important [result] is the raising of the consciousness of the working class."[64]

Through interviews with other Pernambucan textile workers, Leite Lopes showed how participation in the labor court process had an empowering impact, no matter what the outcome, because of its role in fostering a philosophy of rights among rank-and-file workers.[65] Drawing on long-term studies of sugar workers in Pernambuco, anthropologist Lygia Siguad also emphasized the "representation that workers have of their rights, based on a situation in which brokerage by the union is almost always indispensable for them to become real." Rank-and-file workers' participation in labor court cases, she went on, is based not only on their "legalism" but also "on the deep repercussion these [legal] rights have had in revealing to [workers] an alteration in their relationships with the landowners, at the same time that it points to the illegitimacy they attribute to the actions of their employers."[66] Furthermore, according to Siguad, the trade unionists see their role as brokers between workers and the court system as fundamental because it "favors the creation of social bonds" between workers and union leaders, thus generating a debt that fosters participation in union mobilizations.[67]

In the midst of a long exposition about the labor courts, Braz surprised his

North American interviewer by saying that "there is always that *first* measure to be taken. The thoughtful and intelligent leader will try first to resolve the problem through contact with the employer."[68] Braz's reasoning is revealing for what it says about the logic of the Brazilian pattern of deferred grieving identified by Mericle. The labor courts were not to be avoided because of their institutional shortcomings but because of what would happen on the shop floor: "If a worker loses in the first instance, he could well win in the higher ones, but as long as there is no decision there, he finds himself a marked man in the factory, picked on by the foreman, who begins to punish him. They give him a suspension, another suspension, time passes, he's made to feel inferior. His situation [throughout] is very difficult."[69] In other words, precisely because of employer reprisals, trade union leaders insisted that an ideal labor court system would operate on the basis of summary judgments, arrived at with dispatch. The nature of employer-employee relations had not changed between Braz's time and 1972, when Mericle interviewed thirty-five presidents of local unions in Greater São Paulo: 80 percent reported that reprisals were common against workers who had filed cases with the labor courts while still employed (what Mericle called "offensive grieving," which was as rare then as now).[70]

Braz's emphasis on face-to-face contact regarding workers' grievances is worth emphasizing given the facile claims advanced by some external observers. As part of the culturalist argument, Kalman Silvert claimed that the logic of Brazil's corporatist labor relations system was to discourage or avoid direct contact between the two parties in the employment relation. Given the central role accorded government and the courts on paper, such foreign observers were blinded to the daily give-and-take among factory managers, trade unionists, and workers. That this is not peculiar to Braz's union is suggested by Mericle's 1972 finding that 91 percent of the labor leaders interviewed met directly with employers to resolve grievances and that 71 percent of these interviewees listed this as an effective means of resolving grievances. This finding was all the more surprising to Mericle given the absence, under Brazil's labor legislation, of shop floor union representatives and the lack of specific union staff charged with such a responsibility.[71]

Although busy, top union leaders such as Braz and Andreotti often handled such grievances through personal meetings with factory foremen, managers, or personnel department heads. Andreotti recalled the case of an Indústria Sul Americana de Metais worker who was personally disliked by his section foreman. The worker received a three-day suspension because he used some woolen fabric to clean himself when he found no toilet paper in the bathroom. In defending the man, Andreotti argued that the company was responsible for providing toilet paper, and he asked the plant manager, "What did you expect him to do? Use his socks?" The man was allowed to return two days later with no deduction from his pay.[72] In another case handled by Andreotti, a Pirelli worker had been caught red-handed at the factory gate with a spool of electrical wire he was planning to sell outside. Anxious to discourage thievery, management not only fired the worker for cause and refused to pay any severance but also "dirtied" his working papers (that is, noted the cause of dismissal on his *carteira de trabalho*) and sent his case to the police for prosecution. Although Andreotti agreed that some punishment was in order, he objected vigorously to the harshness with which the man was treated. Andreotti's biggest argument was the man's low salary as an unskilled worker: "If he had a remuneration that was adequate to meet his family responsibilities, he wouldn't have needed to take that spool." After prolonged and heated discussion, the two sides worked out a compromise in which the company agreed to fire the worker without dirtying his papers, to pay half his severance, and to drop the police charges.[73]

Such incidents, full of human foibles and often marked by humor, were part and parcel of union leaders' daily lives, but the larger structural significance should not be overlooked. Whatever its grotesque distortions and biases, the CLT provided the basis for the claim to legitimacy through which these working-class labor leaders could seek an audience with those who ran factories (although some managers refused to allow union representatives past the front gate and others, as in the case of Laminação Nacional de Metais, allowed entry by noncommunist unionists like Braz but refused to admit known communists like Andreotti). When this informal process of grievance settlement went well, it did so because individual representatives from both sides had found a common ground for understanding based on shared notions of reciprocity and simple human fairness. And finally, the CLT's definition of the problems—and the possibility of a resort to the labor court (even for an unfounded grievance)—provided union representatives with what little leverage they had with employers. What they achieved beyond that depended on their wit, their skill at human interaction, and similar factors.

Yet these considerations should lead us neither to praise the CLT nor to exaggerate the power it afforded the weak. As perceived with total clarity by

Braz and Andreotti and other activists, the structural imbalances of power were so large, in both the workplace and the courts, that working-class struggle was always a labor of Sisyphus. The importance of small successes lay in their confirmation of individual activists' sense of personal competence. Although such victories often proved Pyrrhic or insignificant, they did attract followers, even though positive outcomes were never large enough to change an accurate perception of the odds by those who knew the system well. This is well illustrated by Braz's discussion of the type of cases that automatically went to the labor courts, especially "disciplinary punishments, because it's a fait accompli [*fato consumado*], it can't be reversed. . . . In that situation, you had to go to court." But even when dealing with a strong court case against an arbitrary firing (one without just cause as defined by the law), "we would still seek to engage in dialogue with the enterprise for it to pay the employee [what he was owed]." "Why would we do so?" Braz asked out loud. His answer was simple: "The labor courts are very slow, unfortunately, and given that, the worker might well prefer to receive two today rather than four in five or six months."[74] As was often said, even "a bad conciliation settlement is worth more than a good demand" in a labor court case.[75]

Braz went on to describe the various legal steps involved with each stage of the process and the likely time frame for their occurrence. Yet Braz's narrative of a worker's saga in the courts ended with an eminently practical bottom-line observation: "The whole thing is transformed into a soap opera. [And] if the worker does not get a new job soon, he'll never be able to believe that he'll get what he's due or that the case [even if won] will allow him to resolve his problems, to pay his bills, [or] to meet his commitments."[76] In 1966 a U.S. graduate student, Joseph Springer, wrote about the "frail fiction" of Brazil's labor law after interviewing seventy-one São Paulo metalworkers.[77] Viewed from their vantage point, one must ask how workers could ever be simply grateful for Getúlio Vargas's magnanimous gift of the labor law.

The illegal actions of employers, coupled with systematic antiworker bias within the labor courts, produced what I have called justice at a discount. It is true that justice at a discount is still some sort of justice rather than a total denial of it. Yet perhaps law and justice should not be approached as something that either does or does not exist; perhaps it should be measured, in its multiple dimensions, in light of the quantities of law at the disposal of different individuals, social classes, and groups. What quantities of law, in other words, are available to the weak and the subaltern of any given social order?

Calculated in this fashion, perhaps justice can be discounted so deeply that it becomes a distortion to use the term. Yet long before we reach that point, all but the most blind will have stopped praising the creators and propagandists of such laws for their enlightened contributions to the triumph of justice and the supremacy and majesty of the rule of law.

We do not exaggerate when we recall that, in the predominant mentality of the previous regime, the labor problem in Brazil was simply a matter for the police. The just demands of the proletariat could not fit within the circle of such a narrow conception, [not even those] contemporary conquests that had [already] been incorporated into the social legislation of the majority of civilized countries.

—GETÚLIO VARGAS, 1931

seven

The Politics of Aphorism
The Social Question as a Police Matter (*Caso de Polícia*)

In 1976, political scientist Luiz Jorge Werneck Vianna opened his influential book, *Liberalismo e Sindicato* (*Liberalism and the Union*), with a discussion of the durable *getulista* mythology that hailed the Revolution of 1930 as a decisive rupture in government treatment of labor. In this view, 1930 was the symbolic moment when the social question ceased to be treated "as a 'police matter,' with the state coming to discipline the labor market in favor of salary earners."[1] From the outset, the proposition that the "social clause is a police matter" was directly attributed to the deposed president, Washington Luis. At his 1931 inauguration as Brazil's first labor minister, Lindolfo Collor declared that Luis's government believed that "social questions in Brazil are merely problems for the police, susceptible to being solved, at the extreme, through repressive measures."[2]

Quickly emerging as a fundamental trope of *getulista* discourse,[3] the *caso de polícia* aphorism always foregrounded the new regime's enlightened policies and progressive credentials, but the role of the adage changed over the fifteen years after 1930. When facing a 1932 military rebellion in São Paulo that cost thousands of lives, national government forces featured the saying prominently in a printed leaflet dropped from the air over enemy lines. According to the anonymous pamphlet, Luis and his ousted presidential candidate, Júlio Prestes, were "even more ferocious in their practice than in their thought," with any labor mobilization "met with horses' hoofs and shots or by encircling them with sabers."[4] As Vargas consolidated his control, the tone shifted decisively toward self-satisfied celebration of labor policies that were hailed as a sharp rebuke of the "the anachronistic methods of the so-called Old Republic."[5] In 1940, Labor Minister Waldemar Falcão chided earlier government officials for treating the social question as if it were only "a tiny little problem of police repression."[6] Luis's "celebrated" phrase was evidence of "the divorce that existed at that time between the prevailing policies and the factual reality" of the labor question.[7]

Throughout these years, *getulistas* made no effort to conceal their underlying objectives. As Vargas made clear on innumerable occasions, his gestures demanded gratitude and loyalty in return: "The beneficiaries of our social laws, having seen the satisfaction of their most just aspirations, will know how to repay this aid from the state."[8] The promiscuous use of the aphorism by Vargas's propagandists was met by a strong rebuttal on the part of critics. When pressed for proof, *getulistas* claimed that Luis had at one point declared that "in São Paulo at least, worker agitation is a question that concerns public order more than the social order." Yet the distance between this alleged statement and the aphorism led at least one cautious Estado Novo propagandist to speak of Luis's "unconscious phrase:—'the social problem in Brazil is a question for the police.'"[9]

Dispute over the aphorism was consistent from 1930 to 1945, arose again during Vargas's political resurrection from 1950 to 1954, and continued on and off through the remaining years of the Populist Republic and into the late 1960s. When scholarship on Brazilian labor emerged during that decade, it invariably included references to Luis's *caso de polícia*, which became a rhetorical commonplace in all subsequent literature.[10] Academics' deployment of the aphorism, however, remained based on unexamined assumptions regarding its origin, meaning, and implications. Even today, scholars have not resolved the empirical question of whether Luis said the words attributed to him or what those words meant if he did. This is all the more surprising because Luis's supporters had long charged their opponents with gross falsification, which, if true, means that scholars have been unwittingly duped by a *getulista* propaganda ploy. In addition, analysts have failed to investigate what Vargas, his supporters, and others meant when they invoked the aphorism, regardless of its origin, or how it was used in different contexts.

Yet even if scholars had focused on the attribution controversy, they would likely have judged the question insignificant because of Luis's prominent role in antilabor repression during the general strikes of 1917 and 1919.[11] In fact, many scholarly works have unknowingly settled for the modified *getulista* position advanced by Joaquim Pimenta, a lawyer who joined the labor minis-try with Collor but stayed after the minister departed. In his 1948 labor law textbook, Pimenta argued that if Luis did not say the words attributed to him, the aphorism nonetheless accurately "summarized the situation of the work-ing classes and the state" during the First Republic, although Pimenta's for-mula conveniently leaves the impression that things changed after 1930.[12]

This chapter systematically explores the origin, genealogy, and use of the aphorism, because "simple phrases, aphorisms, slogans, [and] dicta" have the notable capacity "to summarize, epitomize, exemplify, or even create com-plex programs of research or action."[13] Although analysts of Brazil have sel-dom used this methodological approach, it reveals unexpected similarities between the discourse of Washington Luis in 1920 and the juridical ideas about the social question associated with Getúlio Vargas after 1930. The com-plex story that emerges is marked by substantial continuity, while efforts to test the aphorism's promise of change reveal that Vargas's accession to power did not produce a rupture with past police practices vis-à-vis workers. Indeed, the years of *getulista* preeminence gave the *caso de polícia* aphorism an en-tirely new meaning—no longer a dispute about the past but a comment on the hypocrisies of the *getulista* capitalist present. The broadening popularity of the aphorism during these years flowed from its succinct and uniquely power-ful insight: that the state's "hard" repressive arm was inextricably bound up with its apparently "softer," co-optive, and progressive arm (the *getulista* labor law empire). The chapter's final section examines how this combination of antilabor repression and ostensibly prolabor legal fictions was experienced as an integral whole by midcentury working-class activists. The profoundly contradictory nature of this encounter between workers and the state will return us, once again, to the central theme of the book: the real, the imagi-nary, and the fight to make the imaginary real. It also prepares us to better understand why the Populist Republic of 1945–64 easily gave way to a twenty-one-year military dictatorship that was simultaneously antilabor and a faithful guardian of the CLT system—at least of its reality, if not its promise.

Getúlio Vargas, the *Caso de Polícia*, and the Social Question before and after 1930

At the height of Vargas's power, the Estado Novo's Press and Propaganda Department (Departamento de Imprensa e Propaganda) hammered home the message that the regime's disinterested benevolence had brought a new day for the nation's working people. Innumerable national broadcasts on the new medium of radio would open with the salutation "Laborers of Brazil,"[14] and a new iconography was born as thousands of workers gathered on May Day to hear Vargas's latest promises. "In packed sports stadiums, May Day became the altar on which Getúlio was thanked for the care and nurturing he had displayed for ordinary Brazilians," with the pageantry "faithfully recorded by [department] cameramen and shown as trailers in cinemas."[15] There was always something new for workers to celebrate during the Estado Novo—the minimum wage one year, the implementation of the labor court system the next, and the creation of the CLT in 1943. This abundance of good news was explained with waggish good humor by lawyer Cupertino de Gusmão, a former member of the federal Conselho Nacional do Trabalho (National Labor Council), the labor system's highest adjudicatory body. "New things always brought hope," he explained in 1945, "because the old ones were already completely demoralized" in the getulian state.[16]

Published during the year when Vargas fell from power, Gusmão's *Do Bojo do Estado Novo: Memórias de um Socialista na República de Trinta e Sete (From the Belly of the Estado Novo: Reminiscences of a Socialist during the 1937 Republic)* was full of deliciously cynical stories about the labor relations system he had served from the late 1930s until his ouster in 1942, when he incurred the disfavor of Alexandre Marcondes Filho, a powerful figure who served as both minister of justice and minister of labor. Although hard-pressed to explain how his "socialism" led him into the government's ranks,[17] Gusmão's frank and humorous vignettes richly revealed the political culture of the government's labor relations empire. His book provides a compelling portrait of the intense competitiveness and unrestrained flattery (*bajulação*) through which rival yes-men sought the favor of *the man* or of those close to *the man* who had single-handedly established "social justice in Brazil."[18]

The "spontaneity of the workers' gestures," Gusmão recalled wryly, was demonstrated at a banquet attended by three thousand trade unionists from around the country. At the table of honor were the "respectable gentlemen of high finance and the lofty dignitaries of the *getulista* court," while the workers were there to offer proof, once again, that the labor issue in Brazil "was no longer a question for the police and that at this banquet at least it was a question of food."[19] The gap between lofty ideals and everyday realities made the *caso de polícia* aphorism an obvious target for humor, even for those who lived off of its spoils. Yet not everyone was laughing, and the unamused included not only those who had lost power to Vargas but also many others who opposed him for any number of reasons, most of them legitimate. In the first serious study of Brazil's labor legislation, Evaristo de Moraes Filho vigorously attacked the *getulista* claims to outstanding advances over First Republic policies in this arena. Still read today, his 1952 book criticized the Estado Novo's deceitful affirmations that "nothing was imagined, conceived, thought, tried, or realized by *anyone* before it was undertaken by the nation's chief." As an opponent of the then newly elected President Vargas, Moraes Filho rejected as "mere electoral propaganda" the continued invocation of Luis's infamous aphorism by so-called laborites (*trabalhistas*).[20]

A labor lawyer in government service, Moraes Filho also disputed Luis's authorship of the *caso de polícia* aphorism. A former São Paulo public official, Luis Tenório de Brito, made a similar case in 1969 on the occasion of the one hundredth anniversary of Luis's birth.[21] Although both Moraes Filho and Brito were antigetulists, they differed in their political outlooks, with the former a moderate socialist and the latter nostalgic for the days before the hecatomb of 1930 that drove São Paulo from national power. Both men agreed, however, that the *caso de polícia* aphorism was a crude and badly executed falsification of the relevant chapter of Luis's 1920 gubernatorial platform (from which both works quoted at length). The demagogues who triumphed in 1930, Tenório de Brito declared, had "adulterated the written words to twist the truth of the concepts" advanced by Luis.[22] Using a more measured academic tone, Moraes Filho insisted that Luis's text revealed the true meaning of his formula "that the labor question, among us, is more one of *public order* rather than, properly speaking, the *social order*."[23]

Moraes Filho also quoted a statement from Luis that not only seemed to acknowledge the existence of the social question but admitted the need for government action: "Work stoppages occur every day; there is no way of denying their existence. If they exist, if they are facts and unfold over a long period of time, then the state should fulfill its duty of regulating them in terms of their causes and effects."[24] To do so, Luis proposed federal conciliation and arbitration courts to be staffed by "magistrates, whose independence and impartiality" would guarantee neutral decisions, which should be delivered in a matter of hours if justice is to be equal for all.[25] In and of itself, these quotes could prompt a reconsideration of Luis's established place as archreactionary in the Brazilian national pantheon. His proposed juridical solution, moreover, raises questions about the degree of originality and innovation to be credited to the labor laws associated with Collor and Vargas. The Liberal Alliance platform of 1930, in other words, was by no means Brazilian politicians' first expression of the need for a legal structuring of the emerging labor problem.[26]

Luis also defended the progressive position on the key legislative battle of the day, whether labor legislation fell within the central government's purview. Such regulatory measures, he insisted, "should be imposed by the law of the republic,"[27] a position that put him at odds with the positivist political boss of Rio Grande do Sul whose patronage had favored Vargas's rise to power in state and national politics. In 1917, Borges de Medeiros and his block of *gaúcho* deputies vocally opposed all proposals to limit the hours of labor as a violation of the federal constitution of 1891. Moreover, Borges was equally emphatic in rejecting, based on French positivist Auguste Comte (1798–1857), any solution to the social problem based on such "an erroneous and condemnable basis." Only retrograde or anarchic individuals, Medeiros claimed, could have "the pretension of regulating through law that which should only be governed by custom."[28] In other words, *gaúchos* like Vargas and Collor may have innovated more in relation to the positivist orthodoxy of Medeiros than they did in relation to the discourse of establishment politicians, like Luis, who shared the generalized inheritance of Brazilian juridicism.

If Luis's rhetoric more closely resembles Vargas's discourse than one would expect, perhaps their differences involve whether they promulgated laws to deal with the social question. Yet Luis proudly claimed in 1920, as did Vargas a decade later, that "some of the aspirations of workers elsewhere are already realities" in the state of São Paulo. In particular, Luis cited the eight-hour day, the regulation of the labor of women and minors, obligatory assistance to labor, and the regulation of work accidents.[29] In fact, the assistant director of the ILO, Fernand Maurette, was impressed by some of the pioneering social features of São Paulo's legal system when he visited Brazil for three weeks in the mid-1930s. He singled out for praise a 1907 *paulista* law that gave debts owed to workers priority over other debts as well as the provision of working papers (*cadernetas*) for those who labored in the state's coffee fields. "The 1907 Decree was a first attempt to give a legal status to the work of the agricultural labourer," he said, although he was eminently realistic in immediately adding, "But the law is one thing and its application quite a different one, especially in the field of agricultural employment."[30] Again, similarities between the discourses of Luis and Vargas are clear: São Paulo's advanced laws, as well as the national 1927 Vacation Law passed when Luis was president, were never effectively enforced by those who boasted so freely of them.[31]

Washington Luis, "Worker Agitation," and the Public and Social Order during the First Republic

Sharing a common juridicist political culture, Luis, Collor, and Vargas were attracted to the political symbolism of "advanced" and "progressive" laws yet worried little about their effective implementation. Consequently, the differences among these men, if they exist, require close analysis of Luis's key formula: "In São Paulo at least, worker agitation is a question that concerns public order more than the social order."[32] To emphasize the importance of this statement, Luis repeated it twice in the six paragraphs devoted to labor in his 1920 gubernatorial platform. Most importantly, the formula's target— which is never accurately rendered in paraphrase—was not the social or labor question but worker agitation. According to Luis, strikes and labor protest concerned the "public order more than the social order" at that time and for the foreseeable future.

The formula's disciplinary thrust is made clear by what follows, which was not quoted by Moraes Filho in 1952: worker agitation "represents the state of some workers but not the state of society" as a whole. And who are the workers whose agitation raises issues of public security that require police action? They are, Luis said, "men coming from other climates, habituated to other laws, martyred by sufferings that are unknown among us, exacerbated by ills that do not thrive here." These foreigners, he said in a reference to the recent general strikes, "get agitated and agitate," demand "rights that have not been denied them," and "protest against situations that do not exist here."[33]

In nullifying the social question in this fashion, Luis's carefully crafted formula offers a publicly articulated rationale for breaking strikes and dispersing labor protests. The profoundly reactionary mentality at work is fully revealed in the imaginary country that Luis juxtaposed with the Europe of his nightmares—the Europe of class struggle, revolution, and threats to private property. Unlike Brazil, European societies were overpopulated, and the land was already divided up and cultivated, while an abundance of labor meant low wages. Moreover, European laws maintained "castes in some countries and classes in others," he said, while Europe's worker "must always be a worker, just as his father was, and as his son and grandson" will be. Luis sharply drew the contrast to Brazil: with its abundant land, the country was so underpopulated that it subsidized European immigration, while its "liberal laws have abolished the rights and privileges of castes which, looked at closely, in fact never existed here." Indeed, social classes did not form in Brazil, he asserted, because men tried out and changed professions, and their labor was the start of their capital.[34]

Luis, perhaps inspired by his North American first name, presented an entirely imaginary vision of Brazil to his Paulista Republican Party compatriots who gathered in São Paulo's ornate European-style Municipal Theater. They heard of a country that had no trace of slavery (abolished in 1888) and that never had a monarchy or a titled aristocracy (Brazil had both until the 1889 advent of the republic). The Brazil that Luis presented was thoroughly bourgeois and was characterized, like the United States, by upward mobility through hard work. This claim was improbably advanced in a country whose dominant class had been both obstinate and successful in preserving its power and privileges. Luis also retained a residual Brazilian distinctiveness based on climate, although in a less grotesque manner than the Brazilian who told ILO director "Albert Thomas with a touch of irony but not without some show of reason: 'Here we have the sun and bananas, and so the social question is solved.'"[35]

Yet the absence of sociological imagination or the excessive attachment to progressive facades was not what marked the backwardness of Brazil's dominant class, its lawyers, and its men of letters in the early twentieth century. Rather, it was the stance enacted through their discourse, which, sustained by power alone, was permeated by a self-satisfied arrogance inherited from their slaveholding past. One 1969 tribute to Luis from an old friend and former Paulista Republican Party deputy is particularly revealing in this regard: The "somber features of [Luis's] personality" included his "authoritarianism, bull-headedness, and intolerance," although the ex-president was not governed by the really despotic tendency that might be expected as a result of "the slavocratic psychological environment" in which he was raised in Macaé, a town in Rio de Janeiro province.[36]

The psychological inheritance and ideological arrogance of the self-styled "conservative classes" provided the broad guidelines for the repressive reflexes of an undemocratic oligarchic state before 1930. Tenório de Brito's 1969 article strikingly illustrates this phenomenon. Immediately after proving that Luis did not say that "the social question is a police matter," this former officer in the fire department (*corpo de bombeiros*) engages in an exaggerated outburst that confirms that the aphorism captured the spirit of Luis's position. When the platform was written in 1920, Tenório de Brito says, Luis's words carried with them "a clear memory of the frightening days, two years earlier," when São Paulo experienced "the horrors of anarchy." When faced with "Red agents, spreading terror," Tenório de Brito declares defiantly, "there was no other alternative" to vigorous repression in defense of public order.[37]

This authoritarian response to worker agitation was not unique to Luis. In 1912, for example, the president of São Paulo state, Rodrigues Alves, declared that there could be no valid motive for working-class disturbances in Brazil given the existence "of full democracy and the complete absence of social classes." (He had supported the crushing of strikes in the port of Santos and among railroad workers.) After entering the country, he went on, immigrant workers like those who had struck "find in the law all of the guarantees that are necessary for their subsistence and for a reasonable remuneration of their labor."[38] If they behaved otherwise, the subtext suggests, "apply the rod" (*meter o pau*, a common and revealing colloquial expression).

As the center of early industrialization, São Paulo stood out because its political and economic establishment was among the first to face a strong challenge to the "no talking back" tradition of unchallenged upper-class rule. As the Italian consul reported in 1906, the police in São Paulo, destination of hundreds of thousands of immigrants, were "violent and aggressive" because even "cultivated and calm people here hardly distinguish between strikes and revolts."[39] Yet these attitudes were not unique to São Paulo. In 1929, for example, a U.S. military attaché witnessed Communist Party leaders addressing a meeting on the steps of Rio de Janeiro's Municipal Theater: "The Rio police never seem to handle such a situation with calmness and moderation, and therefore started clubbing right and left and even used their pistols, although there was no really serious resistance on the part of the communists. Three men were later treated for pistol wounds at the emergency hospital, and numerous others were badly bruised in their encounter with the police. [Communism's few] supporters here understand very little about communist doctrines, but only want to protest against the government."[40]

The public discourse in the print media, the chamber of deputies, and the salon laid down an ideological barrage that justified any and all of these antidemocratic actions. In 1917, the *Correio da Manha* explained what caused labor agitation: foreign agitators "had taken advantage of the good faith of our proletariat and ignorance of the majority of Brazilian workers to spread theories and doctrines whose falsity cannot be understood by our laboring classes." After the 1917 general strike in São Paulo, *O Paiz* affirmed that the Brazilian worker, "disciplined and of a good temperament, is being undermined by the deleterious action of certain strangers who desire to forcefully promote" European issues that "are completely without foundation" in Brazil. And finally, the *Jornal de Comércio* held that foreign anarchists and certain Brazilian intellectuals were "repeating things that, if they're not very reasonable in Europe, are entirely inappropriate here in Brazil."[41]

The dramatic general strikes that occurred between 1917 and 1920 would lead São Paulo's Alves and Luis to grudgingly admit the existence of a social question. Yet what they gave with one hand, they took away with the other. Whatever problems Brazil had in the social field, Alves said, were "unquestionably different problems than the European ones"; thus, the Brazilian social question provided no justification for worker militancy. This apparent inconsistency would frustrate a young U.S. historian, Sheldon Maram, author of one of the first studies of the early labor movement, because Alves's statement "did not correspond to the reality of his deeds," which consisted of the negation of any social problem.[42]

As Gisálio Cerqueira Filho suggested in 1982, "the 'social question' appeared in the dominant discourse [before 1930] only as an exceptional and episodic fact, not because it did not already exist but because the conditions necessary for it to impose itself as a question inscribed in the dominant thought did not yet exist." For this reason, the *caso de polícia* became popular in discussing the First Republic. "To the degree to which the dominant classes (agrarian oligarchies) held a monopoly on power, they also held a monopoly on political power and thus simultaneously a monopoly [in defining] legitimate political questions." Consequently, "the 'social question,' being illegitimate, was not a 'legal' question but rather an illegal and subversive matter that should be treated [as such] within the interior of the state's repressive apparatus."[43]

The effective denial of the existence of a social question, Cerqueira Filho also observed, attracted the attention of marginal anti–status quo thinkers during the First Republic, for whom it became a favorite focus of concern. Among the most famous of these prolabor reformers was Evaristo de Moraes

Sr., a "possibilist socialist" who served as juridical consultant under Collor in the early 1930s. In 1926, Moraes authored a polemical newspaper article that set forth the evidence about Luis's 1920 and 1926 declarations about the social question.[44] Gripped by the insurgent spirit of regime change in 1930, Collor, a journalist, recognized a good hook and picked up the antigovernment libel in his inaugural speech as labor minister; from there, the aphorism would migrate into the hands of others, including many who used it opportunistically.

It matters a great deal that the *caso de polícia* aphorism originated among the First Republic's prophetic dissidents rather than among those men of power and position who did so much to spread the adage after 1930. Over the following decades, the saying would retain its moral force and political coherence only when used by those who were part of, committed to, or authentically sympathetic with workers' collective struggles. Such reformist sympathies and democratic attitudes characterized Evaristo de Moraes Filho, whose 1952 book attacked the aphorism's attribution. A consistent critical thinker, Moraes Filho spent his adult life working in the labor ministry that his father had helped to create.[45] While discomforted by a reactionary outburst like that of Tenório de Brito, Moraes Filho would not have been surprised that such retrograde social postures survived among some members of the União Democrática Nacional (National Democratic Union), the liberal party founded in 1945 to campaign against Vargas.[46]

For Moraes Filho, a progressive-minded intellectual, political alliances in the early Populist Republic, when Vargas was still alive, presented tricky rhetorical demands. To rebut *getulista* propaganda, Moraes Filho used his 1952 book to rescue the reputation of a pre-1930 political establishment that had never been troubled by strikebreaking or the falsified elections that underlay the government's rule. And Moraes Filho was also aware that workers were forced to be silent before 1930 as well as subsequently. He would not have been surprised by the powerful and morally charged 1962 denunciation offered by veteran activist Everardo Dias in the first published memoir of the Brazilian workers' movement:

> In the period [before 1930], which wasn't so long ago, the government's conception could be reduced to the sentence—"The worker issue is a question of greater interest to the public order than to the social order." In the understanding of police authorities, all organization that aimed at obtaining some advantage for the worker, however small it was, or that sought to impart a spirit of popular contention to

society at large was seen as seeking the subversion of the established social order. [To be part of any such organization] was to be involved with creating a dangerous focal point, ready at any moment to explode in riotous manifestations, violent protests in the public square, and disorder. [And the government and the police] acted promptly in aiding the capitalist oligarchy in formation, already very powerful: a bribe for the newspaperman, a firing for the functionary who didn't pray according to the official primer, [and] horses' hoofs, the sword, and the bullet for the worker who sought better wage conditions or hygiene in the workplace.[47]

The Police and the Labor Laws in the Early 1930s

Rio federal deputy Maurício de Lacerda (1886–1959) was the leader of the parliamentary fight for social legislation after World War I, which would lead to his political "beheading" (*degolamento,* or punishment by exclusion) during a subsequent election. As a resolute opponent of the political establishment, Lacerda was repeatedly arrested and imprisoned for his support of strikers, anarchists, and antigovernment military rebels in 1922 and 1924.[48] The opponents of labor laws, he complained in 1960, always insisted that the social question did not exist "in Brazil, where it was a matter of police action [*caso de polícia*] against the activities of 'anarchists and foreigners' who 'exploited' the proletariat." In the end, the government always resorted to labeling such "repressive and intolerant actions as a reaction to 'communism.' "[49] A political radical but often at odds with anarchists and communists, Lacerda campaigned hard for Vargas's election in 1930 but turned down Collor's invitation to join the MTIC. As early as November 1930, Lacerda publicly expressed his worries that "the revolution goes around arresting workers" when what was needed was "less policeism [*policialismo,* meaning repression] and more socialism" in its actions.[50] While referring to Collor's "hurried apparatus of labor laws," Lacerda's 1931 book, *Segunda República* (*The Second Republic*), decried the new men of power for possessing the same repressive mentality as those recently "expelled from power in the name of political liberty and social equality." In the persecution of workers, he feared, the First and Second Republics had proven to be identical twins.[51]

Lacerda was prophetic in his early fears about the new government's disposition toward *policialismo* in labor matters. The new government was willing to follow more conciliatory tactics toward labor at times and eagerly gambled on a new progressive-sounding laborite rhetoric. These new leaders had not, however, given up repressing worker agitation. In São Paulo, for example, those named to command the police continued to work closely with industrialists to suppress threatened or actual strikes. As had been true before 1930, the terms of this cooperation were set forth in a multitude of confidential communications by the leaders of the Center of Weaving and Spinning Industrialists of São Paulo. (Textiles were the city's largest industry.) On 22 July 1931, for example, circular 1084 reported that "the military police will garrison the factories threatened by a disturbance of order, day and night, for at least the next forty-eight hours—that is, until the reestablishment of normal labor." In exchange, "the owners [were] to assume the obligation of feeding the soldiers at their disposition, giving them places to rest, and treating them with the greatest solicitousness."[52]

The grassroots impact of this continuity in police approaches to worker agitation could be seen in the recollections of labor activist Marcos Andreotti (1910–84), the most important working-class leader from the ABC region of greater São Paulo prior to Luis Inácio "Lula" da Silva (elected Brazil's president in 2002). Andreotti remembered hearing the anarchist speakers in São Paulo's Praça da Sé after World War I and grew up reading the anarchist newspaper *A Plebe* to his father. Joining the Communist Party at fourteen, Andreotti began to seriously organize in ABC in the late 1920s and founded the most important local unions in Santo André after the Revolution of 1930.[53]

In interviews in 1982, Andreotti was realistic about Vargas's popularity among workers after 1930 but not at all convinced of the reliability of their judgment. Vargas's government, Andreotti said, brought "organizations like the union and the labor laws that were established, but these laws were not really to the benefit of the worker, although they did lead the [rank-and-file] worker . . . to think that Getúlio was the man who would be the 'workers' father.'"[54] Andreotti had no illusions about Vargas's supposed benevolence: the president "brought us laws that were nothing more or less" than those of Mussolini's Italy. The communists opposed such "purely fascist laws," Andreotti went on, because the workers "had been organizing even before there were such laws. But Getúlio took advantage of the situation and brought the Carta del Lavoro of Italy over to Brazil, and we took advantage of it."[55]

What opportunities, if any, did the post-1930 labor laws offer? Andreotti recalled that the key lay in understanding that during the 1930s "the social question, the worker problem, really was *um caso de polícia*. If the worker occasionally made a demand or revolted against an injustice that he suffered, he was sometimes arrested within the factory itself" for his impertinence. This extremely repressive context, Andreotti's words suggest, made it possible for him to say that the insincere labor laws after 1930 had "improved the workers' situation a bit."[56] Under these circumstances, the delimitation of any area of legitimate union activity as no longer subject to automatic police action represented an advance because it placed some limit, however small, on the scope of the state's repressive role.[57]

The labor reforms of the early 1930s, observed Estado Novo publicist Alcides Rego, had been carried out under the influence of a variety of political currents "identified with the spirit of reaction" against the First Republic. The resulting "movement of opinion, many times contradictory and even antagonistic," proved unsettling to a class of Brazilian industrialists who were beginning their rise to national prominence.[58] As a leftist soldier, Nelson Werneck Sodré, recalled in 1967, the bourgeoisie felt threatened by "the progress of worker demands," which was connected to the climate of "free discussion of problems and mobilization of opinions" in the early 1930s.[59] Any link between reformist views and the central government was especially threatening, and by 1932 most military and civilian dissidents (including Collor and Moraes) had either changed course or found themselves on their way out of power.

The consolidation of a repressive "common sense" among government policy makers was marked by a number of Vargas appointments in 1932. To replace Collor, the president appointed Joaquim Pedro Salgado Filho, who came directly from the DOPS, a specialized force used since the 1920s against labor radicals, military rebels, and other subversives. The new labor minister assured his listeners that the police's part in labor relations would not disappear, as had been charged, precisely because it played a vital "intimidating and preventative role." Forced to maintain some rhetorical contrast to the old regime, however, Salgado Filho claimed that when trouble arose in the workplace, police action would be the last resort rather than the first.[60]

In 1932, Vargas's new police chief in the nation's capital, Filinto Müller, began a ten-year reign that was marked by an "intense dislike for labor organizers and leftist politicians."[61] Müller seized on the political mobilizations of 1934–35 to vigorously repress the leftist threat in defiance of the rights guaranteed in the 1934 constitution. "We are truly in a regime of government terrorism," Álvaro Ventura, an angry prolabor deputy, declared in October 1934, with "shootings, deportations, imprisonments, attacks on unions and workers, jailings of the editors of the *Jornal do Povo*. [Furthermore,] those who are imprisoned for labor conflicts are subject to physical torture in the dungeons of this inquisitorial republic. Militant labor leaders [simply] disappear."[62]

Collor joined the criticism of Müller and his counterparts around the country in a 1934 newspaper article: "Acts of violence occur one after another in Rio, and workers are savaged openly in the streets. The government's newspapers say the victimized workers are communists, but the procedure wasn't any different in the Old Republic: workers who don't agree with the government are always communists." Even when defending legitimate interests, "the worker is never in the right. And when he resolves to protest and make his rights prevail, he's a communist and ends up in jail."[63] The truth of such charges was so clear that even deputy Francisco Antonio Sales Filho, a government propaganda chief, admitted to his parliamentary colleagues in 1935 that "when Dr. Washington Luis was president, some said that the labor question was a matter for the police. Just between us," he went on, "labor problems still are police affairs."[64]

The Social Question as a *Caso de Polícia* during the Estado Novo

Although the dominant class was divided over Vargas at middecade, it was united in its support for his strong-arm policy against lower-class opponents and the Left. After an ineffectual communist-led barracks revolt in 1935, communism became, in Gusmão's words, the great *bicho papão* (an imaginary monster) of Vargas-era politics.[65] The anticommunism and hostility toward popular mobilization shared by members of the dominant class would prove vital to Vargas's greatest victory, the self-administered coup that preempted the 1938 presidential election. As befitted the moment, the repressive configuration of the Estado Novo's early years was only lightly "disguised by its laborite paternalism."[66]

The 1937 dictatorship vastly expanded the role of an increasingly diversified array of police institutions, as shown by Elizabeth Cancelli in *O Mundo da Violência: A Polícia da Era Vargas* (*The World of Violence: The Police of the Vargas Era*). The police acquired ever greater importance, she noted, through the imposition of new punishments, the consolidation of a new approach to crime, and the exercise of varied new forms of social vigilance. Her study also offers abundant evidence, drawn from Brazilian and U.S. archives, about the prevalence of wide-scale informing (*dedo-durismo*, or finger-pointing), on which Andreotti commented extensively. As for the social question, the Vargas regime aimed to extinguish "class struggle" through a two-pronged approach: the "exercise of pure and simple terror," and the establishment of tight police control over the day-to-day lives of workers and their unions.[67] "A powerful anticommunist discourse," massively diffused through government propaganda, made the communist threat "a permanent part of Brazilian urban life during the 1930s and early 1940s."[68]

As a worker militant, Andreotti experienced the full weight of the anticommunism of a succession of Brazilian governments. He was subject to a multitude of interrogations, police harassment, raids on his homes (the last in 1978), and arrests and imprisonments. During his first detention, on 26 October 1938 while engaged in clandestine political activity, Andreotti was held incommunicado by the DOPS for forty-five days and subjected to repeated interrogations: "Four or five hours would pass with them questioning you, always with a cop [*tira*], a bunch of cops, and a large number of tools on the table, pliers for pulling out fingernails and all that, with the cop banging those tools [on the table]. This made an impression on the prisoner, thinking that any moment they would take one of those tools and pull out your nail or shove bamboo under your nail or burn you with a cigarette."[69] He was released after a year in prison but was arrested again in July 1941 when he brought a sick comrade to a doctor under surveillance. Andreotti recalled how torture or the threat of torture was used "to intimidate the new arrivals using various modalities. With some, they tore out their fingernails or pushed pins under their nails, all that. But since I was a low-level prisoner, so to speak, without any real responsibility at the time, I was never [tortured]. The only thing they did was to put me in a chair that closed and squeezed me. . . . As a rank-and-file prisoner, I never got a beating—or, rather, only once. . . . That time, I was brought in, I had nothing to do with that problem [a group arrested with the party mimeograph machine], but the cop gave me a blow to the head [*bofetada*] when I entered."[70]

Convicted by the TSN, Andreotti served several years in prison during the Estado Novo; on one occasion, his release occurred weeks after he had finished his sentence. (Paperwork delays were offered as the official explanation for this arbitrary and illegal harassment.)[71] The TSN had been established in 1936, with full support of Luis's followers in São Paulo, as a military court to combat "crimes with ends subversive of the political and social institutions" of Brazil. Originally created under the constitution of 1934, its repressive characteristics further deepened during the Estado Novo. By the time of Andreotti's condemnation, the TSN was an independent court that operated outside of standard Brazilian legal procedures and that issued decisions that could not be appealed to any other court.[72]

The newly released Andreotti emerged a marked man (*queimado*, or burned, in the jargon of the Left) and struggled to find jobs as an electrician during the late Estado Novo, a period during which he picked up a lasting personal habit. For the rest of his life, he always wore a coat, even when the weather was warm. The police during World War II had once picked him up and put him on a train to Rio Grande do Sul, Brazil's southernmost and coldest state. The cold was the most memorable aspect of his kidnapping—making more of an impression on him than being separated from his family without notice—and he swore he would never again be caught unprepared.[73]

The deeply entrenched nature of these repressive reflexes is graphically illustrated by an unlikely source, the 1939 telegraphic code of the Civil Police of São Paulo.[74] The eighty-page printed code book contained 1,288 entries covering the routine police business thought necessary for statewide communication between subordinate police chiefs (*delegados*) and their superiors in São Paulo. It appeared four years after an armed challenge from the Left (1935) and one year after an attack on the presidential palace by the integralist Right (1938), although both groups had been smashed by 1939. The importance of political repression can be seen in the code's categories for "Integralism and Communism" (39 entries), "Agitations" (22 entries), and "Conspiracies" (24 entries). When the category of "Strikes" is added (48 entries), this repression-related grouping makes up 10 percent of the book's entries.[75] On the basis of numbers alone, any ambitious *delegado* would immediately grasp the importance of anything he could report in terms of social and political subversion.

Strikes occupied a surprisingly large place within the telegraphic code's sixty-nine major categories, ranking third in number of entries, trailing only procedural and bureaucratic matters. The forty-eight strike-related entries are particularly surprising because only a small minority of *delegados* were in charge of *municípios* with significant populations of potentially strike-prone urban wage earners. Strikes thus received pride of place despite their irrelevance to the day-to-day police business conducted by most telegraphers and their commanders. Furthermore, strikes or potential strikes did not loom large during 1939 in the state of São Paulo, however skewed the distribution of workers. In fact, the São Paulo Civil Police's annual report for that year revealed that only five work stoppages had occurred or been attempted during the year. Six cases of threatened strikes were reported, but "preventative policing in threatened establishments" assured that "nothing abnormal occurred."[76] In addition, strikes were illegal under the 1937 constitution, which also banned employer lockouts. Not surprisingly, this neutrality and balance on paper was an unconvincing gesture: not a single entry in the telegraphic code book dealt with lockouts, the employer expedient of class struggle that was equally forbidden.

Once again, the conclusion is inescapable: worker agitation was as much if not more a *caso de polícia* under Vargas as it had been during the First Republic. In discarding legal impediments and hypocritical fig leaves, the Estado Novo regime could be said to have rigorously fulfilled Luis's repressive formula. Indeed, the labor ministry's legal adviser, Francisco José de Oliveira Vianna, criticized the liberality of the prior noninterventionist regime for its inability to control "violent class struggles, with a multiplicity of strikes, sympathy strikes, general strikes, boycotts, and systematized sabotage." Unlike its ineffectual predecessor, the powerful interventionist state of 1930s would put an end to such "generalized disorder harmful to the collective good."[77]

The same repressive spirit could be seen in the 1938 drafting of a new unionization law under Oliveira Vianna's direction. The drafting commission's report vigorously reaffirmed its condemnation of trade unions that served as instruments of "extremist ideologies and social revolution." Such practices of "revolutionary unionism," commission members pledged, would be liquidated through "one of the most rigorous preventive and repressive systems."[78] Indeed, the resulting 1939 unionization law promised repressive action against all who "suspend their work in a lockout or a strike, or who refuse to obey the decisions of the labor courts."[79] The harshest penalties, as Oliveira Vianna emphasized in 1938, were reserved for the agents provocateurs responsible for "the explosion of such conflicts [as well as] those who ostentatiously lead them." Rebel workers such as Andreotti were to be imprisoned for their leadership roles, while mere participants would be punished with "pecuniary penalties and the loss of their right to representation or employment." Such measures, Oliveira Vianna continued, were essential if the state was to eliminate "violent processes of class struggle" such as strikes.[80]

The 1939 telegraphic code was shockingly explicit in its hostility toward collective forms of working-class mobilization or pressure. Standardized entries refer to policemen escorting strikebreakers, using violence against strikers, arresting strikers, and detaining strike leaders. The book even included an entry for closing trade unions, although the organizations that existed in 1939 were tightly controlled and directly incorporated into the *getulista* state.[81] In addition, the code made no attempt to conceal its actively proemployer attitude. While one lonely entry referred to strikers as peaceful, the rest dealt in stereotyped images of strikers burning, attacking, stoning, killing, and kidnaping.[82] While mentioning an abundance of repressive measures, the code book contained no entry for pressuring an employer to settle a strike.

The telegraphic code also continued to blame working-class protest on foreign agitators, although the working class was overwhelmingly Brazilian-born by that time. One four-part sequence of entries begins "The head of the strike is ——." The telegrapher then has the following options: the strike leader is the "Spaniard so-and-so," the "Portuguese so-and-so," or the "Italian so-and-so." The sequence allowed for no possibility that the strike leader might be Brazilian, so that the telegrapher would have to report that information by using the entry "He is the communist so-and-so."[83]

The "ideological cliché" that linked foreign origin with subversion, as Adalberto Paranhos has recently shown, was shared by both "those who governed and the dominant classes" as a whole during the Estado Novo. Within this framework, "the class struggle, an 'exotic plant,' was [always] linked to the action of small groups of foreign agitators" and was therefore "an imported phenomenon estranged from the 'pacific temperament' of the Brazilian worker."[84] This antiforeign reflex would survive the advent of electoral democracy in 1945, as suggested by a 1948 courtroom exchange in São Paulo recalled by Elias Chaves Neto, a communist journalist. When Chaves Neto admitted his beliefs, the judge was infuriated because the subversive was Brazilian-born: "I can admit that misery exists. I can admit that discontent exists and even a spirit of revolt. What I cannot admit is that Brazilians would seek out foreign ideologies to apply them to our country."[85]

This older repertoire of images and postures figured prominently in the discourse of Labor Minister and Justice Minister Alexandre Marcondes Filho, the *paulista* lawyer who ordered the legal standardization of the labor laws in the 1943 CLT. In October of that year, the minister offered his personal reminiscences of the "bad old days" in a speech to trade unionists at the army's General Command School: "My first encounter with the social problem happened in São Paulo. The year was 1916 [1917]. A general strike had been declared, with conflicts in the street and marauding, so that repression by the police was required to assure public order. There was a shoot-out between workers and soldiers, with dead among both groups. . . . The agitation at that time, which disturbed urban life for several days, constituted a portrait of the first industrial phase in São Paulo. In that period, the worker, the machine, the raw material, all came from Europe; the only thing national about our industry was the climate. For that reason, the strike was also a transplantation of a European mentality and European agitations. It had arrived in the baggage of the immigrant."[86] In a pattern that continued from before 1930, this ambitious and well-connected São Paulo bankruptcy lawyer rejected all that was foreign as inappropriate and blamed foreign immigrants for strikes, while the subtext indirectly expressed a certain pride that Brazil was becoming modern (European), even with the problems created in the wake of this process (such as worker agitation).

Mouthing words to which he was not committed, Marcondes Filho demonstrated the discomfort that he shared with his industrialist friends from São Paulo when faced with some of the regime's laborite rhetoric and propaganda. He would have disapproved of the short 1941 book entitled *Getúlio Vargas: O Reformador Social* (*Getúlio Vargas: Social Reformer*) when it drew an unsavory portrait of the recent past: "Before 1930, what prevailed? The right of the strong over the proverbial weak: the rights of the bosses over the interests of the workers. No rights of the worker were recognized, and their class interests were left to be resolved through police inquiries; to demand a right was a misdemeanor, to insist on it was a crime."[87] Marcondes Filho would have disapproved because even if the recipient of such a message agreed that things had previously been worse, it would be hard to believe that all had changed, in one decade, through a simple "wave of the magic wand"[88] of social reform through law. Exaggerated claims that Vargas had "resolved the social question" likewise implied that class struggle had once existed, even if only before 1930. Such an admission directly contradicted the upper-class mythology about the pacific nature of Brazilian social relations (a discourse to which Marcondes Filho was committed).

The Estado Novo's labor minister even felt constrained to explain away the *caso de polícia* aphorism, which did not indicate, he insisted, any animosity toward employers because that "would be improper." If anything negative or sad happened to workers before 1930, he claimed, it had never resulted from any "sentiment of cruelty on the part of employers." The saying, he said, merely highlighted the Old Republic's "unforgivable legislative backwardness," which had been caused by the state's absence from labor relations.[89] Although his excuses were unconvincing, the promulgator of the CLT and his subordinates were certain that Brazil's social laws had only one valid objective: to establish "unity, order, and discipline."[90] In the words of a government May Day banner, "The Unionized Worker Is a Disciplined Worker"; if not, there was always recourse to the rod (*pau neles*).

Rally at Pacaembu stadium in São Paulo, May Day, 1944. The main banner says: "The Unionized Worker Is a Disciplined Worker." (Courtesy Iconographia/Cia. da Memória/Brazil)

While some observers have seen ideological confusion or fluidity within the ruling circles between 1930 and 1945, many opponents and some scholars have interpreted the Estado Novo's antiliberalism and repressive practices as the culmination of a totalitarian project linked to Vargas. Cancelli, for example, sees clear evidence of "a very well articulated set of ideas with a common [totalitarian] origin."[91] Yet this one-sided characterization underestimates powerful continuities from Brazil's inheritance of despotism, paternalism, and juridicism.[92] Far from being the fruit of imported European ideologies, the Estado Novo's antidemocratic outlook was an expression of the Brazilian dominant class's deeply rooted authoritarian political culture. Viewed in the larger sweep of Brazilian history, the roots of police violence and arbitrariness toward labor in the 1930s and 1940s must be sought in the world of slavery, an institution that had been abolished only fifty years earlier.

The late-twentieth-century literature on Brazilian labor has overlooked the continuities between capitalist free labor and slavery,[93] whether in terms of status hierarchies, broader societal models of authority, or styles of labor management. In contrast, those who wrote about Brazilian labor legislation at midcentury saw this inheritance with greater clarity. In a 1957 interpretive essay, Lídia Besouchet argued that the MTIC's founding could be understood only in light of the country's social history, which was dominated by slavery. Slavery's humiliating conception of manual labor, she suggested, had bred deformed values and undemocratic forms of behavior in the conduct of relations between the subaltern and the superordinate (a group in which she included degree holders [*bacharéis*], government employees, military men, and industrialists). Although she did not develop it further, Besouchet even advanced the hypothesis that the "Brazilian worker could be characterized as a fruit of the system of slavery."[94]

Pimenta, a labor lawyer and MTIC official, made the case persuasively in his discussion of state-society relations in a 1948 labor law textbook (although the placement of his observations consigned them to the years before 1930). Brazilian government leaders, he said, "continued to see the worker as a direct dependent under the incontestable authority of the boss [*patrão*]." Labor in the factory, the mill, and the retail shop, he suggested, may "no longer reflect the somber spirit of the slave quarters," but these work relations "are still saturated with false and disgraceful ideas" from the time of slavery, "a labor regime in which the employer exercised his power without restrictions." Even worse, Pimenta said, the boss does so with impunity, because he is shielded by an equally "false and sinister principle of political authority. The state became accustomed to seeing in the boss an incarnation of discipline, of security in the economic order, and to seeing the worker, the one who diverged from his employer by demanding a right, as an element of disorder and a threat to social tranquility."[95]

José Aranha de Assis Pacheco, a lawyer who represented employers in labor court cases, provided eloquent proof of the living heritage of slavery in mid-twentieth-century São Paulo factories. In his 1945 book, *Prevenção de Dissidios Trabalhistas* (*The Prevention of Labor Dissídios*), Pacheco offered legal and managerial advice on how factories could avoid the expense and hassle of labor law cases by better handling their workers. His stories about shop floor life offer unique access to the employer side of the class divide, but even Pacheco was amazed by one "truly incredible episode" that he recounted under the title "An Apologist for the Whip [*Chicote*]." Pacheco had learned that the general manager (*gerente*) of a large factory the lawyer represented had received a report that a section chief (*encarregado*) had publicly displayed a firearm on the job. Since weapons were strictly forbidden under the factory's regulations, Pacheco assumed that proper measures would be taken "to prevent a repetition of the act and to punish the transgressor." Pacheco was shocked, he declared, when he heard an impassioned and emotional tirade from the general manager: "Well done! Only with a pistol in your belt can you really deal with such scum [*canalhada*]! Those people should be handled with a whip!"[96]

Workers, Cops, and *Trabalhistas* during the Populist Republic

As this chapter has discussed, the *caso de polícia* first emerged from the ranks of a marginalized opposition during the 1920s, although it quickly became common currency with both the *getulista* establishment and its opponents.[97] The saying played an especially important role in the discourse of labor activists and the radical Left over the next half century. These groups deployed the aphorism differently than did Luis's nostalgic champions, hordes of opportunist *trabalhistas*, or even moderate leftists such as Moraes Filho. For such radical activists, the *caso de polícia* expressed the conviction that state violence against and repression of workers' struggles was characteristic of all Brazilian governments, regardless of whether they were oligarchical, "revolutionary," electoral democratic, or dictatorial. From this point of view, the only persistent truth about the Brazilian state was that the enduring mission of a capitalist government, whatever its paternalistic pretenses, was to preserve the social and political order of a violently unequal society through the repression of its victims and opponents.

After a brief period of hopefulness after World War II, the radical Left's pessimistic conclusions were amply confirmed by the violently repressive Dutra administration of 1946–50. Dutra's attack on what he saw as the forces of disorder, anarchy, and communism came less than a decade after a similar crackdown during the somber years from 1935 to 1941. Both twentieth-century episodes of repression showed clear parallels to the upper-class response to the social turbulence and political disorder that had characterized Brazil's first decade after independence. The leaders of the conservative reaction of the 1830s sharply criticized the destabilizing enthusiasm for what they called the "vague and rhetorical doctrines of an exaggerated freedom." According to historian Thomas Flory, "The men of the *Regresso* [return, going back] distrusted elections and democratic forms," as did Vargas and many of his elite, antipopulist opponents. They might lament the backward state of Brazilian civilization and its need for a stable source of authority, but their view of

Brazilian society "was one which assumed the ultimate victory of the elite class and corporate [upper-class] consensus. Political opposition, for the Conservatives, was hard to distinguish from social threats; hence the fear of the mob and the often-expressed worry that an opposition party would try to build a following among blacks, workmen, or other socially disreputable elements. The centralizing laws would presumably make this impossible by uniting the 're-sponsible' or 'conservative' classes in a union of self-interest."[98]

These attempts to maintain upper-class unity against the advance of democracy and the masses failed in the late 1940s, in large part because of the disruptive maneuvers of the now-unsound Vargas who, angered by his ouster in 1945, maneuvered successfully to win election as president in 1950. The breakdown of dominant class unity in the political sphere, combined with changes in the political outlook and understanding of the general populace, would lead to a third and successful conservative counterattack, the 1964 military coup. Within the context of this unresolved struggle, there was no question about police loyalties during these years of mass electoral democracy and labor mobilization. As one Rio policeman recalled in 1981, the democratic opening at the end of World War II brought communist "contractors of disorder" into the streets, inciting the common people to riot (*fazer baderna*) and to insult the police. Despite Dutra's valiant efforts to restore order, Olyntho Scarmuzzi went on, the period from Vargas's 1950 election through 1964 featured "unrestrained political demagoguery" driven by an unholy alliance between malleable opportunists like Goulart and a disorderly and subversive minority. Recycling old ideological commitments at the height of the fight for redemocratization, Scarmuzzi attacked communo-*janguistas* for imposing a demagoguery on the country in which strikes were "officialized and even forged" in the halls of the Labor Ministry.[99]

For the labor Left, the years from 1945 to 1964 confirmed the belief that police truculence toward workers might ebb and flow with the political tides but had not abated. Even in dealing with the most routine labor-management disagreements, the police automatically aligned themselves with employers, as was illustrated in a story told by Philadelpho Braz, a noncommunist. He recounted what happened during a 1950 in-plant stoppage at the Fichet-Schwartz Hautmont factory where he worked: "The local police *delegado* [was from] the social-political order [DOPS]. And I remember the sergeant who commanded the unit [that arrived at my factory], a very fat man named Sergeant Garcia. He arrived, but he's never going to listen to the leaders of the stoppage to find out why it occurred. He's always going to listen to the em-

"Law of Fidelity to the Country [of the] Yankees," a 1953 communist cartoon that criticizes the McCarthyite repression that characterized the Dutra and Vargas administrations (1946– 54). The caption reads, "This dangerous subversive agent asked for a match from a man who telephoned the aunt of a shoeshine boy who did the shoes of someone who knew the neighbor of a communist" (*Notícias de Hoje* [São Paulo], 28 August 1953).

ployer first. Besides, he had already arrived on the scene swaggering, armed, prepared for beatings, prepared psychologically to beat up the worker without even knowing the strike's cause. In that particular situation, it appeared that we were going to go through Christmas without any money in our homes [without receiving their pay]. It was an absurdity. Everybody stopped."[100]

Speaking about the height of the populist era, Braz had no illusions about the state's repressive forces and their attitudes toward labor: "The police don't like unions. Military men in general, those enrolled in any of the branches of the armed forces, they don't like unions either, and then there is the militarized police as well."[101] He had equally little confidence in the worker's ostensible allies in the labor ministry and the labor court system. Although a member and onetime candidate of Jango Goulart's PTB, Braz was profoundly skeptical of the glib professional *trabalhistas* whose speeches inevitably invoked the *caso de polícia* and Vargas's benevolent "gift" of the labor laws: "Now you do occasionally encounter a person of authority in the labor ministry who is willing to give us a hand and enter as a conciliator, but even that person will never clash directly with an employer. He'll stay where he is, there in the middle, for a long time unless there is pressure from the union or the employer. But it is hard—rare in fact—to find cases where the individual will pass over to the union's side and declare hostilities against the employer. [Why?] Because industrialists are the economic force of the nation, they elevate the GNP [gross national product]. It is they who export, who produce, and if they're not producing, the politicians won't be coming."[102]

Asked about the role of repression in workers' struggles during his pre-1964 days in union leadership, Braz was eminently down-to-earth in describing both the police and how they handled strikes:

> To strike, you have to picket. Well, the police are always against the union and against those who are picketing. Why? Because of a question of education, of culture. Because the soldier, military policeman—with the exception of the officers who have a bit more education—these men are all at the same cultural level as the worker. And why is this done? They don't want an educated police force because the police are supposed to beat people. When the employer, the boss, orders the police to give someone a beating, policemen will beat up their own brothers, their brothers of misfortune, because all of us are living badly.
>
> So the big enterprises have control over the repressive power, the police. If we plan a strike at Pirelli tomorrow, they'll have the military police force put up inside. They'll maintain a restaurant, treat them well, and do everything to win them over. By birth, the repressive forces are favorable to the employers, and when they are well treated, the boss is a saint to them. This happens even today. . . . The policeman knows that after the strike is over, at the end of the year, at some point, the employer will send a Christmas basket to the commandant. He doesn't send it to the common soldier but to the commandant of the police detachment. That nice Christmas basket, with imported whiskey, Peruge [a candy]. This is a game of playing for influence. And it's here that the union loses.[103]

Braz also eloquently discussed the many shortcomings of the labor law system anchored in the CLT. When asked if it would not have been better for the labor movement to have based itself more firmly on the workers' strength rather than on the labor law, he replied,

> Look, this is the way it is. No matter what the regime is, no matter what form it takes, what you do has to take into consideration, [has to] be based on some mechanisms of toleration. If what is done isn't legal, it has to at least be tolerated. Such and such a thing happens and is tolerated; this is permitted.
>
> So I think that the CLT was a start [in this context]. After all, how does it advance our struggle when the boss does something [and I say] "Let's go on strike"? Because you have to take into account the power of repression in the hands of the employer. Anything that happens—like a movement in the factory—is a matter for the police [*caso de polícia*]. Moreover, even today—and at that time in a different fashion—there was no right to strike. There was a terrible decree [in my time] against those who went out on strike. There was the National Security Law, and a decree 9.070 that impeded you from striking.
>
> So you had to do everything legally, because the conditions didn't exist to strike. If I organized a strike, [pause]—I've seen many communists proceed in that fashion, and the police would go into the factory just like that, grab the guy, take him to jail, beat him up, and then release him. The guy returns to the factory to ask for his job back, and nobody had done anything in solidarity with him.[104]

Brazilians of all political outlooks have long recognized that the post-1930 flood of labor legislation did not change the truth captured in the famous aphorism that "the social question is a matter for the police [*caso de polícia*]." The question of law has always been inseparable from that of order in a nation whose green, blue, and yellow flag, adopted in 1889, boasted the positivist slogan "Order and Progress."[105] And for working-class activists and trade union leaders after 1931, no amount of time spent dealing with lawyers, judges, and labor ministry officials (most often lawyers) changed the fact that the fate of their organizations and struggles was profoundly shaped by other, more openly repressive state institutions and policies.

The coexistence of the world's most advanced labor legislation with the *caso de polícia* aptly captures the two sides of Brazil's dominant-class rule over the popular majority. For the Vargas regime and all of its successors, the ostensibly paternalistic and highly protective labor law did not stand in contrast to

Philadelpho Braz and Luis Inácio "Lula" da Silva, the old and new generation of ABC's metalworkers, 1982. As founders of the Workers' Party, Braz and Silva shared the fight during the latter's first run for elective office. (Courtesy of the author)

police repression but rather as its necessary complement, its inextricable double. The violent, corrupt, and arbitrary police actions that trade unionists, activists, and rank-and-file workers faced help to explain why the Brazilian popular classes have never bought into illusory notions about the essential "goodness" of law as an expression of their inalienable rights as citizens.

As a social class, Brazilian workers have always known that society must be forced to recognize them as citizens. In acting on that basis, their mobilizations across the decades made possible a previously unthinkable event: the election of a poorly educated manual worker and former trade union leader as Brazilian president. As a leader among ABC's metalworkers, "Lula" da Silva carried forward Andreotti and Braz's tradition of struggle while illustrating its underlying truths. Lula's personal radicalization was fostered by his repulsion for the police after the ferocious 1975 torture of his communist brother, "Frei Chico," Andreotti's friend and comrade who, like Lula, had been elected to union leadership in ABC. After leading massive strikes in 1978, 1979, and 1980, Lula was arrested and prosecuted under the National Security Law first passed under Vargas during the 1930s and revised during his second presidency in the early 1950s. In Lula's case, however, the worker agitation so long deemed a *caso de polícia* proved capable of turning matters on their head as part of a broad coalition that brought a return to democratic rule in 1985. The unparalleled scope and intensity of popular and democratic struggles throughout Brazil since those years has now made a former prisoner the new commandant of the same police and military men who had persecuted Andreotti and put Lula in jail.

The CLT is the AI-5 of the working class.
—LUIS INÁCIO "LULA" DA SILVA, referring to
Institutional Act 5 of 1968, which dismissed
Congress, ended habeas corpus, and inaugu-
rated the most radically repressive period of
the post-1964 military regime

Question: Who makes the laws and what are
the laws good for?
Answer: Today, those legislating are "men
of confidence of the capitalist regime. For example, in relation to the labor laws, we know
that many of the articles of the labor legislation
are conquests of the workers, who, to the extent
to which they carried out their struggles, succeeded in transforming into law a series of
things; that is, they were able to transform
those fights and demands into laws. . . . But
clearly the legislators that are there [now] are
very crafty, and they create laws to weaken that
which the workers have won. The law that
exists [today] is not really favoring the workers
because of the defects that it has acquired with
the passage of time."
—SANTOS DIAS, a member of the São Paulo
metalworkers' opposition killed by police
during the 1979 metalworkers' strike

conclusion

Drowning in Laws and Starving (for Justice)

Workers and the Quest to Realize the Imaginary

Working-class activists in modern Brazil have always been acutely aware of the illusory freedom that exists for the proletarianized "free" laborer. This is clearly illustrated by the epigraph to the introduction to this volume. Even in Brazil, there is no law to prevent a worker from dying of hunger. And the words of the worker Joaquim from Pernambuco (see chap. 6) clearly demonstrate his awareness that the nation still has not fulfilled the promise of freedom given to the worker through the labor law. Using the term "freedman" (*liberto,* or former slave), Joaquim also subtly reminds his listener of the continuities that underlie Brazil's long history of coercing labor, slave and free, whether by the whip or through the threat of hunger. The discourse of this minority of activist workers suggests the limits of the ability of Brazilian bourgeois thought to achieve the ideological illusion possible in the developed industrial world. In a very real sense, these individuals can also be said to see through the illusion underlying labor law itself in a capitalist society:

FIGURE 2. The Law (CLT) Is My Bible

João Dirceu Mota [1916–1969] was a mason and had rough, calloused hands. He came from Uruguaiana and already brought with him some union experience. . . . He arrived in Quaraí in the 1950s. Here, he [encountered] a surprise: the city didn't know about working papers and the labor laws were dead letters. No one knew of them. Or [people] pretended not to know them.

And this was his great [battle] flag, the great challenge for João Dirceu Mota until his death. . . . He founded and was made president of the Union of Construction Workers of Quaraí. This was the [favored] daughter in his eyes. Theater of his combats, mirror of his dreams.

Even now I can still see him: huge, a half-waggish smile, a half-deformed arm, always in a jacket. Simple, humble. But furious when confronting the employers, when he denounced the exploiters of the working class. There he was something else: his voice was strong, harsh, trampling over itself. In defending his companheiros, he was all indignation. . . . Under his arm, always, the Consolidation of Labor Laws. "This is my Bible," he told me once.

Source: Marçal, Comunistas Gaúchos, 95–96.

the belief that "the qualitative differences between social classes could be surpassed juridically" through protective labor legislation.[1]

Condemned to act within the universe of fraud that was the CLT, which was stacked against workers, working-class activists and trade unionists after 1943 would in practice subvert the existing law through a fight to make the law, as imaginary ideal, real. In a Brazil where workers were drowning in laws but starving for justice, it thus makes complete sense for a gaúcho construction worker to confront the bosses with his well-worn copy of the CLT: "This is my bible." Even the soon-to-be-martyred Dias's more reckless characterization of the CLT as a "workers' conquest" makes sense despite its historical inaccuracy. Given the extremely difficult conditions of workers' struggle under the post-1964 military dictatorship, it was sensible for a labor militant like Dias, in his discourse, to valorize the CLT and even to praise the ambiguous and demagogic statecraft of which it was part before 1964.[2] Acting without illusions, this construct would transform the CLT, at least discursively, into a weapon in his fight against powerful enemies for a better future. Yet like other workers before him, Dias's tactic of using the CLT should never be mistaken for a disagreement with Lula da Silva's or Marcos Andreotti's more harshly critical view.

If the CLT produced such ambivalence in the discourse of working-class activists, the ongoing and uncamouflaged antilabor repression, even against the legal unions, produced a sharp and undifferentiated clarity of discourse about the police. Together, the CLT and the police constituted the discursive and material space within which honest working-class activists and union leaders struggled against those above. On the one hand, the government gave the workers the "gift" of the CLT, which had not been requested and could never be used effectively to its declared end. On the other hand, the same government beat the workers. This system of rule was based on the fundamental duality of giving people gifts and beating them up; benevolence and violence; *violence douce* and *violence dure*. Yet neither is to be understood as separable from or in contradiction to the other. As Brazilian political philosopher Roberto Unger has suggested, "legalism and terrorism, the commitment to rules and the seduction of violence, are rival brothers, but brothers nonetheless."[3]

To survive and struggle in industrial Brazil, workers required an outlook that both rejected the law and idealized it. The law as ideal should not be seen, however, as imaginary but rather as "an icon that derives its power from the fact that it is not a person but rather something objective, impersonal, fair, and just. Of course, everyone knows that the law is in fact personal, not fair, and not just. It is thus both a joke and not a joke. It is a serious farce."[4] As for police vexations, arbitrariness, and acts of despotism, the leaders of Brazil's working people have often pondered how long such humiliations might last. "We Brazilians," Romulo Pereira de Souza suggested in his 1998 memoir, "are the children of an authoritarianism that has unhappily been part of our country since the arrival of the caravels of Cabral [in 1500]. A Brazil made miserable from birth because it had police before it had a people. The trauma in our collective unconsciousness perhaps."[5] This chastened meditation by a Rio trade unionist was published four years before an election that offered a brighter prospect: that Brazil's people, no longer fearful of being happy, might take their country a step beyond its history and into its dreams.

appendix

The Man of the Book

"This Is My Bible"

Joan Bak

The conclusion of this book offers a cameo portrait of João Dirceu Mota, a construction worker and militant communist labor activist in Rio Grande do Sul, my area of study, during the 1940s and 1950s. Two things are particularly memorable about this vignette. One is the visual image of Mota, carrying "under his arm, always, the CLT." The other is Mota's description of his relationship to the CLT: "This is my Bible."

If we begin to ask who Mota is, we find that he was born in 1916, at the time of the Bolshevik Revolution and World War I, and that he came of age in the Brazil of Getúlio Vargas during the 1930s. Mota was still a young man of twenty-seven when the CLT was created in 1943, and he was in his thirties when he came to Quaraí in the 1950s.

But of course we see him, not directly or transparently but rather filtered through his representation by João Batista Marçal, himself a fascinating figure and very much a participant in Brazilian labor history. Marçal's 1986 book on the lives of thirty-one communist militants from Rio Grande do Sul—the book from which this vignette is taken—is the product of a labor of love spanning years spent interviewing and collecting photos from labor activists.

Marçal is a committed journalist, a reporter and editor for a long list of leftist, popular, and mainstream papers as well as a well-known and very colorful local radio personality in Porto Alegre. When I visited his tiny dilapidated house in one of the poor, working-class neighborhoods on the city's periphery, I had to walk along a sequence of teetering planks across ditches and mud to get to the door, and the unique labor history archive he kept in an alcove of the main room was in real danger of imminent destruction by any passing storm.

When Marçal wrote this vignette, he was writing it as one portrait in a kind of pantheon of labor heroes, designed to celebrate and inspire the spirit of struggle. His intended audience, like his style, was not academic but popular. His communist militants are represented as heroic rebels, the mythic type or stereotype who dares to question the structures of power and privilege.

Mota is "simple, humble," with the handicap of a "half-deformed arm" to overcome and the "rough, calloused hands" of the manual laborer. Yet at the same time, he is physically and figuratively "huge," a man who assumes the responsibility of defending his *companheiros* (fellow workers), "furious when confronting the employers." Marçal gives Mota the masculinity of the hero: the rough hands, the strong voice, the combative stance, the image of father to the Union of Construction Workers he founded, which is gendered as the "daughter in his eyes." What gives all this a new twist is the unexpected surprise description of what this combative hero uses to defend his *companheiros*: under his arm there is no anarchist's bomb, no revolutionary's gun, just a book.

Here we must pause to consider the cultural and symbolic meanings of this image of labor militant armed with a book. First, this image foregrounds literacy, the power to read, the command of the written word as liberation from ignorance. By extension, it references the power of knowledge and access to books as an implicit challenge to the traditional monopoly of the written word by the *bacharel* and *letrado*. A book in the hands of a labor militant clearly has a very different meaning from a book in the hands of a lawyer.

The book under Mota's arm is a source of authority and of a particular kind of authority—something other than personal charismatic authority. The book is a source of authority both over other workers (and Marçal's book tells us that Mota was not a simple mason but a construction foreman) and to denounce "the exploiters of the working class." Mota references this authority when he tells Marçal (and with how much irony we can only guess), "This is my Bible." He is playing with the dual authority of that other code of moral laws as both a comprehensive set of rules for daily life and promise of a better order to come.

Furthermore, Marçal makes Mota a bringer of laws, an outsider who brought his CLT along with "some union experience" to a "city that didn't know about working papers" where "the labor laws were dead letters. No one knew of them. Or [people] pretended not to know them." Far from "drowning in laws," it seems, the workers of Quaraí were stranded high and dry without them until this working-class Moses came to town.

Thus, Mota arrives as some sort of prophet or preacher of the Word to the ignorant and unenlightened, a teacher as well as a fighter. The laws he carries under his arm are distanced from the bourgeois laws Marx condemned as veils over the workers' eyes. These laws are brought not to blind and exploit but to enlighten and free.

It is interesting how these meanings change within the particular context of the world of Quaraí, of which Marçal, not incidentally, is a native son. This is not a world of factory workers. Though Marçal suggests that the Quaraí of the 1950s was virgin territory, a backwater innocent of labor law, in reality, it was a transnational crossroads with a distinctive place in Brazilian labor history.

Quaraí sits on the north bank of the river that forms Brazil's southern border with Uruguay, separated only by the water from the Uruguayan town of Artigas, which by the start of the twentieth century was already linked by railroad to the struggles of workers in Montevideo. During Brazil's First Republic, all manner of leftist and labor literature crossed through here from the reformist Uruguay of President José Batlle y Ordoñez (1856–1929), just another element in the flood of contraband for which the area has always been notorious. There is particular irony in the image of Mota bringing his copy of Brazil's famous labor laws to Quaraí, since he was bringing them to an area famous for flouting all law—as if legal culture could tame a border's gun-toting and smuggling culture of violence.

There is also a very particular political trajectory in Quaraí that has shaped the terrain into which the CLT suddenly intrudes. As early as the 1890s, when Quaraí's twenty thousand people slaughtered ninety thousand head of cattle to supplement what the inhabitants made on contraband, a mayor who took up the Comtian positivist project of "incorporating the proletariat" not only helped organize local working-class associations but also got a worker elected to the town council, dominated at the time by the usual suspects, local landowners and *coronéis* (local political bosses). During the course of the First Republic, the city produced more than one labor militant who passed through this Comtian positivism on his way to Marxism. I know little about how these early influences were transformed or reworked after 1930, but I do know that during the 1930s, labor activists from the cities of Rio Grande do Sul's eastern seaboard were commonly deported to this border zone, complicating its social geology still further.

This is just a glimpse of the specific social world into which we should insert the image of Mota, with his copy of the CLT "under his arm, always"—almost like some medieval saint, never portrayed without his or her characteristic attribute. Neither Mota nor the CLT came into a vacuum of "virgin territory," and they do not enter the same sort of crucible at issue in John D. French's *paulista* cases. French's book shows us a number of such images of labor activists as "people of the book," armed with law, treating the CLT as their Bible. There is the image of Philadelpho Braz, secretary-general of the ABC metalworkers' union in 1961, who, "when approached by a fellow worker . . . would pull out a well-worn copy of the CLT, and 'look up the answer.'" And there are union vice president Miguel Guilhen and other working-class activists.

These images all seem to align workers not only with the law but also with the state. Mota and the other activists are not appealing to natural rights but to rights created by the state, and in this sense, the state, at least initially, is defining what justice is—the same state we would expect a communist militant to be working to subvert.

These images aligning workers with the law come from the Populist Republic, which spanned the years from the end of World War II to the military coup of 1964. These images are bracketed in time by two contrasting images: a familiar one, from elite visions in the First Republic, pre-1930, that associates militant workers with subversion of the law (in effect, standing Mota on his head), and a later one, Lula's more recent comparison of the CLT to Brazil's 1968 Fifth Institutional Act, which again reverses the relationship, making the law a weapon for repressing workers' rights.

These changes over time can provide another narrative to add to our multiplying narratives of labor history: a narrative of workers' changing relationship to the law. Perhaps one of the most interesting things to come out of this kind of work will be some surprising new visions of how these multiple narratives fit together.

INTRODUCTION

1. Erickson, "Corporatism and Labor," 146.
2. Baer, *Industrialization*, 96, 98. Leaving to one side the CLT's nonapplication to rural labor, Baer also observed, with suitable scholarly understatement, that it was "difficult to measure the extent to which all the legislation on the books was complied with."
3. Albertino Rodrigues, *Sindicato e Desenvolvimento*, 95.
4. Guilherme dos Santos, *Cidadania*, 76.
5. In this regard, the trajectory of labor studies in Brazil mirrored the "three historical stages in the development of the industrial relations literature" in Latin America noted in 1967 by Morris and Córdova, *Bibliography*, xi. Throughout the region, there was an early period of concern for the "social question" and a search for and debate about legislative " 'solutions' to conflict, strikes, violence, and the radical leadership and orientation of the labor movement." The second period, marked by a "more voluminous [scholarly] production," presented the new legal structure to a broader public. And finally, Morris and Córdova suggest, a new stage was reached that is marked by a "more diversified industrial relations literature" although the flood of legal studies continues unabated, at least in Brazil. Honoring its founder in 1998, the specialized Editora LTr proudly hailed the seventeen hundred books it had produced on labor law since it became a publishing house in 1968, in addition to innumerable journals, monthly reference works, and conferences it had sponsored since its founding in 1937 as a legal journal focused on the new labor laws (Ferrari, Nascimento, and Martins Filho, *História*, 7–8).
6. By no means unsympathetic to the moral aspirations or motivations of the "reform-minded ministerial bureaucracy," Loewenstein ends with an image that is close to a whole strain of Brazilian introspection. "Brazil is about to embark on a drugstore civilization. What is needed, however, is one which is firmly grounded in the little red schoolhouse" (*Brazil*, 335, 55, 339–41).
7. Castro Gomes, *Burguesia e Trabalho*, 309.
8. Loewenstein, *Brazil*, 338–39.
9. A recent memoir by a status-quo-oriented trade unionist recalls that speakers at the famous May Day rallies held during the Estado Novo always "pointed to Getúlio as 'father of the poor,' to which his enemies would add, 'and mother of the rich' " (Pereira de Souza, *Memórias*, 44). The use of the conjunction "and" rather than "or" is fundamental to understanding the characteristic wit of Brazilians as well as the politics of *getulismo*.
10. Fischer, "Poverty," 155.

11. Except for six years between 1945 and 1951, Vargas served as chief executive, in a number of guises, from 1930 until his 1954 suicide while serving as a democratically elected president.

12. International Confederation of Free Trade Unions, "Missión de la CIOSL a Rio de Janeiro, Brasil" (in Spanish), January 1958, folder 5368, "Brazil 1958," International Confederation of Free Trade Unions Archive.

13. Córdova, "From Corporatism to Liberalisation," 251, 256. Unlike the United States, however, Brazil has ratified the other fundamental ILO convention (98), which concerns workers' right to bargain collectively.

14. The ranking and 2003 estimates are from Population Reference Bureau, *2003 World Population Data Sheet*, <http://www.prb.org>; U.S. Central Intelligence Agency, *The World Factbook*, available at <http://www.cia.gov>.

15. Hobsbawm, *Age*, 370; Di Tella, *Latin American Politics*, 107; Seidman, *Manufacturing Militance*. See French, "Latin American Labor Studies Boom," for an international and comparative perspective on labor and the Left in contemporary Brazil and Latin America. For the development of the field of study, see French, "Laboring and Middle-Class Peoples."

16. French, *Brazilian Workers' ABC*, 1–16.

17. Paoli, "Labor, Law, and the State," 437. Brazilian and foreign scholars are not alone in their overwhelming focus on the laws that govern the organization and functioning of trade unions. An edited international labor history collection from 2000 also focused solely on "collective labour law (by which we mean the law that governed and regulated the organised presence of labour in a particular society)," although the editors were aware that this "removes important areas from consideration," including the legal regulation of work itself (Linden and Price, *Rise and Development*, 8).

18. Paoli, "Labor, Law, and the State," 437. The pioneering generation of sociologists in the 1960s, such as Leôncio Martins Rodrigues, were not entirely unaware of these gaps in scholarly understanding. As he noted in 1974, "The effects of the labor legislation on the attitudes of the Brazilian proletarian are still not well understood, as is also true of the motives that led to its promulgation" (*Trabalhadores*, 101). However, he and other scholars who were "discovering" the working class at the time were quick to offer bold generalizations that went far beyond existing empirical evidence (especially about history).

19. Castro Gomes, *Invenção*, 23.

20. The analytical terrain began to be reconfigured in the mid-1980s through the works of French ("Industrial Workers" and *Brazilian Workers' ABC*), Castro Gomes (*Invenção*), Leite Lopes (*Tecelagem*), and Paoli ("Labor, Law, and the State"). These works both anticipated and contributed to the emergence of a new revisionist literature in Brazil that placed the question of citizenship and rights at the center of scholarly debate on labor.

21. Herrup, *House*, 153, 8, xv. The CLT's unsettled meanings might also enable us to better understand the system's dynamism, including "how the ideals of a regime could both prevail and fail in a single application" (Herrup, *House*, xiv).

22. Forbath, *Law*, xiii, 6.
23. Paoli, "Labor, Law, and the State," 437–38. The term "legal consciousness" comes from Merry, *Getting Justice*, 5.
24. The quotation from the trade unionist is from a 1970s interview with a leader of the textile workers' union before 1964 in Juiz de Fora, Minas Gerais (Loyola, *Sindicatos*, n.p.).

CHAPTER ONE

1. Vargas, *Nova Política*, 1:26–27.
2. Collor, *Origens*, 179. In 1931–32, national budgetary allocations gave the MTIC just under 1 percent of the national budget; Treasury received 25 percent, Justice received 6 percent, Education received 5 percent, and Agriculture received 3 percent (Barbosa de Araújo, *Batismo*, 71). These figures suggest that if the new ministry was the "Ministry of Revolution," it did not amount to much of a revolution.
3. Barbosa de Araújo, *Batismo*.
4. Wolkmer, *Constitucionalismo*, 64–86; Lucas, *Conteúdo*, 65–71.
5. For the use of the word *outorgada* for the 1937 charter, see Lucas, *Conteúdo*, 72, as well as the memoir by Vargas's daughter, Peixoto, *Getúlio Vargas*, 332, 334, 380, 326.
6. Peixoto, *Getúlio Vargas*, 326.
7. Ibid. As is typical of Brazil's rich tradition of political humor, the joke plays with the contrast between what is and what should be: the boss isn't necessarily right except that he *is* the boss; firing without notice happens all the time (despite any laws); and a floor waxer may have the legal right to *aviso prévio*, but the employee is no more likely to be given a month's advance notice of a layoff by *his* boss, ex-deputy Olegário Mariano, than the latter got when Vargas decided to close Congress from one day to the next.
8. The reference to legal formalisms is from Vargas's national address announcing the establishment of the Estado Novo (Peixoto, *Getúlio Vargas*, 329; see 372 for her use of the term "polaca" for the 1937 constitution).
9. On the *Queima das Bandeiras* (Burning of the Flags), see Williams, *Culture Wars*, 9–10, 177; Peixoto, *Getúlio Vargas*, 329.
10. Peixoto, *Getúlio Vargas*, 329; Brazil, *Constituições*, 1:223 (article 187).
11. In 1952, Moraes Filho, *Problema*, 273, was among the first to make this larger point about the continuity of the CLT, promulgated for a "corporatist fascistizing regime," into the postwar democratic era—a phenomenon he called "truly curious." He was quoted on this point by Francisco Weffort in a famous 1974–75 polemic ("Democracia e Movimento," 10). Similar observations were also made in Albertino Rodrigues, *Sindicato e Desenvolvimento*, 77; and Skidmore, *Politics of Military Rule*, 33.
12. Mericle, "Corporatist Control," 306. Moraes Filho argues against the effort to link "all the evils" of later legislation to the 1931 Unionization Decree 19,770 ("Introdução," 22). Motivated at least in part by a desire to deflect "blame"

from his socialist father, Moraes Filho does admit in his major work of 1952 that 19,770 was "the start of ministry control [of unions], even though well intentioned" (*Problema*, 220).

13. Castro Gomes and Souza, *Trabalho e Previdência*, 57.

14. Erickson and Middlebrook, "State and Organized Labor," 217–18; Medeiros, *Ideologia*, 178–88. For a fine critical treatment of the Estado Novo's ideological production around labor, see Paranhos, *Roubo*.

15. These particular examples of rhetorical commonplaces are taken from recent publications by two intellectuals, with quite different political trajectories, who have held high government positions: on the right, R. Campos, *Lanterna*, 180; on the center-left, Weffort, "New Democracies," 220–21. In 1956, the editor of the Communist Party's *Gazeta Sindical* told Robert Alexander that there was no question that the CLT was "a fascist-inspired document," albeit one that could and did change over time (Motta, interview by Alexander, 21 March 1956, Rio de Janeiro, Alexander Papers, Rutgers).

16. For a side-by-side comparison of the social provisions of the 1934 and 1937 constitutions, see Werneck Vianna, *Liberalismo e Sindicato*, 272–75.

17. Brazilian jurists and Vargas opponents quickly pointed out this flagrant plagiarism of the Carta del Lavoro (Moraes Filho, *Problema*, 243–47).

18. Quotation from F. Campos, *Estado Nacional*, 61, as cited in Lenharo, *Sacralização*, 22. The Brazilian episcopate's aggressive support for the Estado Novo gave regime rhetoric a right-wing Catholic flavor (Lenharo, *Sacralização*, 190). To facilitate its objectives, the regime's "powerful anticommunist discourse targeted," as Eliana Dutra and Adriano Duarte argue, more than merely those who offered a radical political or social threat. "Communism" grouped together under a single label a wide and shadowy array of subversive practices, norms, and values that were thought to threaten the foundations of society in many spheres, including gender (Duarte, *Cidadania e Exclusão*, 108).

19. Vargas, *Nova Política*, 5:311. See also Lenharo, *Sacralização*, 22.

20. Two recent studies have graphically underlined the repressive dimensions of Vargas era, which had begun to be underplayed in many other, more sympathetic, recent treatments; see Cancelli, *Mundo*; and Rose, *Forgotten Things*.

21. Moraes Filho, *Problema*, 265–66.

22. Amad Costa, *Estado e Controle*, 62–63; Castro Gomes and Souza, *Trabalho e Previdência*, 57; Barbosa de Araújo, *Batismo*, 137.

23. Füchtner, *Sindicatos*, 45, 67; Amad Costa, *Estado e Controle*, 62–63.

24. Castro Gomes and Souza, *Trabalho e Previdência*, 9.

25. Castro Gomes, *Burguesia e Trabalho*, 214; Albertino Rodrigues, *Sindicato e Desenvolvimento*, 93.

26. A short list of key legislation can be found in Simão, *Sindicato e Estado*, 84–92, 204–5.

27. Hall and Garcia, "Urban Labor," 171.

28. Barbosa de Araújo, *Batismo do Trabalho*, 60.

29. Lacerda, *Evolução*, 26.

30. Moraes, *Anarquismo*.
31. Moraes Filho, *Problema*, 219–20, 222; Moraes, *Apontamentos* (1905).
32. Cerqueira Filho, *Questão*, 59.
33. Hall and Pinheiro, "Grupo Clarté," 251, 287.
34. The positivist, socialist, Catholic, and Brazilian reformist origins of 19,770 must be given at least equal weight to external influences (Chacon, *Estado e Povo*, 53–57, 118). Nor should one underestimate the impact in legal and political circles of the 1919 decision by Rui Barbosa, Brazil's most famous liberal jurist and politician, to give a speech on the social question (*Questão Social*). A figure of overwhelming prestige, Rui Barbosa's new posture encouraged wide-ranging theoretical discussions in legal circles that meshed nicely with concerns central to Catholic social doctrine (see *Questão Social* by Viveiros de Castro, a member of the Brazilian Supreme Court in the 1920s). Books were still being published in the late twentieth century to claim recognition for pioneering legal and legislative advocacy on behalf of social legislation. (Carvalho-Neto, *Precursor*, deals with a deputy from the small state of Sergipe in the 1920s.) Not surprisingly, none of the juridical works in this vein reflect direct investigation of workers or their labors, lives, or struggles. Discussion has remained overwhelmingly doctrinal, not empirical, in nature.
35. Joaquim Pimenta, "O Sindicato Verdadeiro e o Sindicato Fascista," *Revista do Trabalho*, April 1934, 15–17, cited in Amad Costa, *Estado e Controle*, 64.
36. In "Still the Century of Corporatism?" political scientist Philippe Schmitter took aim in 1974 at the prevalence of narrow understandings of the ideological roots of corporatist forms of interest representation. He particularly castigated the "normative variety and behavioral hypocrisy" of self-righteous critics who, while contributing little in terms of analytical depth and substance, were given to using the corporatist ideological label as a negative reference. Schmitter, author of a valuable 1971 study of Brazil (*Interest Conflict*), offered a nonnormative definition that presented corporatism as a particular modern way of organizing interests in contrast to the pluralist interest group model of the United States. Stripped of polemical fascist associations, he argued, corporatist practices and institutions were widespread in many democratic societies in postwar Western Europe, and corporatist elements could even be found within less state centered political systems such as the United States (Schmitter, "Still," 89, 93, 95).
37. As a participant in the Mexican constitutional assembly of 1917, Deputy Alfonso Cravioto would hail its handiwork as "the most advanced labor code in the world." France after its revolution, he went on, "had the high honor of consecrating the immortal rights of man in the first of its magna cartas, so too does the Mexican revolution have legitimate pride in showing to the world that it is the first to include the sacred rights of workers in a Constitution" (Torre Villar and García Laguardia, *Desarrollo Histórico*, 241, as cited in Wolkmer, *Constitucionalismo*, 18).
38. The overwhelming symbolic importance of the ILO can be seen in one of the preparatory 1929 documents of Vargas's Liberal Alliance. The "Tópicos do

Manifesto" devoted eight paragraphs to the "social question," which the alliance insisted did exist in Brazil and should be seen as a sign of progress. The document contained no discussion of concrete Brazilian realities but devoted half of its text to arguing that membership in the ILO required that Brazil undertake such legislative initiatives. Similar arguments were advanced in Labor Minister Collor's inaugural speech and by Vargas on repeated occasions (Collor, *Origens*, 73; Vargas, "Mensagem Lida Perante a Assembléia Nacional Constituinte, no Ato de Sua Instalação, em 15 de Novembro de 1933," in *Nova Política*, 3:139–40). The ILO continued to serve as a fundamental reference point in Brazilian policy debates throughout the rest of the century, as demonstrated by Noronha in his treatment of these issues in *Entre a Lei*, 105–13.

39. Bastos and Quartim de Moraes, *Pensamento*, 289.

40. Burlamaqui, *Associações*; Bezerra de Menezes, *Homens e Idéias*, 36–41; Ferrari, Nascimento, and Martins Filho, *História*, 220. Union official Ary Campista was also an integralist during the 1930s, although his success at the pinnacle of the trade union structure for the next fifty years depended on his service to whomever controlled the federal government (Campista, "Todos Melhoraram").

41. A famous opponent of state interventionism in socioeconomic affairs, Eugênio Gudin was a *relator* for the first railroad workers' retirement fund and served on a drafting commission at the labor ministry under Collor (Sodré, "Necessidades," 77). On Moraes Filho, see *Problema*, xi.

42. Howes, "Progressive Conservatism," 177.

43. Richard Terdiman, introduction to Bourdieu, "Force," 806.

44. Howes, "Progressive Conservatism," v, 2–3.

45. See the introduction to Moraes, *Apontamentos*, xix; their teacher-student relation at the Faculdade de Direito de Niterói is noted in Macieira, "Oliveira Viana," 226.

46. Ribeiro Costa, "Corporativismo," 131.

CHAPTER TWO

1. R. B. Collier, "Popular Sector Incorporation," 59. For too long, historians of Latin America, Charles Bergquist observed in 1986, had "failed to recognize the decisive historical role of organized labor and the labor movement" in explaining the "very different ideological and political trajectories" of the countries in the region (*Labor*, 1).

2. Abel and Lewis, *Latin America*, 279. In offering a sociopolitical history of the law, this book follows the path set out by the pioneers who discussed Latin American labor law in the 1970s. In 1979, David Collier and Ruth Berins Collier placed particular emphasis on labor law as a "valuable point of reference for analyzing the larger political context" ("Inducements versus Constraints," 971; see also R. B. Collier and D. Collier, *Shaping*). Using formal features in labor law texts from different Latin American countries, the authors examined patterns of corporatist interest representation in terms of

inducements and constraints. Labor law played a central political role, they went on, because it was "a highly visible and concrete policy statement around which political battles are fought, won, and lost, and around which political support is attracted, granted, and withheld" (D. Collier and R. B. Collier, "Who Does What," 98). Yet their study, which covered only "years in which labor law is promulgated or modified," was only a starting point, they admitted, because the analysis should also encompass "the application of law and [even] certain aspects of corporative practice that may never be ratified in law" (D. Collier and R. B. Collier, "Inducements versus Constraints," 971; D. Collier and R. B. Collier, "Who Does What," 495). The Colliers also observed, quite acutely, that "similar structures may have very different functions in different settings" (D. Collier and R. B. Collier, "Who Does What," 295).

A similar analytical approach to the labor laws was advanced in an excellent 1974 historiographical article on labor in Argentina, Brazil, and Chile. The labor laws in the ABC countries, Kenneth Erickson, Patrick Peppe, and Hobart Spalding stressed, were "extremely complex and regulate[d] virtually every aspect of worker activity." Erickson, Peppe, and Spalding's proposed agenda for future investigations, still largely neglected three decades later, was wide ranging and suggestive. "For administrative or political reasons," they observed, the law's "provisions are often selectively or arbitrarily applied. Social scientists could profitably ask: which provisions are consistently enforced or flouted; what determines whether a particular portion of a code is enforced or not; what political, economic or social circumstances govern such selectivity?" Does labor law, they went on, vary by regime? And what effects does it have on the style or intensity of labor mobilization? Does labor law co-opt or politicize labor's leaders? ("Research," 127).

3. Abel and Lewis, *Latin America*, 24–25.

4. R. B. Collier, "Popular Sector Incorporation," 98; Abel and Lewis, *Latin America*, 279.

5. T. Santos, *Brasil*, 51. Even far more prominent and mainstream 1960s Brazilian intellectuals such as Hélio Jaguaribe shared the assessment that Vargas sought "to organize a new political force based on an alliance between two emerging groups: the industrial bourgeoisie and the proletariat" (*Brazilian Nationalism*, 6).

6. Cammack, Pod, and Tordoff, *Third World Politics*, 63.

7. Abel and Lewis, *Latin America*, 24, 278, 279.

8. Erickson, "Corporatism and Labor"; Erickson and Middlebrook, "State and Organized Labor," 214; Wiarda, *Politics*.

9. For the development of the study of labor in Brazil, see Brant, "Bibliographe"; Martins Rodrigues and Munhoz, "Bibliografia"; Dutra and Grossi, "Historiografia"; Paoli, "Trabalhadores"; Batalha, "Historiografia"; French, *Brazilian Workers' ABC*, 1–16; French and Fortes, *Urban Labor History*; Fortes and Negro, "Historiografia."

10. Lahuerta, "Intelectuais," 87, 89.

11. Pinheiro, "Trabalho," 127, 129.

12. Werneck Vianna, *Liberalismo e Sindicato*, 57.
13. Lahuerta, "Intelectuais," 87.
14. Weffort, "Origens," 65.
15. The general presumption underlying the corporatist consensus was that the aims of the framers of the labor laws had been achieved. "In overemphasizing the regime's grandiose aspirations and overarching ideology, both the defenders and opponents of Brazil's corporatist labor system have continued to embrace the particularly bankrupt assumption that law equals reality, that intention equals result, and that rhetoric equals substance" (French, *Brazilian Workers' ABC*, 82).
16. Loewenstein, *Brazil*, 344; Erickson and Middlebrook, "State and Organized Labor," 213–14.
17. Ianni, *Industrialização*, 128; Ferrante, "Legislação," 50–51. On the supposed deradicalizing effects of the government's intervention in labor affairs, see Huntington, *Political Order*, 284–85; Erickson, "Corporatism and Labor," 144; Wiarda, *Politics*, 221, 285.
18. Füchtner, *Sindicatos*, 101, 165; Dean, *Industrialization*, 188; Werneck Vianna, *Liberalismo e Sindicato*, 58–59, criticized the simple exchange model of state-worker relations that was ubiquitous during the 1970s.
19. Basbaum, *História*, 3:182.
20. Munakata, *Legislação*, 78.
21. Erickson, "Corporatism and Labor," 156.
22. Basbaum, *História*, 3:182.
23. For a broader perspective on the larger shift in Brazilian historiography, see French and Fortes, *Urban Labor History*; Santana, "Política"; and Teixeira da Silva and Costa, "Trabalhadores." For recent explorations of the old and the new in Brazilian labor history, see Abreu and Pessanha, *Trabalhador*; Badaró Mattos, *Novos*; Costa, *Busca*; J. Ferreira, *Trabalhadores*; P. Fontes, *Trabalhadores*; P. Fontes, "Comunidade"; Fortes et al., *Luta*; Fortes, " 'Nós' "; Grossi, *Mina*; Lobo et al., *Rio de Janeiro*; Morel, "Empresa"; Morel and Mangabeira, " 'Velho' "; Negro, " 'Via Willyana' "; Negro, "Linhas"; Negro, "Nas Origens"; Pessanha and Morel, "Gerações"; Ramalho, *Estado-Patrão*; Ramalho and Santana, *Trabalho*; Santana, *Homens*; Santana, "Partido"; Santana and Nascimento, " 'Trabalhadores' "; Teixeira da Silva, *Carga*; Teixeira da Silva, *Operários*.
24. For example, in 1982 Erickson and Middlebrook stated incorrectly that "the labor legislation of Vargas' Estado Novo gave Brazilian workers the right to organize for the first time" and that "corporatist legislation and Vargas's authoritarian rule [after 1930] effectively barred nearly all strikes for the next fifteen years" ("State and Organized Labor," 214, 240). Similarly, Koval, a Soviet political scientist, incorrectly claimed that that the 1931 Unionization Law was based on the grouping of employers and workers in the same organizations, as in fascist Italy (*História*, 258, 347). And finally, the literature is full of less significant errors that have been widely circulated in more general historical treatments, including the claim that union membership in Brazil is

compulsory, which originated in an erroneous statement first made in a 1942 book by Loewenstein, a U.S. visitor to Brazil (see Loewenstein, *Brazil*, 343, repeated in Skidmore, *Politics in Brazil*, 11; Skidmore, *Politics of Military Rule*, 40). A recent survey of "Vargas and his era" not only contained inaccuracies (Levine, *Father*, 34, 84, 91) but showed clear evidence of analytical confusion in its arguments (Levine, *Father*, 8, 10–11, 43, in contrast to 106, 131, 11, 46; 84–85 in contrast to 108, 111, 66–67).

25. Castro Gomes, *Invenção*, 22, 195, discusses the symbolic logic of *trabalhismo getulista* in terms of the gift exchange of Marcel Maus.

26. Oliveira Vianna, *Direito*, 65; Cerqueira Filho, *Questão*, 89–90.

27. Medeyros, *Getúlio Vargas*, 21.

28. Paranhos, *Roubo*, 147, 142.

29. Barbosa de Araújo, *Batismo*, 95; Vargas, *Diretrizes*, 211, 212, 214–15, 220. H. Souza Martins, *Estado*, 24–48, offers a fine summary of Vargas's rhetoric on labor, while an insightful and original dissection of the Vargas regime's discourse on labor in the 1930s can be found in Cerqueira Filho, *Questão*, esp. 85–90. See also Paranhos, *Roubo*, 165–67.

30. Motta, *Classes*, 89.

31. Huntington, *Political Order*, 286. In 1970, French scholars Alain Touraine and Daniel Pécaut similarly argued that it was "hard to classify [Latin American] social legislation and the development of political rights as working class achievements" since they were "imposed by the political elites in order to maintain their control." In the face of such initiatives from above, the authors concluded, the "working masses . . . passively adapt," and workers serve as "objects rather than agents" of change ("Working Class Consciousness," 67, 72).

32. In explaining this Brazilian singularity, Oliveira Vianna often evoked the older Brazilian myth of a uniquely conflict-free country that was marked, unlike Europe, by the absence of any "tradition of class struggles" (Oliveira Vianna, *Direito*, 12–13; Paranhos, *Roubo*, 155).

33. For responses by antigetulist politicians in São Paulo, see *Ação da Bancada Paulista*, iii, 346, 306, 308.

34. For examples of such employer rhetoric, see ibid., 361–62, 88–89.

35. Moraes Filho, *Problema*, 212–13.

36. Pinheiro, "Trabalho."

37. Some scholars do admit that this large body of government legislation contains some "positive elements" of interest to the workers and may include some "workers' conquests" (Munakata, *Legislação*, 7–8; Raimundo N. Santos, "Historia," 34).

38. Rodrigues, *Estado*, 106.

39. Mericle, "Corporatist Control," 306. Córdova, "From Corporatism to Liberalisation," 257–58, describes the Brazilian system of industrial and labor relations as having come "into being artificially."

40. Albertino Rodrigues, *Sindicato e Desenvolvimento*, 80. Similar language would appear in descriptions of labor organizations in later periods, even

when they were gaining strength and deepening their roots. Discussing the early 1960s, John W. F. Dulles observed that "it would be a mistake to overlook the considerable amount of artificiality about labor organizations" (*Unrest*, 297).

41. Basbaum, *História*, 3:33.

42. The analytical vocabulary of political scientists has proven richer in its descriptions of variations within this universe of anticipatory, preventative, or co-optive policy making. Schmitter characterized Brazil as "an almost perfect example" of artificial corporatism as part of a broader pattern of "preemptive cooptation" after 1930 (*Interest Conflict*, 112, 124). R. B. Collier, "Popular Sector Incorporation," 63, distinguishes autonomous participation from participation mobilized from above and differentiates between a pluralist model (demand participation) and a preemptive one (extended before demanded and co-opting new participants).

43. Segadas Vianna, interview by Lima, Castro Gomes, and Ramos, 6 October 1983, Rio de Janeiro, 81–82, 49.

44. Skidmore, *Politics in Brazil*, 14. Influenced by the critical literature of the next twenty years, Skidmore would go still further in 1988 and add that Vargas had even "preempted" the question of whether urban workers were "good material for unionization" (*Politics of Military Rule*, 11).

45. Cited in Castro Gomes, *Burguesia e Trabalho*, 27.

46. Quotation from Kubitschek's 1956 presidential message to Congress, as cited by Pazzianotto Pinto, "Sindicatos," 94.

47. Barbosa de Araújo, *Batismo*, 83. In the late 1930s, a frustrated Oliveira Vianna recognized that some Brazilian elites still claimed that the government's efforts to resolve a nonexistent "social problem" had created "a series of purely artificial questions, because they are entirely incompatible with our economic structure" (*Direito*, 11). Brazilian trade unions had been created "artificially, from above, by the government," a Rio *fazendeiro*, Fábio Sodré, complained in 1938, thus upsetting "the natural equilibrium of economic factors." This was not only unnecessary but harmful, he went on, because workers' low cultural level made them easy prey for communists (Sodré, "Necessidades," 70).

48. Cited in Paoli, "Labor, Law, and the State," 412.

49. Saad, interview by Alexander, 13 April 1956, São Paulo, Alexander Papers, Rutgers.

50. Furtado, *Diagnosis*, 71.

51. Vargas, *Nova Política*, 3:144.

52. Lahuerta, "Intellectuais," 73–75.

53. Wanderly Reis, "Apresentação," xiv. Recent research on the industrial bourgeoisie has suggested new models of state-society relations in Brazil after 1930 (Weinstein, *Social Peace*; Draibe, *Rumos e Metamorfoses*, esp. 43–55).

54. Oliveira Vianna, *Direito*, 143.

55. Bello, *Questão*, 27.

56. Oliveira Vianna, *Direito*, 34–35, 291–92, 43–44; Loewenstein, *Brazil*, 339.

57. Oliveira Vianna, *Direito*, 138–39.
58. Motta, *Classes*, 89.
59. Vargas, *Diretrizes*, 226–27.
60. Spalding, *Organized Labor*, 72, 73, 182, 155.
61. Ibid., 184, 153, 180. Elsewhere, however, Spalding indicates some uncertainty about this denial of any material benefits to workers through social legislation. Even if such legislation did produce "shorter hours, better working conditions, minimal rights on the job, and even higher salaries," he argued, "social legislation [would still have] benefitted capitalists more than it harmed them" because increased productivity is "translated into larger profits" (*Organized Labor*, 37).
62. Bernardo, *Tutela*, 86, 58, 159.
63. Spalding, *Organized Labor*, 79; F. Oliveira, "Economia"; Raimundo N. Santos, "Historia," 28. A 1974 article by Rowland, "Classe," was one of the few at the time that dissented from these attempts to directly link the labor laws to capital accumulation, instead proposing a political explanation for their enactment.
64. Flynn, *Brazil*, 100–101.
65. A number of early studies by Brazilian scholars could have led to a revision of dominant views: Gomes's exploration of the industrial bourgeoisie and its relationship to government policy making on labor from 1917 to 1937 (*Burguesia e Trabalho*); Barbosa de Araújo's study of Collor's administration as labor minister (*Batismo*); and Leme's brief summary of the industrialists' thinking about labor and state action prior to 1945 (*Ideologia*). These works had already begun to fill the lacuna identified in 1973 by Roberto Santos, who noted that "the groups involved with the dispute over social laws in Brazil [after 1930] have not yet been identified with rigor" (*Leis*, 21–25). Yet we still lack the Brazilian equivalent of James O. Morris's rich study of the debates associated with the adoption of labor law in the 1920s in Chile (*Elites*) or the fine recent collections dealing with the early history of the social question in Chile and Argentina (Grez Toso, *Cuestión Social*; Suriano, *Cuestión Social*).
66. As suggested in Weinstein, *Social Peace*, 59, 360. It is also important to remember that there will always be strict limits to the "progressive" rhetoric advanced by those industrialists who proclaim their acceptance of "sound social legislation," improved factory conditions, and the raising of low wages. This type of discourse was always more characteristic of the leaders of the industrialists' associations—for example, Roberto Simonsen—especially when, in dialogue with the government, they faced the challenge of casting the immediate economic interests of their fellow employers as essential to the common national good. By the 1950s, populist political rhetoric had become widespread in the increasingly competitive mass politics that characterized urban Brazil. As Weinstein notes, São Paulo industrialists reacted by abandoning the earlier, more daring "progressive" discursive strategy identified with Simonsen and instead espoused a reflexive antipopulism that cast the labor relations system and politicians as a threat (*Social Peace*, 283, 294, 296, 303). Jaguaribe

also identified these dynamics, noting that "industrialists and technocrats were divided in their feelings vis-à-vis the populist governments" and never gave them "full allegiance." While doing business with these governments, industry was simultaneously frightened due to "conscious and unconscious class feelings, by the ascent of the masses, which actually tended to loom much larger in the propaganda of both the government and the opposition than in actual fact" (*Political Development*, 450–51).

67. Weinstein, *Social Peace*, 82.

68. While employer resistance to most measures resulted from simple financial concerns, the opposition to an active trade unionism was a matter of principle. The problem of working-class organization unquestionably serves as the best pivot for any analysis of the broader societal significance of state intervention in industrial relations (French, *Brazilian Workers' ABC*). The characteristic language of employer resistance to effective union organization was well captured in a 1959 book by a lawyer who worked for a Minas Gerais gold mine. The administrators of Morro Velho, Daniel de Carvalho said, had greeted the government's labor laws in the early 1930s with understanding and applause. As in other industrial centers, there were some difficulties, which the companies handled successfully through the "goodwill of those workers who had not yet been poisoned by demagoguery" (Carvalho, *Novos Estudos*, 163; see Grossi, *Mina*, for a splendid account of the workers' movement that was emerging during these years among the Nova Lima workers who had already been "poisoned").

69. Phelps, *Migration*, 216–19.

70. Ibid., 216–17, 219. Those skeptical of Phelps's claims about the modification of the two-thirds law should see the list of decrees in MTIC, *Dez Anos*, 87.

71. Phelps, *Migration*, 219, 226–27.

72. Ibid., 226, 280.

73. A few years after Phelps, another foreign visitor to Rio and São Paulo, ILO official Fernand Maurette, noted that "infringement of labour legislation, with the assent of the authorities and the interested parties," was common, whether for reasons of custom or economics; thus the law's provisions must "be interpreted in the broadest possible way" in such an environment (*Social Aspects*, 54–55).

74. Viotti da Costa, *Brazilian Empire*.

75. Oliveira Vianna, *Direito*, 65. As a vigorous opponent of Vargas by 1934, Brazil's first labor minister, Lindolfo Collor, attacked *getulista* propaganda on the social question precisely in this regard. It would be "a grave injustice to the Brazilian working class," he declared, to affirm that it "did not yet possess, even if only in a chaotic way, a consciousness of its rights." Yet this affirmation was followed almost immediately by statements that coincide with Oliveira Vianna's claim. Given "the great mass of sufferers" in Brazil, Collor said, it was up to the government to act. His initiatives, he said, had the merit of taking "the social question from out of the police stations and dungeons and into the

open air of discussions" (Collor, "A Questão Social no Brasil," *Correio do Povo*, 19 September 1934, in Collor, *Origens*, 210).

76. Segadas Vianna, interview by Lima, Castro Gomes, and Ramos, 6 October 1983, Rio de Janeiro, 258. Schwartzman, *Estado Novo*, 329, offers a related formula, written by government officials during the Estado Novo, about the anticipatory nature of government action in the labor sphere.

77. Oliveira Vianna, *Direito*, 12–13.

78. Fortes, "'Nós.'"

79. Francisco Weffort, in the early 1970s, was speaking to an audience of radical intellectuals distant from the common people but seeking salvation through them. Within this context, Weffort attacked those who doubted the workers' capacity for struggle—at that time or previously—by charging such doubters with manifesting the Brazilian dominant class's traditional belief in the "backwardness" of the popular classes, which he called the "ideologia do atraso" ("Sindicatos e Política," 1:14).

80. See French, *Brazilian Workers' ABC*. On the case of the northeastern states in the early 1930s, see B. C. Ferreira, *Trabalhadores*; and Romão, *Trama*.

81. Bergquist, *Labor*, 132, 158, 165, 167; see also the analogous argument offered in French, *Brazilian Workers' ABC*, 277–79. The absence of serious studies about labor law and its administration in different countries is a serious lacuna in Latin American labor history. The insights that might come from such a comparative analysis remain unfulfilled given the absence of even comparable country-by-country studies of the labor law and its administration. A quick glance at studies of labor law in Argentina, Chile, Mexico, Panama, Guatemala, and socialist Cuba confirms not only the difficulties but also the potential of such systematic comparisons: see Morris, *Elites*; Compa, *Labor Law*; Middlebrook, *Paradox*; Bortz, "'Without Any More Law'"; Collazos, *Labor and Politics*; Adams, "Access"; Fuller, *Work*.

82. For a compelling critique of the mechanistic explanations of the politics of the 1930s that prevailed until recently, see Font, "Failed Democratization."

83. *Legislação do Trabalho* [São Paulo], vol. 2, no. 2: 201, as cited in Simão, *Sindicato e Estado*, 82. "There is an excellent Federal labour inspection service," Maurette wrote diplomatically in 1937, "but the number of inspectors is quite limited and the territory of Brazil is vast," and inspections worked best in Rio de Janeiro (*Social Aspects*, 54). Brazilian observers agreed that the labor ministry met its responsibilities more or less effectively, at least in labor court filings, only in Rio de Janeiro, followed by Minas Gerais and Rio Grande do Sul (MTIC, *Dez Anos*, 60).

CHAPTER THREE

1. An influential analyst in the 1970s and 1980s, New Left sociologist Francisco Weffort, attached fundamental importance to the survival of the fascist-inspired CLT after World War II ("Democracia e Movimento," 10). As Castro

Gomes noted in 1988, the maintenance of a "corporatist union in a liberal-democratic regime" was seen as both anomalous and dubious (*Invenção*, 22–23). That Weffort's contention served for so long as the starting point for discussions of Brazilian labor is a clear demonstration of his ability to set the intellectual agenda for his generation. Alternatively, the persistence of the CLT system—across alternating dictatorial and democratic periods—could be seen as a warning against exaggerating the significance of such institutional and legal continuities.

2. American Chambers, *Consolidation*, article 511.

3. Ibid., articles 73, 59, 67. See articles 76–156 for the minimum wage.

4. Ibid., pp. 62–100.

5. For a better understanding of *dissídios coletivos*, see Sitrângulo, *Conteúdo*, a detailed study of their evolution in São Paulo between 1947 and 1976. From the outset, the CLT also provided for another, if little used, procedure for negotiations between unions and one or more employers. Such collective accords did not cover the workers of an entire industry (*categoria*) in a given geographical area, as in the case of *dissídios coletivos* (Nascimento, "História," 128).

6. Brazil, *Consolidation*. The fastidious attempt to encompass everything within the paper universe of the law has long been a source of humor, as in the case of the management consultant who provided the epigraph to this chapter (Lobos, *Manual*, 63–64).

7. The decision to create the CLT originated, wrote labor ministry functionary Joaquim Pimenta in 1948, in the "ever more imperious need to make uniform a legislation that experience and practice had already shown to be in the condition to form a body of norms" (*Sociologia*, 11). Yet even labor lawyers disagree on the scope and accomplishments of the CLT's drafters. One of the deans of Brazilian labor law, Amaury Mascaro Nascimento, wrote in 1998 that the CLT "was more than simply a compilation because, although called a consolidation, it added innovations, coming close to being a true code" of laws. Yet Nascimento elsewhere presents the CLT "as a mere reunion of already existing texts with a few added brush strokes" and little that was innovative ("História," 158, 95). Such unstable judgments, which are characteristic of legal commentary on Brazilian labor law, remind us that answers to the larger questions posed by these laws will be found only by going beyond the juridical field.

8. Albertino Rodrigues, *Sindicato e Desenvolvimento*, 93. The CLT drafting commission reported that its work was based on "class confraternization" and "sentiments of Christian humanism," principles that reflected "the maturity of a social order" (Nascimento, "História," 158). Fifty-one years later, a former labor minister and TST president, Almir Pazzianotto Pinto, echoed these ambitious claims when he disagreed with those who saw the CLT as merely a technical aspect of the modernization of Brazilian law under Vargas. Doing so, Pazzianotto Pinto argued, ignored "the rounded and ambitious project of socioeconomic development" represented by the CLT. "In approving the CLT,

Getúlio Vargas endowed Brazil with a perfected legislation that accorded individual rights to workers that had not even been thought of yet" ("Sindicatos," 89).

A less grandiose and more convincing explanation for the CLT was offered by another former labor minister, Segadas Vianna, one of the CLT's four drafters. His boss at the time, Alexandre Marcondes Filho, a lawyer who served as minister of both labor and justice, felt that laws on labor issues were chaotic (Segadas Vianna, interview by Lima, Castro Gomes, and Ramos, 6 October 1983, Rio de Janeiro, 134). Moreover, practical and bureaucratic rationales no doubt contributed to the CLT's creation because the "laws, decree-laws, decrees, regulations, instructions, ordinances [*portarias*], circulars, models, and tables referring to the labor legislation" already amounted to 1,278 pages in 1939 (Souza Netto, *Legislação*). Viewed from this perspective, the CLT arose as a result of the appeal of systematization and rationalization to the legal mind (Simão, *Sindicato e Estado*, 208) rather than as some overarching project of hegemony, citizenship, or national development.

9. In her extensive use of press clippings from greater São Paulo, Maria Inês Rosa offers a good sample of the types of labor law violations and employer "illegalities" that labor leaders and journalists alleged were being committed in the 1960s ("Indústria").

10. McMillan, "American Businessman," 74, 69. As an assistant professor at Michigan State University, McMillan helped to establish Brazil's first advanced training in business administration (McMillan, telephone interview by author, 3 June 1996).

11. McMillan, "American Businessman," 70.

12. Shearer, interview by Alexander, 24 September 1958, New Brunswick, N.J., Alexander Papers, Rutgers. For the results of his research, see Shearer, *High-Level Manpower*; Shearer, "Underdeveloped Industrial Relations."

13. McMillan, "American Businessman," 70. See Gordon and Grommers, *United States Manufacturing Investment*, for U.S. employers' complaints about the CLT's job security provisions in the early 1960s.

14. In this regard, the more intriguing analytical problem lies in explaining why a capitalist state that follows a policy of discouraging effective collective representation through trade unions would have sponsored their creation. This question is explored in French, *Brazilian Workers' ABC*. The same paradox serves as the point of departure for Biorn Maybury-Lewis's fine study of rural trade unionism from 1964 to 1986. How did a "huge, progressive trade union organization manage to establish itself" in rural areas under harshly authoritarian conditions despite all the " 'good reasons' why such a trend would not easily have been anticipated when the military took power" in 1964? The answer, he suggests, lies in labor leaders' marshaling of "maximum political creativity" as they exploited the institutional space created by a state apparatus that sought to "coopt, encapsulate, and suppress" workers' struggles (*Politics*, 1–2).

15. Irving Salert, "Labor Minister Goulart and the Enforcement of Brazilian Labor

Laws," 8 December 1953, U.S. Embassy Dispatch 734, Department of State Records, U.S. National Archives and Records Administration, Washington, D.C.

16. Romeu de Lucca (DRT) and Vinicius Ferraz Torres (Serviço Jurídico), "Histórico da D.R.T., São Paulo," included in Airgram A-14 from Daniel M. Braddock, U.S. Consul General in São Paulo, to Department of State, 18 July 1962, Department of State Records. In 1953, the head of the DRT inspection services said that at least three hundred inspectors would be needed to properly inspect workplaces in the city of São Paulo alone (Antônio Barreto, interview by Alexander, 16 June 1953, São Paulo, Alexander Papers, Rutgers).

17. Rosa, "Indústria," 98–99.

18. Barros, *Origens*, 92–93.

19. Salert, "Labor Minister Goulart."

20. Antônio Barreto, interview by Alexander, 16 June 1953, São Paulo, Alexander Papers, Rutgers.

21. Rebouças, *Insalubridade*, 44–46, discusses the sequence of legal measures regarding industrial health and safety. The best and most complete such law dated from the Estado Novo era, although the author's case studies from the mid-1980s demonstrate that even in exceptionally poisonous working environments, such protections were seldom implemented.

22. Braz, interview by author, 17 August 1991, Santo André.

23. Salert, "Labor Minister Goulart."

24. The tendency of labor courts to settle disputes between individuals and enterprises by "stipulating values or rights inferior to those defined in the law," as labor sociologist Eduardo Noronha noted in 2000, encourages employers not to fulfill the law's provisions (*Entre a Lei*, 42).

25. Itaboraí Martins, "Sem Juizes, Processos Trabalhistas Demoram," *Estado de São Paulo*, 8 April 1972, 17, as cited in Mericle, "Conflict Resolution," 172.

26. Ferrante, *FGTS*, 157; B. Calheiros Bomfim, "Defende Teu Direito," *Novos Rumos* (Rio de Janeiro), 27 March–2 April 1959; see also "Individual Conflict in Brazil," in Mericle, "Conflict Resolution."

27. Pereira de Souza, *Memórias*, 69.

28. As early as the 1930s, leftist labor leaders routinely criticized the Vargas regime's newly created labor ministry as the "Ministry of Swindles and Trickery" (*tapeação*) (Munakata, *Legislação*, 86–88).

29. Montenegro, interview by Alexander, 21 February 1956, Recife, Alexander Papers, Rutgers.

30. Moreira Júnior, interview by Alexander, 13 March 1956, Rio de Janeiro, Alexander Papers, Rutgers.

31. Tavares, interview by Alexander, 13 March 1956, Rio de Janeiro, Alexander Papers, Rutgers. During the Populist Republic, the sluggishness (*morosidade*) of the labor courts at all levels became so legendary that it received mention in a labor court functionary's 1998 sketch of the system's history. In 1952, for example, the TST had four thousand cases (*processos*) awaiting a scheduled judgment date, while one TST minister had seven hundred cases awaiting his

evaluation (Silva Martins Filho, "Breve História," 200). Looked at more broadly, this problem should not be viewed as essentially bureaucratic, procedural, or financial in origin (the usual explanation offered by insiders). Rather, it reflected an absence of political will by the executive branch combined with the indifference of Brazil's legislative leadership.

32. Andreotti, interview by author, 20 September 1982, Santo André. Andreotti's observation about the routine perversities of the labor courts was echoed by labor lawyer Carlos Eduardo Bosísio. Before the mid-1960s, he recalled, the period of the time in which a worker could seek legal redress was very short. If someone lost his job and went to court to demand overtime owed for ten years of work, "he would immediately lose eight of those years [because the statute of limitations had expired], and even in the case of the two years for which he did have a legal right, he would receive the payment at a loss, because there was no monetary correction" for inflation until 1965 (Bosísio, "Justiça," 52).

33. Caio Plinio Barreto, interview by Alexander, 17–18 June 1953, São Paulo, Alexander Papers, Rutgers.

34. Andreotti, interview by author, 29 November, 2 December 1982, Santo André.

35. For a description of the structure of the labor court system and the process of appointment of class judges, see Gomes, "Justiça," 185.

36. Giglio, *Direito*, 26, as cited in Mericle, "Conflict Resolution," 163–65, which also draws on Mericle's April 1972 interview with Giglio. Radical Pernambucan lawyer Francisco Julião, who led the Peasant Leagues of the early 1960s, also emphasized the class basis of the Brazilian legal system: "Judges, state attorneys, and appeals court judges are descendants of *fazendeiros*, not peasants. They are formed in a feudal atmosphere and rarely free themselves from the spirit of those environments." As a result, he said in 1963, judicial officials in rural areas work closely with the police, who are really the armed thugs (*capangas*) of landowners who get their way by threatening peasants with a "technical application of democracy." Although he insisted that "the law in Brazil is a tacit conspiracy of the powerful against the humble," Julião nonetheless explained that the mobilization of peasants and rural workers must be based on the law and its dubious protections. Although the Civil Code is "a monument erected in defense of private property," it still represents "a promise of liberation," he went on, because of the miserable state of relations between peasants and landowners. And rural wage earners' fight must, in a similar fashion, be based on the labor laws, although the CLT "does not and never has functioned fully" (Fonseca, *Assim Falou*, 36, 73, 38).

37. Drummond, interview by Alexander, 27 March 1956, Belo Horizonte, Alexander Papers, Rutgers.

38. Andreotti, interview by author, 29 November, 2 December 1982, Santo André.

39. Giglio, interview with Mericle, April 1972, cited in Mericle, "Conflict Resolution," 163–65.

40. Drummond, interview by Alexander, 27 March 1956, Belo Horizonte, Alexander Papers, Rutgers. It has been argued that despite its original intent, the participation by class judges made little difference as labor court delibera-

tions were increasingly modeled after and based on legal principles with which nonlawyers were unfamiliar. As Orlando Gomes noted in 1972, the result was the "ascendancy of the *juiz togado*," while the class judges, "lacking juridical knowledge," were limited to either "subscribing to a decision with which they are incapable of agreeing" or making a decision, without legal support, on behalf of their economic or professional group ("Justiça," 201). The institution of class judges in the labor courts was finally abolished in 2002.

41. Mericle, "Conflict Resolution," 164.

42. *Folha do Povo* (Santo André), 13 April 1951. For Poletto's earlier complaints about *assiduidade integral*, see *Folha da Manhã* (São Paulo), 26 March 1950.

43. For an account of the incident, see French, *Brazilian Workers' ABC*, 175.

44. Working papers also served, in the words of Brodwyn Fischer, to divide the popular classes into those with *carteiras* and those without. "The kind of social exclusion engendered by the merger of citizenship rights with the documents that signified them was both subtle and graduated: an exclusion that did not operate through legally explicit interdictions, but rather through a kind of procedural myopia, a refusal to recognize that the burdens of establishing formal, documentary relationships with the various branches of governments would weigh more heavily on the shoulders of lower class or rural Brazilians than they would on the more privileged or urban" ("Poverty," 124, 164). As a sign of status or protection against police harassment, *carteiras* came to play a fundamental role within urban working-class life (Machado da Silva, "Significado," 164).

45. Andreotti, interview by author, 27 September 1982, Santo André. Couldn't the worker who had been prejudiced in this way simply get a new *carteira*, I asked Andreotti. Yes, "but that just made things worse because then he'd arrive at a factory with a new *carteira* and they'd say, 'This one here never worked'" and not hire him.

46. Puech, *Direito*, 131–33.

47. Springer, *Brazilian Factory Study*, chap. 2, p. 7.

48. C. Grandi, "Official Report on Labor, Year 1958," in U.S. Embassy Dispatch 1449, 16 March 1959, p. 5, Department of State Records.

49. *Folha do Povo*, 25 May 1951.

50. Ibid., 10 March 1950.

51. Lopes de Almeida, *Política Salarial*, 21, 59.

52. The TST's disposition to follow the lead of the powerful might be explained, in part, by the fact that "all the judges [on the TST] were named freely by the president [and for life], without approval by the Senate being necessary" (Moreira Júnior, interview by Alexander, 13 March 1956, Rio de Janeiro, Alexander Papers, Rutgers).

53. Richard P. Butrick and Benjamin Sowell, "Supreme Labor Court Alters Decision on October Strike," U.S. Embassy Dispatch 262, 24 January 1958, pp. 1–3, Department of State Records.

54. Butrick and Sowell, "Supreme Labor Court," 5, 7, 4.

55. Even in São Paulo, the refusal to pay the minimum wage was not unknown, although it was even more common in less developed regions of the country. In 1956, the DRT in Pernambuco, Antônio Luis Lins de Barros, told Alexander that there were "many cases in this state, and city where employers actually pay less than the sixteen hundred cruzeiros a month called for by the minimum wage and then make the employees sign receipts for sixteen hundred cruzeiros. However, unless a worker comes in and denounces such a situation, there is nothing the Delegado Regional can do about it. He has the power only to look at the books, at the vouchers and receipts for wages paid, not to make sure that these represent the true situation. Workers are in many cases afraid of their employers and so do not come in to expose such situations" (Lins de Barros, interview by Alexander, 18 February 1956, Recife, Alexander Papers, Rutgers).

56. David P. Mann, "Social Security in Brazil," U.S. Embassy Dispatch 230, 15 September 1960, pp. 1, 8, Department of State Records.

57. *Folha do Povo*, 13 April 1951.

58. Fuerstenthal, interview by Alexander, 15 March 1956, Rio de Janeiro, Alexander Papers, Rutgers. For Fuerstenthal, the situation was particularly unjust because "if the same things were done by foreign companies and they were denounced in the labor courts, the book would be thrown at them, so they are forced to obey the labor law."

59. Hollanda de Cavalcante, interview by Alexander, 9 March 1956, Rio de Janeiro, Alexander Papers, Rutgers. The title of J. A. Oliveira and Teixeira's 1986 book on the Brazilian social welfare and pension plans is apropos: *(Im)Previdência*, thus combining the word for the social welfare function (*previdência*) and a word (*imprevidência*) that means carelessness or negligence. U.S. political scientist Barbara Geddes missed the sordid reality of the IAPI and its functioning in her superficial discussion of the politics of pension reform. Eager to criticize *trabalhista* president Jango Goulart, who was overthrown in 1964, Geddes, "Building 'State' Autonomy," 231, naively presents IAPI in 1960 as having "a reputation for competence and honesty." Unaware of its checkered past, she hails the pre-Goulart IAPI as efficient and professional before it was ruined by "political intervention and consequent subversion of agency performance."

60. Gusmão, *Bojo*, 137.

61. Sigaud, *Clandestinos*, 227; Amad Costa, *Estado e Controle*, 28.

62. Wimmer, *Michaelis Diccionário*, 445; Nogueira, "Working"; Chaves de Mello, *Dicionário Jurídico*, 77.

63. Wimmer, *Michaelis Diccionário*, 1186, 194.

CHAPTER FOUR

1. ILO, "Labor Legislation," 217.
2. Ibid., 228. A 1956 article by two scholars of U.S. businesses in Peru and Venezuela noted that the "sudden development of comprehensive labor legislation" was common throughout Latin America at midcentury. "The characteristic pattern has been for the Latin-American reformers to study the most
   'advanced' types of legislation that have been developed over a period of
   many years by more industrialized (and particularly European) countries."
   The result has been a tendency "to enact such model legislation, providing for
   detailed regulation of employer-worker relations, for labor courts, and for
   other forms of government intervention" (Whyte and Holmberg, "Human
   Problems," 27). The reasoning behind the Latin American approach can be
   seen in the parliamentary exchanges at the 1934 Brazilian Constituent Assembly recounted in Wolkmer, *Constitucionalismo*, 69–71.
3. In 1942, Loewenstein suggested that the Vargas government had set labor
   standards and social benefits at unrealistic and incongruously high levels,
   thereby bestowing "on a country scarcely emerged from feudalism one of the
   most advanced systems of social legislation in existence anywhere" (*Brazil*,
   339, 57). The resulting legislation, observes labor sociologist Adalberto Moreira Cardoso, was "advanced and anachronistic for a country that was still
   attempting to consolidate an urban capitalism worthy of that name. This
   means that the labor legislation in Brazil preceded the massive growth of
   salaried labor [and] that many of these rules were destined to remain on
   paper for many years" (*Sindicatos*, 29).
4. Marcondes, "Social Legislation," 399, 386. The chasm between the labor legislation and the imperfectly understood realities of working-class life opened
   the way for rival forms of nonjuridical knowledge. In the 1930s, for example, a
   school of empirical studies of working-class living standards began to develop
   in São Paulo. These sociologists believed that only field research and surveys
   offered the "objective and detailed knowledge of the environment" that was
   needed to guide policy making (Egídio de Araújo, "Pesquisa," 10–11).
5. Goodman, "Legal Controls," 233–34.
6. R. B. Collier, "Popular Sector Incorporation," 73.
7. Alba, *Politics*, 258.
8. Mericle, "Corporatist Control," 303.
9. Morse, "Heritage"; Silvert, "Politics"; Wiarda, "Law."
10. Silvert, "Politics," 162. Silvert was one of the cruder and more arrogant ana-
    lysts identified with this culturalist approach. If we are to understand "anti-
    developmental political patterns in Latin America," he argued, it is crucial to
    grasp the underlying "value system" that explains why "this part of the West-
    ern world is so prone to the excesses of scoundrels, so politically irrational in
    seeking economic growth, and so ready to search for gimmicks." The answer,
    he went on, can be found in "the Mediterranean ethos [which] is dedicated to
    hierarchy and order and absolutes" ("Politics," 162–63).

11. These theories of Latin American patrimonialism, long in vogue in the United States and Europe, are closely identified with Morse, a historian of Brazil. His work is clearly marked by a simple-minded and unself-conscious Anglo-Protestant smugness and self-satisfaction disguised as cultural critique. In Morse's 1974 projection of a future for the region, for example, he wrote of the first "erratic, sometimes timid, sometimes melodramatic" steps that Latin American nations were taking as moves toward achieving "greater maturity" and "national self-images of deeper coherence. A Protestant civilization," he went on, "can develop its energies endlessly in a wilderness, as did the United States [with its] strong and viable national structure. [But] a Catholic civilization stagnates when it is not in vital contact with the diverse tribes and cultures of mankind" ("Heritage," 67).

12. Wiarda, "Law," 209–10. Wiarda summarized the findings of the culturalist school: "Spain, Portugal, and their New World colonies were established upon a base that was Catholic, corporate, stratified, elitist, authoritarian, hierarchical, patrimonialist, and semifeudal to its core. Largely untouched by those great revolutionary" developments "that we associate with the emergence of the modern order, the Iberic and Latin American nations remain locked in this traditional pattern of values and institutions that has postponed and retarded their development." Going from the ridiculous to the sublime, he informs the reader that "a volume of canon law, the writings of Seneca or Thomas Aquinas, or the encyclicals of a long-forgotten pope . . . probably tell us more about the nature and functioning of the Iberic-Latin nations than the bulk of the textbooks of modern political and sociological analysis" ("Social Change," 269, 285).

13. Winston, *Workers*, 260–61.

14. Wiarda, "Law," 209–10, 212–13; Wiarda, "Corporative Origins."

15. Silvert, "Politics," 162–63. Like the ethnocentric Silvert, U.S. scholars Whyte and Holmberg also idealized what they called "our [U.S.] cultural emphasis on local face-to-face problem solving." In the United States, they said, labor legislation helped set the legal framework, but workers and unionists "do not expect [that] the details of their relations with management shall be subjected to the scrutiny of government officials or adjudicated in the courts." Rather, "the development of the union-management grievance procedure," conducted in the private sphere, stands "at the heart of the U.S. system of industrial relations." For the manager of a North American enterprise in Latin America, they wrote, the conduct of labor relations may seem "quite similar" but "with one significant exception. In many situations, he gets the impression that, while he is in face-to-face discussion with the union officials, the pattern of the resulting agreement is being influenced, if not completely determined, by people who are not in the room: government officials" ("Human Problems," 27).

16. Martinho, "Populismo," 44, 46, is one of the few students of the Brazilian workers' movement to advance such ideas.

17. French, *Brazilian Workers' ABC*, 1–16. For a critique of the historiography that

makes many parallel points, see the introduction to Paoli, "Labor, Law, and the State."

18. M. H. M. Alves, *State and Opposition*, 45.

19. Boito, *Sindicalismo*.

20. La Rochefoucauld, *Reflections*, maxim 218.

21. Lothian, "Political Consequences," 1009–10. (This is called a "legislated model" in an excellent recent book by labor sociologist Eduardo Noronha, *Entre a Lei*.) For a sympathetic critique of Lothian's work, see Gacek, "Revisiting"; for Lothian's provocative response, see her "Reinventing."

22. Lothian, "Political Consequences," 1003.

23. This peculiarity was aptly posed by Cohn, *Previdência*, 30.

24. Viotti da Costa, *Brazilian Empire*. This classic motif in Brazilian political and cultural history has given rise to a long tradition of commentary. For a superb historical study of this process, see Flory, *Judge and Jury*.

25. Anthropologist Peter Fry offers a brief discussion of the expression "para Inglés ver" that suggests other origins and uses. All revolve around "the basic idea that formal rules can be *burladas* [cheated on] to the degree that the 'other' does not perceive it." In its various versions, he says, the key is that the relationship is a hierarchical one in which the weaker party "elaborates strategies of survival" and hides "its 'resistance' through the construction of a facade of conformity" (*Para Inglês Ver*, 17). On strategies of dissimulation by the subaltern, see J. Souza Martins, *Chegada*, 25.

26. Bethell, *Abolition*. For a discussion of characteristic imperial Brazilian responses to foreign criticism of the illegal slave trade, see Bosi, "Arqueologia," 205, 218.

27. L. Martins, "Gênese," 74, offers a particularly insightful definition of the role and characteristics of the *bacharel* in Brazilian culture and society, as do Adorno, *Aprendizes*; Junqueira, "Bacharel"; and Kirkendall's fine recent study, *Class Mates*.

28. Schmitter, "Development and Interest Politics," 115, 174. Schmitter went on to say that formalism could also be found in the " 'popular' electoral sphere," where it took the form of "an extensive use of stereotypical phrases and vague, 'demagogic' promises of comprehensive, definitive and simple solutions." Both "are equally formalistic in that they are more-or-less calculatedly divorced from the complexity of real political and social processes." Although the phenomenon is indeed characteristic of Brazilian politics, formalism is by no means unique to Brazil but rather is characteristic, to varying degrees, of all modern political systems. Schmitter's Brazilian foray occurred at the outset of his career as an influential theorist of corporatism, with a primary focus on Western Europe rather than on Brazil.

29. Wright and Wolford, *To Inherit*, 19–22, offers a rich discussion of the specialized slang for the various forms of legal fraud and influence peddling that have long marked the world of rural Brazil.

30. See Kant de Lima, "Bureaucratic Rationality," for a comparative perspective on the nature of law and the legal process in Brazil and the United States.

31. Viotti da Costa, *Brazilian Empire*.

32. Barcellos, *ROTA 66*; Blat and Saraiva, *Caso*, 43–44; Chevigny, *Edge*; Pinheiro, "Violência"; Pinheiro, *Escritos*; Pinheiro, *Crime*.

33. The de facto toleration of abortion, despite its formal illegality, led to a peculiar strategy debate within the Brazilian women's movement during the drafting of the 1988 Brazilian Constitution. In the end, the feminist movement decided not to press for the inclusion of a right to abortion in the constitutional text. Instead, they preferred to leave the issue entirely untouched rather than risk the inclusion of a constitutional prohibition of the practice. In other words, despite the suffering entailed, the status quo in which abortion was tolerated but officially illegal under the Criminal Code was considered preferable to the risks of trying to change abortion's de jure legal status (Verucci and Patai, "Women," 562–63).

34. Schwarz, *Misplaced Ideas*, 19–32.

35. Simonsen, *Indústria*, 276. Loewenstein, *Brazil*, 340, cited Simonsen on the appeal of social reform ideas among Brazilian law students.

36. Morena, interview by Alexander, 28 August 1946, Rio de Janeiro, Alexander Papers, Rutgers.

37. Labor Minister Marcondes Filho entrusted the task of consolidating the labor law to a commission headed by MTIC Consultor Jurídico Oscar Saraiva, although the task itself was carried out by the four *procuradores do trabalho* appointed: Dorval Lacerda, Rego Monteiro, Arnaldo Süssekind, and Segadas Vianna (Silva Martins Filho, "Breve História," 195). Both Süssekind and Segadas Vianna would serve as labor ministers, the latter during Vargas's second government and Süssekind after the 1964 military coup (Silva Martins Filho, "Breve História," 195).

38. Segadas Vianna, interview by Alexander, 26 August 1946, 16 March 1956, Rio de Janeiro, Alexander Papers, Rutgers. At the outset of the First Republic, an early advocate of labor legislation discussed the passage of laws benefiting government employees in 1889–91. Such measures, Deodato Maia said, were for "external use in diplomatic matters," with the aim of "conquering European public opinion" (Barbosa de Araújo, *Batismo*, 38).

39. For public praise of Collor by Segadas Vianna, see the 1969 speech he delivered at the inauguration of Collor's portrait in the office of the minister of labor ("Discurso do Ex-Ministro," in Mello, *Legislação*, 24–25).

40. During the crisis that began with the famous Strike of the 300,000 in São Paulo in 1953, Vargas had replaced Segadas Vianna in labor ministry with his rival, João "Jango" Goulart. In the same period, Segadas Vianna also lost control of the PTB's most powerful state affiliate, in Rio de Janeiro, to Vargas's son, Lutero. Deeply embittered by his loss of influence in the PTB, Segadas Vianna became a virulent personal enemy of Goulart and closely allied with the rightist antilabor governor of Guanabara, notorious anti-*getulista* Carlos Lacerda (Kornis and Junqueira, "Segadas Viana"; D'Araújo, "PTB"; Irving Salert, "Letter from Former Labor Minister [Segadas Vianna] Attacking Goulart," 14 October 1955, U.S. Embassy Dispatch 499, Department of State Records; V. R. Lima, *Getúlio*, 304).

41. Moura, interview by Alexander, 20 April 1956, São Paulo, Alexander Papers, Rutgers.

42. Alexander, *ABC Presidents*, 154.

43. Moraes Filho, *Problema*, 212–13.

44. Middlebrook, *Paradox*, 41–71.

45. Holston, "Misrule," 697–98.

46. Sady, *Direito*, 33.

47. Bodea, *Greve*; Bosi, "Arqueologia," 273–307; Tejo, *Jango*, 90.

48. Loewenstein, *Brazil*, 337, noted that *empreguismo* (the avid search for government jobs to give out or receive) was an important factor in understanding the expansion of the state during the Estado Novo. A similar argument has also been advanced about the growth in government functions and employment in Latin America as a whole during the Great Depression. The principal aim, in the words of Abel and Lewis, "was to maximize employment in the bureaucracy and to cushion professional groups against job losses in the external sector. No more sophisticated construction need be placed upon the proliferation of interventionist agencies and the quest for new forms of taxation than the mere expedient of bureaucratic survival." Abel and Lewis also note, however, that this explanation alone is insufficient without also looking into "questions of policy determination" (*Latin America*, 276).

49. Tavares de Almeida, "Estado," 24, 160–62. This judgment is shared, in essence, by Paoli, "Labor, Law, and the State," 172. The initiative for the new social legislation of the 1930s, sociologist Leôncio Martins Rodrigues has also suggested, came from the government, and he emphasized that government and industry should not be conflated with each other ("Sindicalismo," 516). For one of the few studies that engages these earlier arguments, although it does not do so in a fully developed fashion, see Lopes da Silva, *Domesticação*, 56.

50. Howes, "Progressive Conservatism," 81. On the cynicism of Segadas Vianna, see French, *Brazilian Workers' ABC*, 313.

51. Although outside the scope of this work, this subject is explored in detail in French, *Brazilian Workers' ABC*; and Castro Gomes, *Invenção*.

52. Paoli, "Labor, Law, and the State," 250.

53. A month-to-month grassroots examination of this period can be found in French, *Brazilian Workers' ABC*. This postwar upsurge has also been the focus of a great deal of the new labor history literature of the mid- to late 1990s (Costa, *Busca*).

54. Oliveira Vianna, *Direito*, 165, 168–69.

55. Ibid., 177.

56. Ibid., 35, 41–43.

57. Ibid., 23–24, 177.

58. See the personal recollections by Oliveira Vianna's friend and neighbor (Macieira, "Oliveira Viana") as well as Medeiros, *Ideologia*; and Needel, "History." The reformist dimension of Oliveira Vianna's thought is a recurring theme in recent revisionist works. See Bastos and Quartim de Moraes, *Pensamento*, esp. Ribeiro Costa, "Corporativismo."

59. Werneck Vianna, *Liberalismo e Sindicato*, 374, attributes this quotation to a 1943 book by Oliveira Vianna, *Princípios de Direito Sindical*, but its source is most likely Oliveira Vianna, *Problemas do Direito Sindical*.
60. Howes, "Progressive Conservatism," 136–37.
61. Ribeiro Costa, "Corporativismo," 131.
62. Quartim de Moraes, "Oliveira Vianna," 117.
63. Talarico, interview by Guido and Roels Júnior, [September 1978–July 1979], Rio de Janeiro, 71–72.
64. Carvalho, *Novos Estudos*, 188–90.
65. Trigueiro do Vale, *Supremo Tribunal*, 32.
66. Montenegro, interview by Alexander, 21 February 1956, Recife, Alexander Papers, Rutgers. Both employers and trade unionists often mentioned the unconstitutional nature of Dutra's restrictive 1946 antistrike Decree 9,070, although to different ends. On the equally confusing jurisprudence of strikes during the Populist Republic, see Ribeiro, *Problema*, which argues that workers should be fired for their participation in stoppages that occurred before all legal steps had been exhausted. The 1946 constitution's guarantee of the right to strike was given legal form only in June 1964, although the long-awaited "right-to-strike decree" was an *abacaxi* (literally, a pineapple; a mess), in the words of São Paulo union leaders. It had been drafted so that everyone gained the right to strike in theory "but nobody could strike in practice," thus negating the constitutional decree that was ostensibly being implemented (H. Souza Martins, *Estado*, 118–20). See also Pinheiro, *Estratégias*, 119–20.
67. Adorno, *Aprendizes*, 245–46. An excellent recent monograph by Pena, *Pajens*, explores the proslavery practice of the most famous legal opponents of slavery in nineteenth-century Brazil. Pena provides a striking illustration of what could be seen as either the moderation and good sense of the *bacharel* or his rank opportunism. (See also Grinberg, *Fiador*, 29.) Kirkendall, *Class Mates*, 136–37, 142, 144, 162, 170, similarly shows the strict limits that governed the "advanced" republican and abolitionist ideas embraced by many law students during late imperial Brazil.
68. The destabilizing potential of a refusal to tolerate the gap was aptly illustrated by an agitational pamphlet, written in 1963 by a militantly leftist jurist, Osny Duarte Pereira, that asked "whether that which is in the letter of the constitution [*letra da Constituição*] and of the laws exists in the reality of facts." If not, he suggested, then it must be made so (*Quem Faz*, 14).
69. Fontes, *Corumbas*, 63–66.
70. Ibid., 67–71.
71. Cerqueira Filho, *Questão*, 85, 113.
72. Adorno, *Aprendizes*, 246; Lucas, *Conteúdo*, 77; Besouchet, *História*, 19. The findings of an excellent recent study of the 1871 sexagenarian emancipation law, and how slaves used it, sound like a description of the dynamics, flaws, and injustices of Brazil's CLT system in the mid–twentieth century (Mendonça, *Entre a Mão e os Anéis*, 317, 323–24, 261, 269, 271). For at least one foreign observer of slavery, the distance between the institution's law and its

practices and customs was marked by "an opposition so absolute" as to demonstrate law's absurdity in Brazil (Rugendas, *Viagem*, 270). Another commented more wryly that "law is worn very loosely" there (Carneiro da Cunha, "Silences," 427).

73. Cerqueira Filho, *Questão*, 91.

74. Holston, "Misrule," 708.

75. Siqueira Neto, *Direito*, 205. Like Siqueira Neto, a former DRT in Minas Gerais noted with deep irony in 2001 that the word "flexibilization" "might not provoke desperation among many workers and union leaderships if they took into account that the labor legislation adopted in Brazil is among the most flexible in the world," even to the point of paradox. In a passionate book, *Cativos na Liberdade*, 19, Marilton Velasco discusses the labor law's alternation between intense rigidity and excessive flexibility that seems, for most of the time, to come at the expense of social justice.

76. French, *Brazilian Workers' ABC*, 74–75, 288–89, 292–93.

77. Segadas Vianna, interview by Lima, Castro Gomes, and Ramos, 6 October 1983, Rio de Janeiro, 126–27.

78. Holston, "Misrule," 723.

79. Ibid., 708.

80. Segadas Vianna, interview by Lima, Castro Gomes, and Ramos, 6 October 1983, Rio de Janeiro, 82–83, 328, 432, 218.

81. Lobos, *Manual*, 94–95, 63–64 (chapter epigraph). Refreshingly partisan in its outlook, Lobos's *Manual de Guerilla Trabalhista para Gerentes e Supervisores* (*Manual of Labor Guerrilla Warfare for Managers and Supervisors*) deserves a far wider audience for its wonderful cartoons, outrageous humor, and acute social insights from the employers' side of the proverbial barricades. The Chilean-born Lobos is also the author of scholarly works on industry and labor in Brazil ("Technology"; *Sindicalismo*). See former vice president João Café Filho's memoir, *Sindicato*, 221, 225, for his comments about the European reactions to Brazil's advanced labor law he encountered during a trip to Sweden in the early 1950s.

CHAPTER FIVE

1. Paoli, "Labor, Law, and the State," 236–37, 440.

2. Having abandoned inherited visions, the revisionist pendulum on midcentury labor relations has now swung so far that a few analysts have recently hailed Vargas, the PTB, and even the CLT as a new day for workers. Breaking with dark visions of Vargas and his handiwork, a 2001 edited volume (J. Ferreira, *Populismo*) explicitly takes up the defense of *trabalhismo*, which the book's editor insists has been incorrectly labeled as "populism," a term taken to be both derogatory and inaccurate (J. Ferreira, "Nome"). At its most polemical and least researched, these authors credit the term "populist" to right-wing enemies of Vargas and the PTB who set out after 1964 to destroy the *trabalhista* tradition of "reformist social struggles [that were] given rhythm

through collective bargaining [*dissídios coletivos*], arbitrated by the Labor Courts, [and] mediated when possible by the [workers'] leaders" (Reis Filho, "Colapso," 346–47). "The trajectory of trabalhismo and the PTB," Lucília Neves Delgado goes on, is bound up with a redistributive program that was linked to an "effective national project of economic and social development" ("Trabalhismo," 175, 202). Although only a minority of Brazilian scholars embrace such propositions, the *trabalhista* polemic derives its key terms from Angela de Castro Gomes's innovative 1988 book, *A Invenção do Trabalhismo*, and has led to an interesting exchange of views (see Teixeira da Silva and Costa, "Trabalhadores," for a broad historiographical survey closer to my critical perspective on these matters).

3. Silva and Carneiro, *Os Presidentes*, 47; Vargas, *Campanha*, 68–69, 97. On Barros, see "Workers and the Rise of Adhemarista Populism in São Paulo," in French, *Brazilian Workers' ABC*, 199–224.

4. Vargas, *Campanha*, 67–69; D'Araújo, *Segundo Governo Vargas*, 88–89.

5. Vargas, *Campanha*, 70; D'Araújo, *Segundo Governo Vargas*, 89.

6. Vargas, *Campanha*, 67–69.

7. Café Filho, *Sindicato*, 193.

8. V. R. Lima, *Getúlio*, 169; D'Araújo, *Sindicatos*, 54–55; Silva and Carneiro, *Os Presidentes*, 112; Neves Delgado, *PTB*, 108–10; Talarico, interview by Guido and Roels Júnior, [September 1978–July 1979], Rio de Janeiro, 76. In July 1951, the U.S. labor attaché, Henry S. Hammond, reported that "labor opinion with regard to Minister Coelho remains somewhat indefinite" in São Paulo ("Labor Conditions in the São Paulo Consular District, Second Quarter 1951," 24 July 1951, p. 6, Department of State Records).

9. Neves Delgado, *PTB*, 117, 119.

10. Ibid., 97.

11. Ibid., 108.

12. The term *mergulhadores de tapete* (carpet divers) comes from an interview with Coelho's successor, Segadas Vianna (interview by Lima, Castro Gomes, and Ramos, 6 October 1983, Rio de Janeiro, 138), as a description of the extremes of subservient behavior toward superiors common within the MTIC.

13. Hammond, "Labor Conditions," 6.

14. Romeu de Lucca and Ferraz Torres, "Histórico," 1, gives the number of employees at the São Paulo DRT at 1,422 in 1953.

15. Ibid.; Henry S. Hammond, "Annual Labor Report 1950," 19 February 1951, p. 5, FSD 81, Department of State Records.

16. In the case of the Rio metalworkers, Marco Aurélio Santana has examined the lists of suspect union members sent back and forth between the MTIC and the union *interventor* in the Rio metalworkers' union in the late 1940s. The aim was to certify whether the individuals in question were "communist agitators," although the union often sent additional names with the notation "not on the list but they are communists." His careful examination of the individuals listed, which included many future union leaders, showed that the unifying feature among these "communists" was not ideology but rather their

opposition to the junta running the union ("Trabalhadores," 171). Moderate socialist João Mangabeira denounced the same union *interventor* in June 1948 for his expulsion of eight hundred union members as "communists or crypto-communists," including a leader of the Catholic Worker Youth (F. Barbosa, *Idéias*, 154–55).

17. For an introduction to the DOPS archives, see Aparecida de Aquino, Leme de Matos, and Swenssen, *Coração*. Robert Alexander, among others, has commented that the "one aspect of SESI's work about which there is not much talk, but of which there is considerable awareness among the workers, is its espionage activities. The organization keeps a very extensive intelligence network going among the workers. Just who serves as its informants, I do not know, but they try to keep abreast of what is going on in all of the unions, and particularly in those in which there is some Communist influence. The SESI works with the police and other authorities in this connection. This is an aspect of the organization's activities which makes it suspect among many of the workers, even those who are anti-Communist" ("General Observations of Labor-Management Relations in São Paulo," 28 April 1956, Alexander Papers, Rutgers).

18. Neves Delgado, *PTB*, 110, 117.

19. Vargas's Olympian posture in these passages also speaks to his conception of the role of president as a leader responsible only to the people and standing above his appointees.

20. "Portaria N.o 36, de 1 de Maio de 1951 [sobre Eleições nas Entidades Sindicais]," *Gazeta Sindical,* 2a Quinzena de Agosto (1951); "Lei N.o 1.667 de 1 de Setembro de 1952 [sobre Revogação do Atestado de Ideologia nas Eleições Sindicais]," *Gazeta Sindical,* 1952; Neves Delgado, *PTB*, 110, 117.

21. "Portaria N.o 36"; "Lei N.o 1.667"; Neves Delgado, *PTB*, 110, 117.

22. A description of the labor ministry's post-1950 internal reorganization can be found in Lobo et al., *Rio de Janeiro*, 231–36, which also lays out the union-related political dilemmas Vargas's administration faced.

23. V. R. Lima, *Getúlio*, 179; Benevides, *PTB*, 107; D'Araújo, *Sindicatos*, 63, 71–72, 89; Neves Delgado, *PTB*, 116–17; Talarico, interview by Guido and Roels Júnior, [September 1978–July 1979], Rio de Janeiro, 76.

24. Getúlio Vargas, "Comemoração do Dia do Trabalho: Discurso do Presidente," 5 May 1952, p. 3, attachment to U.S. Embassy, M1487, roll 7, Department of State Records.

25. Neves Delgado, *PTB*, 120.

26. Talarico, interview by Guido and Roels Júnior, [September 1978–July 1979], Rio de Janeiro, 76.

27. Segadas Vianna, interview by Lima, Castro Gomes, and Ramos, 6 October 1983, Rio de Janeiro, 388, 399, 216, 153–54; Talarico, interview by Guido and Roels Júnior, [September 1978–July 1979], Rio de Janeiro, 76, 79.

28. Neves Delgado, *PTB*, 101–5; Hippólito, *Raposas*, 87–103.

29. Neves Delgado, *PTB*, 125; Brandi et al., *Vargas*, 267–68; H. Silva, *1954*, 170; V. R. Lima, *Getúlio*, 184.

30. V. R. Lima, *Getúlio*, 292–93.

31. José Gomes Talarico, "Relatório de José Gomes Talarico, como Observador do Ministério do Trabalho, Indústria e Comércio das Greves de São Paulo," presented to President Vargas on 29 April 1953, attachment to Irving Salert, "São Paulo Strike Report," U.S. Embassy Dispatch 1678, 11 May 1953, Department of State Records; José Gomes Talarico, "Relatório Levado pelo Ministro do Trabalho ao Presidente da República no Despacho de 8 de April de 1953," 7 April 1953, attachment to Irving Salert, "São Paulo Strike—A Report by Labor Minister Segadas Vianna Submitted to President Getúlio Vargas," U.S. Embassy Dispatch 1547, 14 April 1953, Department of State Records.

32. Salert, "São Paulo Strike—A Report," 1; Talarico, "Relatório de José Gomes Talarico," 1.

33. Talarico, "Relatório de José Gomes Talarico," 1, 7–11.

34. Ibid., 2; Talarico, "Relatório Levado," 7–11.

35. Talarico, "Relatório de José Gomes Talarico," 7–9.

36. Salert, "São Paulo Strike—A Report," 3.

37. Talarico, "Relatório de José Gomes Talarico," 10.

38. Salert, "São Paulo Strike—A Report," 2–3.

39. V. R. Lima, *Getúlio*, 178–179; Neves Delgado, *PTB*, 120–21; Irving Salert, "Quarterly Labor Review—First Quarter 1953," p. 3, Department of State Records; Brandi et al., *Vargas*, 268.

40. Ibid.

41. V. R. Lima, *Getúlio*, 179; Neves Delgado, *PTB*, 122, 132.

42. V. R. Lima, *Getúlio*, 180.

43. Salert, "São Paulo Strike—A Report," 2–3.

44. French, *Brazilian Workers' ABC*, 274–75.

45. D'Araújo, *Sindicatos*, 91; M. Ferreira and Benjamin, "João Goulart," 1504–5; Robert J. Alexander to Jay Lovestone (International Affairs Department, American Federation of Labor), letter [B], 23 June 1953, p. 3, Alexander Papers, Rutgers.

46. M. E. A. T. Lima, *Construção*, 68.

47. Boito, *Golpe*, 77.

48. Wolfe, *Working Women*, 184.

49. For an accurate but unflattering portrait of the PTB, see D'Araújo, *Sindicatos*.

50. D'Araújo, *Segundo Governo Vargas*, 115–18.

51. Delgado, *PTB*, 135–36. She also cites Kenneth Erickson, who characterized Goulart's brief 1953 ministry as being "radical-populist" in nature (Erickson, *Brazilian Corporative State*; Erickson, *Sindicalismo*, 85). It is probably best, however, not to rely on the judgments in Erickson's pioneering but weakly researched work: his schematic periodization of labor ministry policy labeled the entire period from 1930 to 1953 (as well as 1954–55) as "classical populist."

52. See Tejo, *Jango*, 82, 100, 106, for observations about how Goulart's stance and discourse were rooted in the ranching world of Rio Grande do Sul.

53. Ibid., 100.

54. Goulart, interview by Alexander, 5 June 1972, Maldonaldo, Uruguay, Alexander Papers, Rutgers; Alexander, *ABC Presidents*, 154.

55. Barsted, *Mediçao*, 26–27, 54–55, 111, 122, 130, 132.

56. Ibid., 165–70. If Bonfante and his counterparts in the militant wing of the labor movement did not break with Goulart, it was not for lack of valid complaints. At that point, Goulart and his policies in the MTIC were the best that could be hoped for given a rising right-wing insurgency aimed at Vargas.

57. Hammond reported in 1951 that *paulista* unions "seem virtually certain that the establishment of a federal delegacy in São Paulo will bring with it increased union participation in the Labor Inspection Service" ("Labor Conditions," 5).

58. Salert, "Labor Minister Goulart"; Brandi et al., *Vargas*, 275.

59. Ibid.

60. Segadas Vianna, interview by Lima, Castro Gomes, and Ramos, 6 October 1983, Rio de Janeiro, 332.

61. Cerqueira Filho, *Questão*, 178, 113.

62. Tejo, *Jango*, 40–44, 146. Looking back at the pre-1964 period, São Paulo's famous Marxist historian Caio Prado Júnior offered the harsh judgment that Goulart had all of Vargas's defects but none of his qualities ("É Preciso," 314).

63. D'Araújo, *Segundo Governo Vargas*, 98–99.

64. Brandi et al., *Vargas*, 266; Irving Salert, "Communists, Brazilian Labor Movement," 8 February 1954, p. 2, U.S. Embassy Dispatch 973, Department of State Records; L. Fontes and Carneiro, *Face Final*, 141.

65. L. Fontes and Carneiro, *Face Final*, 94, 120, 107; Salert, "Communists," 1; Gossett, "March and April 1953 Strikes," 2–3. The constitution of 1946 had changed the status of the labor court system, which was incorporated into the regular judiciary, thereby providing independence from the executive branch and greater privileges for its members (Bosísio, "Justiça," 50).

66. Levine, *Father*, 151.

67. Ibid.

68. Irving Salert, "Memorandum of Conversation with João Oliveira Santos, Undersecretary of Labor, Industry, and Commerce, on August 24, at Noon," 24 August 1953, pp. 1–2, U.S. Embassy Dispatch 225, Department of State Records; Segadas Vianna, interview by Lima, Castro Gomes, and Ramos, 6 October 1983, Rio de Janeiro, 435.

69. Welch, *Seed*, 187; D'Araújo, *Sindicatos*, 93.

70. Lessa, *Getúlio Vargas*, 87, 129.

71. This point was made in the memoirs of Vargas's vice president, Café Filho, *Sindicato*, 307–8.

72. Lessa, *Getúlio Vargas*, 129.

73. Jesus, *Antologia*, 135; Jesus, *Estranho Diário*, 70.

74. Lessa, *Getúlio Vargas*, 77, 87, 84.

75. Negro and Fontes, "Trabalhadores," 163.

76. J. Ferreira, *Trabalhadores*, 36, 42, 49, 65.

77. Lessa, *Getúlio Vargas*, 84–85.

78. Macedo, *Fazendas*, 53.

CHAPTER SIX

1. Paoli, "Labor, Law, and the State," 440.
2. Alexandre Fortes, personal communication, 29 January 1998.
3. French, *Brazilian Workers' ABC*, 93, 96–97.
4. E. Martins, *Depoimento*, 89–91. Discussing the 1930s, Andreotti echoed Couto's moral in his explanation of why the labor laws were not satisfactory: "The labor law would give a right to the worker, but the same law would take that right [away] and give it to the boss" (Andreotti, interview by author, 20 September 1982, Santo André).
5. Leite Lopes, *Tecelagem*, 367.
6. Andreotti, interview by author, 3 November 1982, Santo André.
7. Leite Lopes, *Tecelagem*, 367.
8. Löwy and Chucid, "Opinões," 157.
9. Weffort, "Raízes Sociais," 45. Interviewing São Paulo metalworkers in 1966, Springer noted a greater degree of hopefulness among workers born elsewhere. This finding led him to the hypothesis that "besides being highly critical, perhaps the *paulistano* [resident of the city of São Paulo] is a cynical realist. . . . He knows what to expect, and he anticipates even less" (*Brazilian Factory Study*, 33). In a strange twist, the distrust felt by so many rank-and-file workers in São Paulo toward the labor court system could facilitate their victimization by specialized hustlers who preyed on those who filed labor complaints. Known as *paqueiros*, slang for dogs that know how to sniff out game, these disreputable labor lawyers or their employees would frequent the lines where workers gathered to directly file grievances with the court (a right under the labor law). The *paqueiros* solicited business by telling workers that they had "no chance of winning without a lawyer since the courts are *really* run by employers." After signing up the complainant, however, the lawyer in question did no work and, at the first opportunity, pressured the individual to settle for the least expensive settlement, abandoning the case if the worker refused to settle. (Mericle, "Conflict Resolution," 172–73, which draws on "Conversa de Paqueiro é Sobre Causa Perdída," *Jornal da Tarde*, 27 March 1968, and I. Martins, "Sem Juizes").
10. Marcondes, *Radiografia*, 67–68.
11. This is distinct from my earlier call for specialized technical research on the various labor relations institutions, such as labor courts, to understand when and how they worked (French, *Brazilian Workers' ABC*, 309–10).
12. Merry, *Getting Justice*, 5.
13. In the Brazilian case, Vera Lúcia B. Ferrante undertook a 1966 survey of labor courts in the interior city of Araraquara, São Paulo, but only part of her findings found their way into her book (*FGTS*, 152–57, 317). In 1972, Kenneth Mericle carried out research in São Paulo precisely along the lines proposed by Erickson, Peppe, and Spalding in 1974 ("Research"), but later researchers did not follow up on Mericle's pioneering results, most of which remained unpub-

lished (Mericle, "Conflict Resolution"). Maria Hermínia Tavares de Almeida also recognized the importance of the topic ("Estado," 269), although Sonia Avelar is one of the first scholars to have carried out detailed research using union or judicial records regarding labor court complaints ("Social Basis"). In terms of recent work along these lines, Cliff Welch's superb book, *The Seed Was Planted*, offers a fascinating study of a rural labor court established in Ribeirão Preto, São Paulo, before 1964. In addition, see the fine piece by Morel and Mangabeira, "'Velho.'" Samuel Fernando de Souza's recent master's thesis, "Esteira," suggests the potential of labor court filings as primary sources.

14. Montenegro, interview by Alexander, 21 February 1956, Recife, Alexander Papers, Rutgers.

15. Mericle, "Conflict Resolution," 154. The importance of the individual labor contract, whose terms are set by law, will lead Brazilian labor sociologist Eduardo Noronha to argue that the Brazilian labor relations system is best described not as corporatist but as "defined essentially by law and secondarily by the discretionary power of the employer; the latter, for his part, is influenced by the law even while disrespecting it. It is this that we call the *legislated model . . .* in contrast to countries with contractualist models. By legislated we mean a model where the law is more important than collective contract" (*Entre a Lei*, 15, 12).

16. MTIC, *Dez Anos*, 60.

17. In 1969, Neuma de Aguiar Walker attempted to correlate union membership, the industrial labor force, and the number of labor court filings in 1940, 1950, and 1960 ("Mobilization," 245; see also Ferrante, *FGTS*, 154–55). Far more could and clearly should be done in this regard.

18. Kahil, *Inflation*, 64.

19. Pochmann, "Mudança," 291.

20. Morel and Mangabeira, "'Velho.'" In 1974, at the height of the New Left, Robert Rowland criticized the labor courts because they "took away the unions' initiative regarding the conditions of labor and impeded the outbreak of conflicts at the only level—that of the enterprise—favorable to the development of a strong rank-and-file [labor] movement" ("Classe," 32). This assessment met skepticism, even if only on purely empirical grounds, in French, *Brazilian Workers' ABC*, 309.

21. For a fuller discussion of the logical interrelationship between direct action, such as strikes, and indirect action, such as legal and political struggle, see French, *Brazilian Workers' ABC*, 28–32, 45, 60–62, 72, 85–88, 96–97, 152–53, 178, 228, 252–54.

22. Avelar, "Social Basis," 212, 238–39, 241. In their study of the radical leadership of the union at the Volta Redonda steelworks, Morel and Mangabeira ("'Velho'") documented a particularly striking and conscious use of mass labor court filing to achieve the leadership's objective of mobilizing the membership in collective struggle.

23. Camargo, Amadeo, and Gonzaga, "Brazil," 9.

24. Mericle, "Conflict Resolution," 158, 160.

25. Ibid.
26. Andreotti, interview by author, 13 October 1982, Santo André.
27. Aguiar Walker, "Mobilization," 129. Criticisms of the outrageous results of individual cases were ubiquitous among employers and businessmen. See Fuerstenthal, interview by Alexander, 15 March 1956, Rio de Janeiro, Alexander Papers, Rutgers; Winslow, interview by Alexander, 8 July 1954, São Paulo, Alexander Papers, Rutgers; Moraes, *Indústria*.
28. Marcondes, *Radiografia*, 68; Mericle, "Conflict Resolution," 195.
29. This preliminary figure is based on research conducted, as of 1999, by French and Jody Pavilack. The number of consultations given is an understatement, for there are many days on which Braz simply stated that he was busy with too many workers to record their individual data. Definite figures and conclusions are forthcoming based, in part, on a systematic review of each consultation with Braz.
30. The final results of systematic coding of the diary entries and their comprehensive analysis results will be published in French and Pavilack, "What Workers Want."
31. Paoli, "Labor, Law, and the State," 240.
32. Weffort, *Populismo*, 75.
33. Bourdieu, "Force," 833.
34. Braz, interview by author, 6 August 1991, Santo André.
35. Wolfe, *Working Women*, 184.
36. Almeida, interview by author, 20 August 1991, Santo André. Union leaders of the 1950s often expressed pride in their mastery of the intricacies of the labor laws. This competency also eased the certain status boundary between the world of *letrados* and those who did manual labor. A leader of the textile workers' union of Juiz de Fora, Minas Gerais, cited his practical studies of this matter, while noting that "in this, putting modesty aside, I became a *doutor*"— that is, a lawyer, a degree holder (Loyola, *Sindicatos*, 69).
37. Braz, interview by author, 17 August 1991, Santo André. In many ways, Braz's description of the division of labor between himself and the union's lawyers sounds like Judge Giglio's idealized description of how the relationship between career and class judges in the labor courts was supposed to work (Mericle, "Conflict Resolution," 162–63). It made all the difference, however, that Braz, as the union's secretary-general, could fire the lawyers whom he had hired to serve his members. This power dynamic between social classes offered not only a symbolic but a real inversion of Brazil's typical hierarchies of class and education.
38. Almeida, interview by author, 20 August 1991, Santo André.
39. Nogueira, "Working." This language about looking for rights is echoed in a 1974 interview conducted by anthropologist Lygia Siguad with a twenty-year-old rural worker in Capela, Pernambuco. Although he was legally registered, the sugar mill fired him and "gave him nothing!" (failed to pay what he was legally owed with a *carteira assinada*). Asked if he had complained, he responded that he had not: "If you complain, you get a bad reputation." Asked

what that meant, the worker explained, "It's like this: to get a bad reputation, if one does something, if one complains, they order us to go hunt for our rights, but then we go searching, here, there, but it's no use." His mother interjected, "You don't get anywhere. Only if one were to search for one's rights in Recife [the state capital]," a statement that was followed by the worker's pessimistic final observation about the possibility of legal recourse: "If one looks for a lawyer, the sugar mill greases his palm [*o advogado come bola da Usina*; the lawyer eats the sugar mill's cake]" (Sigaud, *Clandestinos*, 97).

40. Simão, "Sindicato." The notion of having the "right to the [labor] laws" (*direito às leis trabalhistas*) has, as its counterpart, a language of the powerful giving *direitos*. In interviews conducted in 1967 in semi-industrialized Bahia, Moreira de Carvalho asked workers to define a good employer: "For most of them, the good boss [*bom patrão*] is the one who treats you well [*que trata bem*], that helps when you are in need, [and] that understands and 'gives' rights [*'da' os direitos*], that fulfills the labor laws." The workers interviewed most strongly emphasized good treatment (Moreira de Carvalho, *Operário*, 61).

41. See French, "Metalworkers," on the struggles of the ABC's metalworkers between 1950 and 1980 (from Andreotti and Braz to the rise of Luis Inácio "Lula" da Silva).

42. Löwy and Chucid, "Opiniões," 156.

43. São Bernardo's expanding auto industry fell within the jurisdiction of the metalworkers' union of Santo André, and Braz had been in charge of the union's office there. Although São Bernardo's union would become independent in 1960, Braz's diary shows that he was still helping dozens of workers from that city in 1961. For a comprehensive examination of the emergence of the new union in São Bernardo within the context of struggles in Santo André, see Negro's superb doctoral dissertation, "Linhas."

44. Martins Rodrigues, *Industrialização*, 103.

45. Ibid., 107. In some factories in Rio de Janeiro in the 1940s, Hercules Corrêa dos Santos noted in a recent memoir, union membership was dangerous: "If the company knew the employee was unionized, he would be fired immediately. Thus, the collection of union dues had to be done on the sly," not automatically through the employer (*Memórias*, 50). This pattern was not universal, at least in São Paulo in the same period.

46. Martins Rodrigues, *Industrialização*, 80.

47. Brandão Lopes, "Ajustamento," 397. An argument to the contrary is made in Wolfe, *Working Women*, although it is far from convincing (French, review).

48. Brandão Lopes, "Ajustamento," 398, 402.

49. Ibid., 397.

50. Ibid., 397, 400. Even today, Braz observes, fifty years after the creation of the labor court system, many workers are at a loss. "When something happens to him in the factory and he presents himself to the union leader or lawyer, the man is, as they say, 'an orphan in everything. His salvation is here.' Because he doesn't know how to proceed. Sometimes he may even be knowledgeable, but

since he's never had a problem before, he's without a compass. So you [the union leader] are a type of confidante or mediator, 'Do this, don't do that'" (Braz, interview by author, 17 August 1991).

51. Andreotti, interview by author, 2 December 1982, Santo André.

52. Martins Rodrigues, *Industrialização*, 71; Moreira de Carvalho, *Operário*, 61.

53. Brandão Lopes, "Ajustamento," 399.

54. Andreotti, interview by author, 2, 9 December 1982, Santo André. That this attitude toward unions was not unique to Santo André is suggested by Robert Alexander's detailed first-person account of two 1956 consultations between workers and their union leader ("Observations on São Paulo Textile Union," [24 April 1956], Alexander Papers, Rutgers).

55. Andreotti, interview by author, 2, 9 December 1982, Santo André.

56. Brandão Lopes, "Ajustamento," 397.

57. For a discussion of why *imediatismo* is a more accurate and revealing term than "individualism," a label used by early sociologists who studied workers in São Paulo, see French, "'They Don't Wear Black-Tie.'"

58. Andreotti, interview by author, 7 December 1982, Santo André.

59. Ibid.

60. Leite Lopes, *Tecelagem*, 367.

61. Ferrante, *FGTS*, 157.

62. Even opening a labor court case was a daring move for many workers. In 1977, anthropologist Merida H. Blanco, "Race and Face," 30, documented the social vulnerability and psychological insecurity that plagued the urban poor. Her Bahian informant Alaide's "crazy mother," Blanco reported, stood "little chance of collecting the wages which the textile factory neglected to pay her for the last four of the 34 years she worked there; she lacks the face to 'defend herself' in court. In order to receive anything at all, Vandete had to agree to pay a public official half the compensation due to her husband when he was disabled in Salvador."

63. Merry, *Getting Justice*, 5.

64. J. C. Lima, *Trabalho*, 169.

65. Leite Lopes, *Tecelagem*, 359–68.

66. Sigaud, "Direito," 225. Welch, *Seed*, 215–17, 222–28, explores the relationship between union struggle and labor court participation in the countryside in the 1950s and 1960s in Ribeirão Preto in the interior of São Paulo.

67. Sigaud, *Clandestinos*, 367.

68. Braz, interview by author, 17 August 1991, Santo André.

69. Mericle, "Conflict Resolution," 158, 160; Braz, interview by author, 17 August 1991, Santo André.

70. Mericle, "Conflict Resolution," 179.

71. Mericle, "Conflict Resolution," 176. The preference for handling grievances directly with employers rather than through the labor courts has also been reported for many other unions in the 1950s: Lombardi, interview by Alexander, 17 April 1956, São Paulo, Alexander Papers, Rutgers; Fonseca, interview by Alexander, 14 April 1956, São Paulo, Alexander Papers, Rutgers.

72. Andreotti, interview by author, 10 December 1982, Santo André.

73. Ibid. Although he understood why workers stole from their employers, Andreotti disapproved of the practice because it was an individualistic rather than collective response to low wages (Andreotti, interview by author, 10, 13 December 1982, Santo André).

74. Braz, interview by author, 17 August 1991, Santo André.

75. I. Martins, "Sem Juizes," as cited by Mericle, "Conflict Resolution," 172.

76. Braz, interview by author, 17 August 1991, Santo André.

77. Springer, *Brazilian Factory Study*, 1–12.

CHAPTER SEVEN

1. Werneck Vianna, *Liberalismo e Sindicato*, 57.

2. Collor, *Origens*, 179.

3. As used by the Vargas's speechwriters, the *caso de polícia* aphorism quickly acquired a fixed and formulaic form, as can be seen in Vargas's 1933 address to the National Assembly that repeated almost word for word his 1931 statement in the epigraph of this chapter: "In the predominant political mentality that oriented the government [before 1930], there had crystallized a judgment that the labor problem in Brazil was simply a matter for the police [*caso de polícia*]. In an environment with such an impoverished social vision, it was natural that labor's demands encountered no echo, not even in the case of the most elementary demands, conquests that had already been incorporated into the legislation of the majority of cultured countries" (Vargas, "O Primero Ano do Governo Provisório [Manifesto à Nação, Lido, Em Sessão Solene, no Teatro Municipal, a 3 de Outubro de 1931]," in Vargas, *Nova Politica*, 1:233–344; Vargas, "Mensagem Lida Perante a Assembléia Nacional Constituinte, no Ato de Sua Instalação, em 15 de Novembro de 1933," in Vargas, *Nova Política*, 3:137).

4. "Aos Operários Paulistas" (leaflet), *Jornal de São Paulo*, 29 July 1932, as reproduced in De Paula, *1932*, 113–14.

5. Rego, *Vitória*, 12.

6. "Discurso do Ministro do Trabalho, Dr. Waldemar Falcão, Saudando o Presidente Getúlio Vargas, em Nome da Massa Trabalhadora, no Dia 9 de Novembro de 1940, na Esplanada de Castelo," in MTIC, *Dez Anos*, ix.

7. Schwartzman, *Estado Novo*, 328.

8. Quoted from press interviews of 19 February and 22 April 1938 published as "Problemas e Realizações do Estado Novo," in Vargas, *Nova Política*, 4:171.

9. Pimpão, *Getúlio Vargas*, 55.

10. The continued power of the reference is well illustrated by a 1990 book in which the Washington Luis aphorism appears in the first sentence of a chapter, "The Nature of State Intervention in the Labor Market" (Lopes da Silva, *Domesticação*, 45). In 1982, Cerqueira Filho would title chapter 2 of his book on the discourse about labor legislation in the 1930s "The Social Question: A Police Matter [*Caso de Polícia*]" (*Questão*, 55). The phrase also provided the subtitle for

Negro and P. Fontes's recent article about police surveillance and harassment of trade unionists, "Trabalhadores em São Paulo: Ainda um Caso de Polícia."

11. Beiguelman, *Companheiros*, 46–48, 51–52.

12. Pimenta, *Sociologia*, 187. A version of this argument about the aphorism appeared in French, *Brazilian Workers' ABC*, 202–3.

13. Merton, Sills, and Stigler, "Kelvin Dictum," 319.

14. See the collection of radio addresses by the Estado Novo's labor minister, Alexandre Marcondes Filho (*Trabalhadores*); the addresses are analyzed in Castro Gomes, *Invenção*, 238–46.

15. Rose, *Forgotten Things*, 83.

16. Gusmão, *Bojo*, 73.

17. Ibid., 33, 88–89. Before 1930, Gusmão noted, the relationship between trade unions and the "government was exercised through the intermediary of the police." After that date, the trade unions—along with many "socialists" of convenience, like Gusmão—placed themselves on the government's side "to achieve the demands that they hoped to obtain" (11, 160–61).

18. Ibid., 71–73. Gusmão provided a fine example of *bajulação* in his 1944 book, *Recursos na Justiça do Trabalho*, which appeared two years after he had been dismissed from government service. Published with an introduction by Pimenta, Gusmão's book opened with a tribute to Vargas as the "eminent statesman" who had personally laid the groundwork for resolving the social question "in all of its aspects" (9).

19. Gusmão, *Bojo*, 52–53. With expenses covered by union funds, the delegates arrived in Rio de Janeiro expecting to stay in hotels, to be served, and to savor the perks. At least on this occasion, however, the visiting trade unionists suffered a bitter disappointment. They were housed offshore in facilities used for newly arrived immigrants and were provided with bad food. The conclusion seemed clear: the social question was clearly not a police matter, "at least on dry land," but perhaps the social question was a concern for the maritime police in this instance. In the same vignette, Gusmão also assures his reader, with a wink, that the visiting delegates, having bathed in the atmosphere of social peace, left satisfied that the "providential man had resolved all [of Brazil's] problems, including immigration. After all, hadn't they, for a few days, been immigrants in their own country?" (Gusmão, *Bojo*, 52–53).

20. Moraes Filho, *Problema*, 210, attempted to salvage the First Republic's reputation by emphasizing that some modest legal progress had occurred during the 1920s. Thus, it was not strictly true, he insisted, that "Brazil possessed nothing in this terrain" before Vargas.

21. Tenório de Brito, "Washington Luis."

22. According to Tenório de Brito, "Washington Luis," 88, the person who fabricated the aphorism added insult to injury by failing to realize that a great stylist of Portuguese like Luis would never have used the "humiliating and impoverished vocabulary" employed in the *caso de polícia* aphorism. Tenório de Brito gave no source for the 1920 Luis platform he cited.

23. Moraes Filho, *Problema*, 210–11, quotes Luis's platform as cited by Carvalho Neto, *Legislação*, 238.

24. *Jornal do Comércio*, 29 December 1925, as cited in Moraes Filho, *Problema*, 210.

25. Luis declared that no one could be silent on or disinterested in the worker issue. For the full text of his 25 January 1920 platform, see Egas, *Washington Luis*, 31–32. I thank Joseph Love for providing this citation.

26. The 1921 presidential platform of Arthur da Silva Bernardes, who held office from 1922 to 1926, endorsed social legislation, including "mixed arbitration courts to settle/put an end to [*dirimir*] conflicts between workers and employers" (Pinheiro and Hall, *Classe*, 1:298; Pinheiro, *Estratégias*, 109).

27. Egas, *Washington Luis*, 32. The Brazilian constitution of 1891 was amended in September 1926 to give the national congress the exclusive competency to legislate on labor matters (Nascimento, "História," 151).

28. Medeiros as quoted in Collor, *Origens*, 40, 65. The complex twists and turns of ideological currents are suggested by the fact that Medeiros's favored solution, based on positivist doctrine, was the "incorporation of the proletariat." For a variety of reasons, including a progressive regional self-image, most scholars have focused on that discourse as a precedent for post-1930 legislation and ignored Medeiros's principled opposition to federal government regulation of the terms and conditions of the sale of labor power. This postwar episode is far more than a curiosity, however, because Collor served as editor of Medeiros's party newspaper in Porto Alegre. At the time, labor reformer Evaristo de Moraes criticized the congressional "positivists inspired by Mr. Borges de Medeiros" for misinterpreting positivist doctrine as set forth by its Brazilian founders during the struggle against slavery (Evaristo de Moraes, "Ainda a Propósito do Código do Trabalho: Os Postivistas da Câmara de Acordo com os Escravocratas!" *O Imparcial*, 8 October 1918, as reproduced in Moraes Filho, *Socialismo*, 109–12).

29. Egas, *Washington Luis*, 31–32. While these claims are exaggerated, a recent sketch of the labor justice system has made a point of citing Luis's initiative, as governor of São Paulo in 1922, to create rural courts to judge contract disputes between landowners and foreign tenants. This "advanced" proposal included participation in court proceedings by both interested parties, although the author notes that Luis's initiative failed to take root given the "economic and social inferiority" of rural working people (Silva Martins Filho, "Breve História," 178–80).

30. Maurette, *Social Aspects*, 51–52. During the First Republic, São Paulo was also the first to establish a state labor department, the DET. For a detailed DET report on wage levels and factory conditions in 1912, see Pinheiro and Hall, *Classe*, 2:63–91.

31. See Bolsonaro de Moura, *Mulheres*; Castro Gomes, *Burguesia e Trabalho*, 233.

32. Moraes Filho, *Problema*, 210.

33. Egas, *Washington Luis*, 31.

34. Ibid.

35. Maurette, *Social Aspects*, 8. Although diplomatic, Maurette's report referred to the banana-and-sun aphorism about the social question as "a lazy half-truth to which day-by-day reality is more and more giving the lie."

36. Instituto Histórico e Geográfico de São Paulo, *Washington Luis*, 134–35, 107–8. In 1924, another old friend, Eugenio Égas, described the behavioral norms of paternalistic lordship that characterized Washington Luis. Aristocratic in his style of dress and worldly in his sophistication, Luis was "smooth and affectionate when meeting with friends or dealing with subalterns, family members, or the poor [*subalternos, domésticos, ou pobres*]." Luis gave the impression, Égas said, of wishing the world to be "an enchanted dream, society a paradise, and government a constant good that was never obliged to use force," although Luis was resigned to the fact that it was not so. "The prestige of power," Égas suggested, could only gain "in force and shine" under the guard of a man whose wide intellectual culture included a touch of Nietzsche (*Washington Luis*, 20).

37. Tenório de Brito, "Washington Luis," 88, even cites his experience during the 1917 São Paulo general strike, in which he commanded the firemen defending the city's gas plant from the "anarchic action of wrongdoers." Anarchy, "with its assassinations, robberies, depredations, [and] the suppression of the provision of public services," must be met with all of the force at the government's command.

38. Maram, *Anarquistas*, 60–62.

39. Hall and Garcia, "Urban Labor," 163; Pinheiro, *Estratégias*, 117.

40. Ibid., 171. A manuscript prepared by the Ministry of Justice in 1943, under the Estado Novo, offered an enlightened and progressive observation about the vices of police behavior "in the old days." The repressive function of the police force "imprinted it with a naturally antipathetic physiognomy," they began, generating hostility and a "lack of confidence on the part of the population." Given the absence of a "perfect and adequate legislation," police "activities were almost always oriented toward the use of violent procedures, which made the police increasingly incompatible with the social environment." The other problem, the ministry suggested, was that the police department, staffed by "individuals without culture," was not attractive to "capable citizens" because of its negative image and low pay. In a subsection, "The Police and the Social Question," the report stated matter-of-factly that "when the proletariat attempted, even through peaceful means, to defend its rights" before 1930, "it was subject to violent repression by the police, who coerced them into desisting, thus instigating their hate and pushing the workers toward a reaction." At the same time, the anonymous authors did not deny the need for police intervention to prevent a disturbance of the social order. They warned, however, that such actions would contribute to popular malaise and antipathy toward the security forces if they were not carried out in a "reasonable and opportune" fashion. The post-1930 regime's social legislation, the report concluded sycophantically, "had definitively stopped such clashes between the workers and the police" (Schwartzman, *Estado Novo*, 111–13).

41. Maram, *Anarquistas*, 60–62.
42. Ibid.
43. Cerqueira Filho, *Questão*, 59.
44. Albertino Rodrigues, *Sindicato e Desenvolvimento*, 68. Moraes admitted in a 1926 article that some observers thought that the *caso de polícia* aphorism was a distortion of Luis's position. By way of proof, Moraes urged his readers to look at Luis's consistently repressive response to "anarchic or libertarian agitation in São Paulo or Santos" ("A Questão Operária em São Paulo e no Resto do Brasil," *Correio da Manhã*, 15 January 1926, 4). For the heavily persecuted anarchist Left, Luis's aphorism was a commonplace, as can be seen in a 1925 letter to ILO chief Albert Thomas denouncing police persecution of workers' struggles (Pinheiro and Hall, *Classe Operária*, 1:133). Luis's *caso de polícia* saying, a Vargas supporter wrote in 1929, was at least semiofficial (*officioso*). The article, which set forth the social and political platform of Vargas's Liberal Alliance, claimed that the aphorism had already resulted in notoriety for Brazil in Europe ("Tópicos do Manifesto," 325).
45. In the 1978 postscript to a new edition of *O Problema do Sindicato Único*, Moraes Filho referred to himself humorously as a "cria autêntica" of the Labor Ministry (a *cria* is someone, usually poor, who is raised in someone else's home). Joining the ministry after finishing high school in 1934, he was promoted to *procurador* (state attorney) in the labor court system in 1941 and served until his retirement in 1966. He departed voluntarily, he adds, and this statement can be seen as a gesture of respect for the thousands of government employees who were fired for their beliefs by the military dictatorship that came to power in 1964 (*Problema*, 323).
46. Along with his associates in the post–World War II Democratic Left Party (later rechristened the Brazilian Socialist Party), Moraes Filho had made common cause with Vargas's liberal constitutionalist enemies in 1945, although the alliances would shift over the next fifteen years as the União Democrática Nacional came to harbor the hard core of the militant antidemocratic and antigetulist right. For more on these liberals, see Benevides, *UDN*.
47. Dias, *História*, 49–50.
48. Lacerda, *História*. P. Alves, *Verdade*, 85–92, provides a discussion of Lacerda and Moraes's activities on behalf of strikers and anarchists between 1917 and 1920.
49. Lacerda, *Evolução*, 279. This detailed and useful account of the ins and outs of his legislative struggles after 1917 was published by the MTIC in 1960, during a more propitious and progressive era.
50. *Diário de Notícias*, 2 November 1930, as quoted in Barbosa de Araújo, *Batismo*, 77.
51. Lacerda, *Segunda República*, 25, 344; Pinheiro, *Estratégias*, 127.
52. Foot and Leonardi, *História*, 213–16. Circular 1157 issued by the Center of Weaving and Spinning Industrialists of São Paulo in January 1932 reported to its members on a "very confidential" basis that the specialized police "Dele-

gacy of Social Order will post a large number of agents in the factories of this city, assigned a special mission. The factories where these police auxiliaries are in service should feed and house them comfortably, for the greater efficiency of the work that they are undertaking."

53. French, *Brazilian Workers' ABC*, 47–52.

54. Andreotti, interview by author, 1 October, 20, 22 September 1982, Santo André.

55. Ibid.

56. Ibid., 22 September 1982, Santo André.

57. See the discussion of the concept of union legalization in French, *Brazilian Workers' ABC*, 61, 110, 253–55, 303.

58. Rego, *Vitória*, 12.

59. Werneck Sodré, *História*, 301–2.

60. Castro Gomes, *Burguesia e Trabalho*, 225.

61. Conniff, *Urban Politics*, 138–39.

62. Ventura cited in ibid., 139.

63. Collor, "A Questão Social no Brasil," *Correio do Povo*, 19 September 1934, in Collor, *Origens*, 210.

64. Sales Filho cited in Conniff, *Urban Politics*, 141. The government deposed in 1930, recalled communist intellectual Leôncio Basbaum in 1962, was accused of "many crimes, including the beating and torture of workers or communists or simply those suspected." Yet he insisted bitterly that before 1930, such actions had been the exception, whereas under Vargas they became the rule (*História*, 2:37).

65. Gusmão, *Bojo*, 21.

66. Werneck Sodré, *História*, 370.

67. Cancelli, *Mundo*, 27.

68. Ibid., 5. Even more polemically than Cancelli, U.S. scholar R. S. Rose, *Forgotten Things*, has criticized the scholarly literature for its cultivated forgetfulness about the crimes, violent repression, and human rights violations of Vargas and his henchmen.

69. Andreotti, interview by author, 1 October 1982, Santo André.

70. Ibid., 28 September 1982, Santo André.

71. Andreotti came to police attention after the confiscation of a leaflet in a local factory (French, *Brazilian Workers' ABC*, 70–73, 91). The details of Andreotti's arrest and conviction by the TSN are amply detailed in Processo 705 (1939), TSN Records. A glimpse of the intensity of police scrutiny of Andreotti during his long life of labor and communist militancy can be found in Prontuário de Polícia 4980 (2 vols.) on Marcos Andreotti, Acervo Departamento de Ordem Política e Social Records. The scale of the DOPS archive covering the state of São Paulo is immense, with at least two million documents organized in 9,626 files covering 1924 to 1983 (Aparecida de Aquino, Leme de Matos, and Swenssen, *Coração*, 19).

72. Pompeu de Campos, *Repressão*, 125, 132, 173. When it was abolished in 1945 with the end of the Estado Novo, the TSN had condemned 4,099 individuals, 782 of them in São Paulo.

73. Andreotti, interview by author, Santo André. When he was put off the train, the penniless Andreotti went into a local trade union, explained his plight, and bought a return ticket with their donations. Although Andreotti's deportation to another state occurred in the 1940s, this type of police action was routine decades earlier. Loading suspect "foreigners" on ships was a common police action before 1930. With Brazilian-born subversives, noted Boris Fausto, police "frequently used the expedient of making arrests that were not communicated to the juridical authorities, and the arrestees would be later released, without means, outside of their native state." As one of his examples, Fausto cited a leader of the São Paulo printers' union who was deported to Rio Grande do Sul in 1917, just like Andreotti nearly three decades later (*Trabalho*, 240).

74. Polícia, *Código*. An opening note praises *bacharel* Venancio Ayres "for the brilliant manner with which he fulfilled the duty conferred upon him." The code was to go into effect within sixty days of 9 June 1939.

75. Ibid., 56–59, 7–9, 28–30, 42–45.

76. Bernardo, *Tutela*, 159.

77. Oliveira Vianna, *Problemas*, 164.

78. Bernardo, *Tutela*, 190.

79. Simão, *Sindicato e Estado*, 120–21.

80. Oliveira Vianna, *Problemas*, 291–92.

81. The 1939 telegraphic code aptly captured the socially repressive common sense that had long permeated the São Paulo Civil Police. A local police *delegado* in 1939 was no more likely to be enlightened than he had been in 1931, when a young lawyer was dispatched to Ribeirão Preto, São Paulo, to investigate the abuses of the old regime. A young worker complained to Caio Prado Júnior that the local *delegado* had closed the small union that the worker was organizing, confiscated the furniture, and prohibited the union's functioning. When the future Marxist historian asked the *delegado*, the man replied, " 'In fact I did go there and close the union. Just imagine, there were communists meeting there.' When he perceived that his explanation didn't convince me, he exclaimed: 'But Doctor (at that time I was already a *bacharel*), they were communists and were there defending that stuff about wages. Now then, you're not going to allow something like that!' " (Prado Júnior, "É Preciso," 304).

82. Polícia, *Código*, 42–45.

83. Ibid., 44.

84. Paranhos, *Roubo*, 150.

85. Chaves Neto, *Minha Vida*, 107.

86. Paranhos, *Roubo*, 149.

87. Medeyros, *Getúlio Vargas*, 10.

88. Pimenta, *Sociologia*, 189.

89. Paranhos, *Roubo*, 151.

90. Ibid., 153.

91. Unlike Cancelli, *Mundo*, 5, Pinheiro, *Estratégias*, 322, downplays foreign influence.

92. Pinheiro, *Estratégias*, 328–29. As a Marxist military man in the 1930s, Nelson Werneck Sodré had no affection for Vargas's Estado Novo, where the workers' movement was treated as "a *caso de polícia* and the social question was to be overseen by special police agencies, with an apparatus of torture and intimidation." Yet in 1967 he insisted that "those who see the Estado Novo only through its sad and infamous" repressive facade "commit a profound mistake. It was that, but it was much more than that" in its continuation of the reforms begun in the early 1930s (*História*, 304).

93. Lara, "Escravidão," 35–38.

94. Besouchet, *História*, 29, 45–46.

95. Pimenta, *Sociologia*, 187.

96. In Portuguese, the factory manager declared, "Pois faz muito bem! Para tratar com aquela canalhada só mesmo de trabuco na cinta. Aquela gente devia ser tratada a chicote." Pacheco, *Prevenção*, 93–94, goes on to rebuke this "apologist for the whip" by citing Carlyle's claim that a great man reveals his greatness in how he treats the little people (*pequenos*). Offering another quote from a different author, Pacheco emphasizes that his industrialist reader should realize that underneath "the modest clothing . . . and rough appearance," the "humble worker" is also a human being, and his dignity should be respected: "He is not simply an animal. He is not simply a machine moved by money."

97. As the social clause aphorism became entrenched in political discourse, it could even be applied to the problems of nonworkers. In 1948, São Paulo state deputy Herbert Levy complained that the national government had ordered banks to purchase bonds. To make his point, he declared that economic questions, "just like social questions, are not and never have been solved by violence or arbitrariness" (*Batalha*, 63).

98. Flory, *Judge and Jury*, 149, 182. The explicitly reactionary class mentality of those who rallied around Dutra is well illustrated by the rhetoric of Daniel de Carvalho, a *dutrista* politician and longtime employer attorney from Minas Gerais. Although his book appeared in 1959, during the centrist conservative presidency of Juscelino Kubitschek, Carvalho lamented the fact that workers had become "the object of electoral exploitation by unscrupulous and ambitious politicians, *pelegos*, and demagogues." He also attacked the false prophets of *trabalhismo*, who talked incessantly about rights to the detriment of production. These demagogues, he said, enthroned "laziness [as] the mother of all virtues" by failing to teach workers their duty and obligation to work assiduously and with care. Such a lax approach had already led to unjustified reductions in working hours, the lengthening of vacations, paid rest on Sunday even for those who skipped work (with the end of *assiduidade integral*), and retirement benefits available even to the young and able. It is hardly surprising, he concluded, that such irresponsible men admitted the validity of strikes in cases where the legal avenues for resolving worker grievances had not yet been exhausted (*Novos Estudos*, 191).

99. Scarmuzzi, *Memórias*, 57, 69, 84, 86. Scarmuzzi was a member of an elite Rio

Special Police unit founded in 1932 to combat subversives. In 1945 he was deployed at a street parade to honor Brazilian soldiers returning from fighting fascism in Italy. As he recalls in his memoir, the unit's longtime chief, João Alberto, advised his men to take care: "We perceived what he was trying to say. The times had changed. The environment would no longer countenance police authoritarianism," as it had during the dictatorship (47–48).

100. Braz, interview by author, 17 August 1991, Santo André.
101. Ibid.; Badaró Mattos, *Greves*.
102. Ibid.
103. Ibid.
104. Ibid., 6 August 1991, Santo André.
105. On the circumstances leading to the adoption of the Brazilian flag with the positivist "Order and Progress" motto, see Murilo de Carvalho, *Formação*, 110–21.

CONCLUSION

1. Simões, *Direito de Trabalho*, 229.
2. Nosella, *Por Que Mataram*, 108–9. This interview with Santos Dias was conducted on the eve of the 1979 metalworkers' strike in which he was killed by a policeman while picketing outside of the Sylvânia plant in São Paulo.
3. Unger, *Knowledge and Politics*, 75.
4. Deborah Levenson-Estrada, personal communication, January 1998; see also her existentialist labor history, *Trade Unionists*.
5. Pereira de Souza, *Memórias*, 58.

Armadilha Trick or swindle

Assiduidade integral Total attendance clause, a 1948 TST ruling that enjoyment of wage increases and benefits by individual workers depended on a 100 percent attendance record

Atestado de ideologia Required certificate from the DOPS attesting to an individual's "political-social antecedents"

Aviso prévio Prior or advance warning before dismissal

Bacharéis Holders of bachelor's degrees, especially lawyers

Bacharelismo That which pertains to or is characteristic of degree holders or lawyers

Bajulação Fawning flattery of the more powerful

Bicho papão An imaginary monster that Brazilian parents use to keep children in line

Bilhete Short informal note

Burlar To cheat, dupe, to swindle

Carteira assinada Signed working papers, an individual working in government regulated employment

Carteira do trabalho Working papers issued to individual workers in government-regulated employment

Caso de polícia A police case, a matter for the police

Companheiro Fellow worker or mate

Dedo-durismo Finger-pointing, informing

Delegados Delegates; a position of command whether in the police force (as its commander in a given município) or in the labor ministry (as head of a DRT)

Direitos Rights, privileges, or entitlements

Dissídios Disputes between workers and employers under the CLT's labor court system. Divided into individual and collective (*dissídios individuais* and *coletivos*)

Dutrista Supporter of or pertaining to President Eurico Dutra

Empreguismo The avid search for government jobs to give out or to receive

Esperteza Cunning(ness), astuteness

Estabilidade Job tenure based on seniority

Estado benefactor The paternalistic "benefactor state"

Estado Novo"New State," the name given to the dictatorship led by Getúlio Vargas between 1937 and 1945

Fazenda Plantation, ranch, or large landholding

Fichado To be on a filing card in the DOPS; to be suspected of subversive activity

Fiscalização Inspection services

Fraudada Cheated on, defrauded

Gaúcho Of or pertaining to the state of Rio Grande do Sul

Getulista Supporter of or pertaining to Getúlio Vargas

Interventor Official appointed to take over a union in which the federal government had intervened

Jeito A knack or maneuver, a way of getting around a bureaucratically or legally difficult problem

Juizes classistas Class judges; worker or employer representatives who served on the labor courts

Junta de Conciliação e Julgamento Junta of Conciliation and Judgment; the lowest-level court within the labor justice system

Laudo Expert opinion, as in the inspection process

Letra morta Dead letter; a written promise not kept

Meter o pau "Apply the rod" as in a beating; repression

Municípios Municipalities; the Brazilian equivalent of a U.S. county

Outorga, Outorgada A grant, gift, or award; something bestowed or conferred

Paulista Of or pertaining to the state of São Paulo

Pelego Literally saddle blanket between the rider and the horse; slang for union officials, often at higher levels, who were nonmilitant and tied to the government or employers' interests rather than those of union members

Pistolão The good word, connections, and pull that comes with being a big shot

Policialismo Literally, policeism; repression

Povo The people, especially the common people

Previdência Welfare/social security

Processo Legal case or complaint proceeding, as with a filing with a government agency

Procurador State attorney

Queimado Literally, burned or exposed; in leftist jargon, known to the police for political or labor militancy

Reclamação Complaint or protest

Reivindicação Demand

Sonegar To withhold or conceal unlawfully; to defraud, cheat

Tapeação Swindle or trickery

Trabalhista Laborite, from *trabalhador* (laborer)

Tutela Tutelage, protection

Varguismo/varguista Supporter of or pertaining to Getúlio Vargas

bibliography

MANUSCRIPT COLLECTIONS

Robert J. Alexander Papers: Interview Collection, 1947–1994, microfilm, IDC Publishers.
Robert Jackson Alexander Papers, Special Collections and University Archives, Rutgers University, New Brunswick, N.J.
Departamento de Ordem Política e Social Records, Arquivo Público do Estado de São Paulo, São Paulo.
Department of State Records, U.S. National Archives and Records Administration, Washington, D.C.
International Confederation of Free Trade Unions Archive, International Institute of Social History, Amsterdam.
Tribunal de Segurança Nacional Records, Arquivo Nacional do Brasil, Rio de Janeiro.

INTERVIEWS

By Robert J. Alexander, in Robert Jackson Alexander Papers, Special Collections and University Archives, Rutgers University, New Brunswick, N.J.
Barreto, Antônio (director of inspection services [*fiscalização*]) of the Delegacia Regional do Trabalho de São Paulo), 16 June 1953, São Paulo.
Barreto, Caio Plinio (lawyer), 17–18 June 1953, São Paulo.
Drummond, Herberto de Magalhães (TRT president in Minas Gerais), 27 March 1956, Belo Horizonte.
Fonseca, Nivaldo (second secretary of São Paulo Textile Union), 14 April 1956, São Paulo.
Fuerstenthal, Achim (Brazilian management consultant for foreign firms), 15 March 1956, Rio de Janeiro.
Goulart, João (ex-president of Brazil), 5 June 1972, Maldonaldo, Uruguay.
Hollanda de Cavalcante, Deocleciano (president of Confederação Nacional dos Trabalhadores na Indústria), 9 March 1956, Rio de Janeiro.
Lins de Barros, Antônio Luis (Delegado Regional do Ministério do Trabalho in Pernambuco), 18 February 1956, Recife.
Lombardi, Aldo (secretary-general of São Paulo Metalworkers Union), 17 April 1956, São Paulo.
Montenegro, Pedro de Albuquerque (judge of TRT of Recife), 21 February 1956, Recife.
Moreira Júnior, Delfim (president of TST), 13 March 1956, Rio de Janeiro.
Morena, Roberto (PCB leader), 28 August 1946, Rio de Janeiro.
Motta, Renato (editor of PCB labor newspaper *Gazeta Sindical*), 21 March 1956, Rio de Janeiro.
Moura, Paulo de Campos (PTB leader), 20 April 1956, São Paulo.

Saad, E. G. (director of Orientação Social, Serviço Social da Indústria in São Paulo), 13 April 1956, São Paulo.

Segadas Vianna, José de, 26 August 1946, 16 March 1956, Rio de Janeiro.

Shearer, John (professor of industrial relations, Princeton), 24 September 1958, New Brunswick, N.J.

Tavares, Manoel Passos (TST statistician), 13 March 1956, Rio de Janeiro.

Winslow, William (U.S. businessman), 8 July 1954, São Paulo.

By Maria Cristina Guido and Reinaldo Roels Júnior

Talarico, José Gomes, [September 1978–July 1979], Rio de Janeiro. In "José Gomes Talarico (Depoimento)." Rio de Janeiro: Centro de Pesquisa e Documentação de História Contemporânea do Brasil/Fundação Getúlio Vargas.

By Valentina da Rocha Lima, Ângela Maria de Castro Gomes, and Plínio de Abreu Ramos

Segadas Vianna, José de, 6 October 1983, Rio de Janeiro. In "Depoimento de José de Segadas Vianna." Centro de Pesquisa e Documentação de História Contemporânea do Brasil/Fundação Getúlio Vargas, Rio de Janeiro, 1987.

By author

Almeida, João de, 20 August 1991, Santo André.

Andreotti, Marcos, 20, 22, 27, 28, 29 September, 1, 13 October, 3, 29 November, 2, 7, 9, 13 December 1982, Santo André.

Braz, Philadelpho, 6, 17 August 1991, Santo André.

McMillan, Claude, Jr., 3 June 1996, by telephone.

THESES AND DISSERTATIONS

Aguiar Walker, Neuma Figueiredo de. "The Mobilization and Bureaucratization of the Brazilian Working Class, 1930–1964." Ph.D. diss., Washington University, 1969.

Avelar, Sonia Maria. "The Social Basis of Workers' Solidarity: A Case Study of Textile Workers in São José dos Campos, Brazil." 2 vols. Ph.D. diss., University of Michigan, 1985.

Blanco, Merida Holderness. "Race and Face among the Poor: The Language of Color in a Brazilian Bairro." Ph.D. diss., Stanford University, 1978.

Fernando de Souza, Samuel. "Na Esteira do Conflito: Trabalhadores e Trabalho na Produção de Calçados em Franca (1970–1980)." Master's thesis, Universidade Estadual de Campinas, 2003.

Fischer, Brodwyn M. "The Poverty of Law: Rio de Janeiro, 1930–1964." Ph.D. diss., Harvard University, 1999.

Fontes, Paulo. "Comunidade Operária, Migração Nordestina e Lutas Sociais: São Miguel Paulista (1945–1966)." Ph.D. diss., Universidade Estadual de Campinas, 2001.

Fortes, Alexandre. " 'Nós do Quarto Distrito . . . ' A Classe Trabalhadora Porto-Alegrense e a Era Vargas." Ph.D. diss., Universidade Estadual de Campinas, 2001.

French, John D. "Industrial Workers and the Origin of Populist Politics in the ABC Region of Greater São Paulo, Brazil, 1900–1950." Ph.D. diss., Yale University, 1985.

Howes, Robert William. "Progressive Conservatism in Brazil: Oliveira Vianna, Roberto Simonsen, and the Social Legislation of the Vargas Regime, 1930–1945." Ph.D. diss., Cambridge University, 1975.

Lobos, Júlio Alejandro. "Technology and Organization Structure: A Comparative

Study of Automotive and Processing Firms in Brazil." Ph.D. diss., Cornell University, 1976.

Mericle, Kenneth S. "Conflict Resolution in the Brazilian Industrial Relations System." Ph.D. diss., University of Wisconsin at Madison, 1974.

Negro, Antônio Luigi. "Linhas de Montagem: O Industrialismo Automotivo e a Sindicalização dos Trabalhadores (1945–1978)." Ph.D. diss., Universidade Estadual de Campinas, 2001.

Paoli, Maria Célia Pinheiro-Machado. "Labor, Law, and the State in Brazil, 1930–1950." Ph.D. diss., Birkbeck College, University of London, 1988.

Rosa, Maria Inês. "A Indústria Brasileira na Década de 60: As Transformações nas Relações de Trabalho e a Estabilidade." Master's thesis, Universidade Estadual de Campinas, 1982.

Schmitter, Philippe Charles. "Development and Interest Politics in Brazil, 1930–1965." Ph.D. diss., University of California at Berkeley, 1968.

Tavares de Almeida, Maria Hermínia. "Estado e Classes Trabalhadoras no Brasil (1930–1945)." Ph.D. diss., Universidade de São Paulo, 1978.

Weffort, Francisco Corrêa. "Sindicatos e Política." Ph.D. diss., Universidade de São Paulo, 1971.

OTHER SOURCES

Abel, Christopher, and Colin M. Lewis, eds. *Latin America, Economic Imperialism, and the State: Political Economy of the External Connection from Independence to the Present*. London: Athlone, 1984.

Abreu, Alice Rangel de Paiva, and Elina Gonçalves da Fonte Pessanha, eds. *O Trabalhador Carioca: Estudos sobre Trabalhadores Urbanos do Estado do Rio de Janeiro*. Rio de Janeiro: J. C. Editora, 1994.

A Ação da Bancada Paulista "Por São Paulo Unido" na Assembléia Constituinte. São Paulo: Imprensa Oficial, 1935.

Adams, Richard Newbold. "Access to Law: Labor and Justice." In *Crucifixion by Power: Essays on Guatemalan National Social Structure, 1944–1966*, 422–37. Austin: University of Texas Press, 1970.

Adorno, Sérgio. *Os Aprendizes do Poder: O Bacherelismo Liberal na Política Brasileira*. Rio de Janeiro: Paz e Terra, 1988.

Alba, Victor. *Politics and the Labor Movement in Latin America*. Translated by Carol de Zapata. Stanford: Stanford University Press, 1968.

Albertino Rodrigues, José. *Sindicato e Desenvolvimento no Brasil*. 1968; reprint, São Paulo: Símbolo, 1979.

Alexander, Robert J. *The ABC Presidents: Conversations and Correspondence with the Presidents of Argentina, Brazil, and Chile*. Westport, Conn.: Praeger, 1992.

Alves, Maria Helena Moreira. *State and Opposition in Military Brazil*. Austin: University of Texas Press, 1985.

Alves, Paulo. *A Verdade da Repressão: Práticas Penais e Outras Estratégias na Ordem Republicana (1890–1921)*. São Paulo: Editora Arte e Ciência/UNIP, 1997.

Amad Costa, Sérgio. *Estado e Controle Sindical no Brasil (Um Estudo sobre Três Mecanismos de Coerção—1960/64)*. São Paulo: T. A. Queiroz, 1986.

American Chambers of Commerce in Brazil, ed. *Consolidation of the Brazilian Labor Laws as Promulgated by Decree-Law No. 5452 Brought Up-to-Date February 1960*

[Portuguese and English text]. Rio de Janeiro/São Paulo: American Chambers of Commerce in Brazil, 1960.

Andreotti, Marcos. Untitled typescript on the history of the Sindicato dos Metalúrgicos de Santo André, n.d. (pre-1981). In possession of author.

Aparecida de Aquino, Maria, Marco Aurélio Vannucchi Leme de Matos, and Walter Cruz Swensson Jr., eds. *No Coração das Trevas: O DEOPS/SP Visto por Dentro*. São Paulo: Arquivo do Estado de São Paulo/Edições Imprensa Oficial, 2001.

Araújo, Angela Maria Carneiro. "Estado e Trabalhadores." In *Do Corporativismo ao Neoliberalismo: Estado e Classe Trabalhadora no Brasil e na Inglaterra*, edited by Angela Maria Carneiro Araújo, 29–57. São Paulo: Boitempo, 2002.

Badaró Mattos, Marcelo. *Novos e Velhos Sindicalismos: Rio de Janeiro (1955–1988)*. Rio de Janeiro: Vício de Leitura, 1998.

——, ed. *Greves e Repressão Policial ao Sindicalismo Carioca, 1945–1964*. Rio de Janeiro: Arquivo Público do Rio de Janeiro/Fundaçao Carlos Chagas Filho de Amparo à Pesquisa do Estado de Rio de Janeiro, 2003.

Baer, Werner. *Industrialization and Economic Development in Brazil*. Homewood, Ill.: Richard D. Irwin, 1965.

Barbosa, Francisco de Assis, ed. *Idéias Políticas de João Mangabeira*. Vol. 3, *Da Esquerda Democrática ao Ministério da Justiça*. Brasília/Rio de Janeiro: Senado Federal/Fundação Casa de Rui Barbosa, 1980.

Barbosa, Rui. *A Questão Social e Política no Brasil (Conferência Pronunciado no Teatro Lírico, do Rio de Janeiro, a 20 de Março de 1919)*. São Paulo/Rio de Janeiro: Editora LTr/Fundação Casa de Rui Barbosa, 1983.

Barbosa de Araújo, Rosa Maria. *O Batismo do Trabalho: A Experiência de Lindolfo Collor*. 1981; revised ed., Rio de Janeiro: Civilização Brasileira, 1990.

Barcellos, Caco. *ROTA 66: A História da Polícia Que Mata*. São Paulo: Globo, 1992.

Barros, Alberto da Rocha. *Origems e Evolução da Legislação Trabalhista*. Rio de Janeiro: Laemmert, 1969.

Barsted, Dennis Linhares. *Medição de Forças: O Movimento Grevista de 1953 e a Época dos Operários Navais*. Rio de Janeiro: Zahar, 1981.

Basbaum, Leôncio. *História Sincera da República (Tentativa de Interpretação Marxista)*. Vol. 2, *De 1889 a 1930*. 2d ed. São Paulo: Edições LB, 1962.

——. *História Sincera da República (Tentativa de Interpretação Marxista)*. Vol. 3, *De 1930 a 1960*. 2d ed. São Paulo: Edições LB, 1962.

Bastos, Elide Rugai, and João Quartim de Moraes, eds. *O Pensamento de Oliveira Vianna*. Campinas: Editora da Universidade Estadual de Campinas, 1993.

Batalha, Cláudio. "A Historiografia da Classe Operária no Brasil: Trajetória e Tendências." In *Historiografia Brasileira em Perspectiva*, edited by Marcos Cezar de Freitas, 145–58. São Paulo: Contexto, 1998.

Beiguelman, Paula. *Os Companheiros de São Paulo*. São Paulo: Símbolo, 1977.

Bello, José Maria. *A Questão Social e a Solução Brasileira*. Rio de Janeiro: n.p., 1936.

Benevides, Maria Victoria de Mesquita. *O PTB e o Trabalhismo: Partido e Sindicato em São Paulo, 1945–1964*. São Paulo: Brasiliense/Centro de Estudos de Cultura Contemporânea, 1989.

——. *A UDN e o Udenismo: Ambiguidades do Liberalismo Brasileiro, 1945–1965*. Rio de Janeiro: Paz e Terra, 1981.

Bergquist, Charles. *Labor in Latin America: Comparative Essays on Chile, Argentina, Venezuela, and Colombia*. Stanford: Stanford University Press, 1986.

Bernardo, Antônio Carlos. *Tutela e Autonomia Sindical: Brasil, 1930–1945*. São Paulo: T. A. Queiroz, 1982.

Besouchet, Lídia. *História da Criação do Ministério do Trabalho: Ensaio de Interpretação*. Rio de Janeiro: Serviço de Documentação do Ministério do Trabalho, Indústria, e Comércio, 1957.

Bethell, Leslie. *The Abolition of the Brazilian Slave Trade*. Cambridge: Cambridge University Press, 1970.

Bezerra de Menezes, Geraldo. *Homens e Idéias à Luz da Fé*. 1942; reprint, São Paulo: Instituto Nacional do Livro/Fundação Nacional Pró-Memória, 1983.

Blat, José Carlos, and Sérgio Saraiva. *O Caso da Favela Naval: Polícia Contra o Povo*. São Paulo: Contexto, 2000.

Blay, Eva Alterman. *Eu Não Tenho Onde Morar: Vilas Operárias na Cidade de São Paulo*. São Paulo: Nobel, 1985.

Bodea, Miguel. *A Greve de 1917 e as Origens do Trabalhismo Gaúcho (Ensaio sobre o Pré-Ensaio de Poder de uma Elite Política Dissidente a Nível Nacional)*. Porto Alegre: L & PM Editores, n.d.

Boito, Armando, Jr. *O Golpe de 1954: A Burguesia Contra o Populismo*. São Paulo: Brasiliense, 1982.

———. *O Sindicalismo de Estado no Brasil: Uma Análise Crítica da Estrutura Sindical*. Campinas/São Paulo: Editora da Universidade Estadual de Campinas/Hucitec, 1991.

Bolsonaro de Moura, Esmeralda Blanco. *Mulheres e Menores no Trabalho Industrial: Os Fatores Sexo e Idade na Dinâmica do Capital*. Petrópolis: Vozes, 1982.

Borges, Stella. *Getúlio e o Mar de Lama: A Verdade sobre 1954*. Rio de Janeiro: Lacerda, 2001.

Bortz, Jeffrey L. " 'Without Any More Law Than Their Own Caprice': Cotton Textile Workers and the Challenge to Factory Authority during the Mexican Revolution." *International Review of Social History* 42, no. 2 (1997): 253–88.

Bosi, Alfredo. "A Arqueologia do Estado-Providência." In *Dialética da Colonização*, 273–307. São Paulo: Companhia das Letras, 1992.

Bosísio, Carlos Eduardo. "Justiça do Trabalho e Política do Trabalho." In *Trabalho e Previdência: Sessenta Anos em Debate*, edited by Angela Maria de Castro Gomes and Amaury de Sousa, 46–55. Rio de Janeiro: Editora da Fundação Getúlio Vargas/Centro de Pesquisa e Documentação de História Contemporânea do Brasil, 1992.

Bourdieu, Pierre. "The Force of Law: Toward a Sociology of the Juridical Field." *Hastings Law Journal* 38 (1987): 805–53.

Brandão Lopes, Juarez Rubens. "O Ajustamento do Trabalhador à Indústria: Mobilidade Social e Motivação." In *Mobilidade e Trabalho: Um Estudo na Cidade de São Paulo*, edited by Bertram Hutchinson, 360–440. Rio de Janeiro: Centro Brasileiro de Pesquisas Educacionais/Instituto Nacional de Estudos Pedagógicos do Ministério de Educação e Cultura, 1960.

Brandi, Paulo, Mauro Malin, Plínio de Abreu Ramos, and Dora Flaksman. *Vargas, da Vida Para a História*. Rio de Janeiro: Zahar, 1983.

Brant, Vinicius Caldeira. "Bibliographie Commentée: Ouvriers et Syndicats du Brésil." *Sociologie du Travail* 9, no. 3 (1967): 352–61.

Brazil, United States of. *The Consolidation of Brazilian Labor Laws*. Rio de Janeiro: Imprensa Nacional, 1944.

——. *Constituições do Brasil: De 1824, 1891, 1934, 1937, 1946 e 1967 e suas Alterações.* 2 vols. Brasília: Senado Federal, 1986.

Burlamaqui, Paulo L. *As Associações Profissionais.* Rio de Janeiro: Laemmert, 1936.

Café Filho, João. *Do Sindicato ao Catete: Memórias Políticas e Confissões Humanas.* Vol. 1. Rio de Janeiro: José Olympio, 1966.

Camargo, José Márcio, Edward J. Amadeo, and Gustavo Gonzaga. "Brazil: Institutions and Its Effects on Employment Quality." *Economia, Capital, e Trabalho* (1994): 8–10.

Cammack, Paul, David Pod, and William Tordoff. *Third World Politics.* Baltimore: Johns Hopkins University Press, 1988.

Campista, Ary. "Todos Melhoraram mas Alguns Muito Mais." In *A História Vivida,* edited by Lourenço Dantas Mota, 2:37–56. São Paulo: O Estado de São Paulo, 1981.

Campos, Francisco. *O Estado Nacional.* Rio de Janeiro: José Olympio, 1940.

Campos, Orlando. *Você Sabia, Trabalhador? As Conquistas do Trabalhador Brasileiro de Getúlio à Jango.* São Paulo: Editora Fulgor, 1964.

Campos, Roberto. *A Lanterna na Popa (Memórias).* Rio de Janeiro: Topbooks, 1994.

Cancelli, Elizabeth. *O Mundo da Violência: A Polícia da Era Vargas.* Brasília: Editora Universidade de Brasília, 1993.

Carneiro da Cunha, Manuela. "Silences of the Law: Customary Law and Positive Law on the Manumission of Slaves in Nineteenth Century Brazil." *History and Anthropology* 1 (1985): 427–43.

Carvalho, Daniel de. *Novos Estudos e Depoimentos.* Rio de Janeiro: José Olympio, 1959.

Carvalho-Neto, Paulo de. *Um Precursor do Direito Trabalhista.* São Paulo: Carthago, 1989.

Carvalho Neto, Antônio. *Legislação do Trabalho: Polêmica e Doutrina.* Petrópolis: Editora Vozes, 1926.

Castro, Augusto Olympio Viveiros de. *A Questão Social.* Rio de Janeiro: Candido de Oliveira, 1920.

Castro Gomes, Angela Maria de. *Burguesia e Trabalho: Política e Legislação Social no Brasil, 1917–1937.* Rio de Janeiro: Campus, 1979.

——. *Estado, Corporativismo y Acción Social en Brasil, Argentina, y Uruguay.* Buenos Aires: Editorial Biblos/Fundación Simón Rodríguez, 1992.

——. "Ideologia e Trabalho no Estado Novo." In *Repensando o Estado Novo,* edited by Dulce Pandolfi, 53–72. Rio de Janeiro: Editora da Fundação Getúlio Vargas, 1999.

——. *A Invenção do Trabalhismo.* São Paulo/Rio de Janeiro: Vértice/Instituto Universitário de Pesquisas do Rio de Janeiro, 1988.

Castro Gomes, Angela Maria de, and Amaury de Souza, eds. *Trabalho e Previdência: Sessenta Anos em Debate.* Rio de Janeiro: Editora da Fundação Getúlio Vargas/Centro de Pesquisa e Documentação de História Contemporânea do Brasil, 1992.

Central Intelligence Agency. *The World Factbook.* 1 August 2003. <http://www.cia.gov>. 13 October 2003.

Cerqueira Filho, Gisálio. *A "Questão Social" no Brasil: Crítica do Discurso Político.* Rio de Janeiro: Civilização Brasileira, 1982.

Chacon, Vamireh. *Estado e Povo no Brasil: As Experiências do Estado Novo e da Democracia Populista, 1937–1945.* Brasília/Rio de Janeiro: José Olympio/Câmara dos Deputados, 1977.

———, ed. *História dos Partidos Brasileiros*. Brasília: Editora da Universidade de Brasília, 1981.

Chaves de Mello, Maria. *Dicionário Jurídico Português-Inglês Inglês-Português*. Rio de Janeiro: Elfos, 1998.

Chaves Neto, Elias. *Minha Vida e as Lutas do Meu Tempo: Memórias*. São Paulo: Alfa-Omega, 1978.

Chevigny, Paul. *The Edge of the Knife: Police Violence in the Americas*. New York: New Press, 1995.

Cohn, Amélia. *Previdência Social e Processo Político no Brasil*. São Paulo: Editora Moderna, 1980.

Collazos, Sharon Phillipps. *Labor and Politics in Panama: The Torrijos Years*. Boulder, Colo.: Westview, 1991.

Collier, David, and Ruth Berins Collier. "Inducements versus Constraints: Disaggregating 'Corporatism.'" *American Political Science Review* 73, no. 4 (1979): 967–86.

———. "Who Does What, to Whom, and How?: Toward a Comparative Analysis of Latin American Corporatism." In *Authoritarianism and Corporatism in Latin America*, edited by James M. Malloy, 489–512. Pittsburgh: University of Pittsburgh Press, 1977.

Collier, Ruth Berins. "Popular Sector Incorporation and Political Supremacy: Regime Evolution in Brazil and Mexico." In *Brazil and Mexico: Patterns in Late Development*, edited by Sylvia Ann Hewlett and Richard S. Weinert, 57–109. Philadelphia: Institute for the Study of Human Issues, 1982.

Collier, Ruth Berins, and David Collier. *Shaping the Political Arena: Critical Junctures, the Labor Movement, and Regime Dynamics in Latin America*. Princeton: Princeton University Press, 1991.

Collor, Lindolfo. *Origens da Legislação Trabalhista Brasileira: Exposições de Motivos*. Edited by Mário de Almeida Lima. Porto Alegre: Fundação Paulo do Couto e Silva, 1990.

Compa, Lance. *Labor Law and the Legal Way: Collective Bargaining in the Chilean Textile Industry under the Unidad Popular*. Working Paper 23. New Haven: Yale Law School Program in Law and Modernization, 1973.

Conniff, Michael L. *Urban Politics in Brazil: The Rise of Populism, 1925–1945*. Pittsburgh: University of Pittsburgh Press, 1981.

Córdova, Efren. "From Corporatism to Liberalisation: The New Direction of the Brazilian System of Industrial Relations." *Labour and Society* 14, no. 3 (1990): 251–69.

Corrêa dos Santos, Hercules. *Memórias de um Stalinista*. Rio de Janeiro: Opera Nostra, 1996.

Costa, Hélio da. *Em Busca da Memória: Comissão de Fábrica, Partido, e Sindicato no Pós-Guerra*. São Paulo: Scritta, 1995.

Central Única dos Trabalhadores—Brasil. *Precarização e Leis do Trabalho nos Anos FHC*. São Paulo: Central Única dos Trabalhadores—Brasil, 2001.

D'Araújo, Maria Celina Soares. "O PTB na Cidade do Rio de Janeiro—1945–1955." *Revista Brasileira de Estudos Políticos*, no. 74–75 (1992): 183–231.

———. *O Segundo Governo Vargas, 1951–1954: Democracia, Partidos, e Crise Política*. Rio de Janeiro: Zahar, 1982.

———. *Sindicatos, Carisma, e Poder: O PTB de 1945 a 1965*. Rio de Janeiro: Editora da Fundação Getúlio Vargas, 1996.

Dean, Warren. *The Industrialization of São Paulo, 1880–1945*. Austin: University of Texas Press, 1969.

De Paula, Jeziel. *1932: Imagens Construindo a História*. Campinas: Editora da Universidade Estadual de Campinas/Centro de Memoria—Universidade Estadual de Campinas/Editora Universidade Metodista de Piracicaba, 1999.

Dias, Everardo. *História das Lutas Socias no Brasil*. 1962; reprint, São Paulo: Alfa-Omega, 1977.

Di Tella, Torcuato S. *Latin American Politics: A Theoretical Framework*. Austin: University of Texas Press, 1990.

Draibe, Sônia. *Rumos e Metamorfoses: Um Estudo sobre a Constituição do Estado e as Alternativas da Industrialização no Brasil, 1930–1960*. Rio de Janeiro: Paz e Terra, 1985.

Duarte, Adriano Luiz. *Cidadania e Exclusão: Brasil, 1937–1945*. Florianópolis: Editora da Universidade Federal de Santa Catarina, 1999.

Dulles, John W. F. *Unrest in Brazil: Political-Military Crises, 1955–1964*. Austin: University of Texas Press, 1970.

Dutra, Eliana de Freitas, and Yonne de Souza Grossi. "Historiografia e Movimento Operário: O Novo em Questão." *Revista Brasileira de Estudos Políticos*, no. 65 (1987): 101–30.

Egas, Eugénio. *Washington Luis: Presidente de S. Paulo (1920–1924), Vice Presidente (1891–1920)*. São Paulo: n.p., 1924.

Egídio de Araújo, Oscar. "Uma Pesquisa de Padrão de Vida." *Revista do Arquivo Municipal* (São Paulo), no. 80, suppl. (1941).

Erickson, Kenneth Paul. *The Brazilian Corporative State and Working-Class Politics*. Berkeley: University of California Press, 1977.

———. "Corporatism and Labor in Development." In *Contemporary Brazil: Issues in Economic and Political Development*, edited by H. John Rosenbaum and William G. Tyler, 139–66. New York: Praeger, 1972.

———. *Sindicalismo no Processo Político no Brasil*. São Paulo: Brasiliense, 1979.

Erickson, Kenneth Paul, and Kevin J. Middlebrook. "The State and Organized Labor in Brazil and Mexico." In *Brazil and Mexico: Patterns in Late Development*, edited by Sylvia Ann Hewlett and Richard S. Weinert, 213–63. Philadelphia: Institute for the Study of Human Issues, 1982.

Erickson, Kenneth Paul, Patrick Peppe, and Hobart Spalding. "Research on the Urban Working Class and Organized Labor in Argentina, Brazil, and Chile: What Is Left to Be Done?" *Latin American Research Review* 9, no. 2 (1974): 115–42.

Fausto, Boris. *Trabalho Urbano e Conflito Social (1890–1920)*. São Paulo: Difusão Européia do Livro, 1976.

Ferrante, Vera Lúcia B. *FGTS [Fundo de Garantia por Tempo de Serviço]: Ideologia e Repressão*. São Paulo: Ática, 1978.

———. "A Legislação Trabalhista e a Ideologia do Estado Populista." *Estudos Históricos*, no. 15 (1976): 47–61.

Ferrari, Irany, Amauri Mascaro Nascimento, and Ives Gandra da Silva Martins Filho, eds. *História do Trabalho, do Direito do Trabalho, e da Justiça do Trabalho: Homenagem a Armando Casimiro Costa*. São Paulo: Editora LTr, 1998.

Ferreira, Brasília Carlos. *Trabalhadores, Sindicatos, Cidadania: Nordeste em Tempos de Vargas*. São Paulo/Natal: Ad Hominem/Cooperativa Cultural Universitária do Rio Grande do Norte, 1997.

Ferreira, Jorge. "O Carnaval da Tristeza: Os Motins Urbanos do 14 de Agosto." In

Vargas e a Crise dos Anos 50, edited by Angela Maria de Castro Gomes, 61–96. Rio de Janeiro: Relumé-Dumará, 1994.

———. "O Nome e a Coisa: Populismo na Política Brasileira." In *O Populismo e Sua História: Debate e Crítica*, edited by Jorge Ferreira, 59–124. Rio de Janeiro: Civilização Brasileira, 2001.

———. *Trabalhadores do Brasil: O Imaginário Popular*. Rio de Janeiro: Fundação Getúlio Vargas, 1997.

———, ed. *O Populismo e Sua História: Debate e Crítica*. Rio de Janeiro: Civilização Brasileira, 2001.

Ferreira, Marieta de Morais, and César Benjamin. "João Goulart." In *Dicionário Histórico-Biográfico Brasileiro, 1930–1983*, edited by Israel Beloch and Alzira Alves de Abreu, 1504–21. Rio de Janeiro: Forense-Universitária, Fundação Getúlio Vargas—Centro de Pesquisa e Documentação de História Contemporânea do Brasil, 1984.

Flory, Thomas. *Judge and Jury in Imperial Brazil, 1808–1871*. Austin: University of Texas Press, 1981.

Flynn, Peter. *Brazil: A Political Analysis*. Boulder, Colo.: Westview, 1978.

Fonseca, Gondin da. *Assim Falou Julião . . .* São Paulo: Fulgor, 1962.

Font, Mauricio A. "Failed Democratization: Region, Class, and Political Change in Brazil, 1930–1937." In *Political Culture, Social Movements, and Democratic Transitions in South America in the Twentieth Century*, edited by Fernando J. Devoto and Torcuato S. Di Tella, 119–66. Milan: Fondazione Giangiacomo Feltrinelli, 1997.

Fontes, Amando. *Os Corumbas*. 1933; reprint, Rio de Janeiro: José Olympio, 1999.

Fontes, Lourival, and Glauco Carneiro. *A Face Final de Vargas (Os Bilhetes de Getúlio)*. Rio de Janeiro: O Cruzeiro, 1966.

Fontes, Paulo. *Trabalhadores e Cidadãos: Nitro Química: A Fábrica e as Lutas Operárias nos Anos 50*. São Paulo: Anablume, 1997.

Foot, Francisco, and Victor Leonardi. *História da Indústria e do Trabalho no Brasil (Das Origens aos Anos Vinte)*. São Paulo: Global, 1982.

Forbath, William E. *Law and the Shaping of the American Labor Movement*. Cambridge: Harvard University Press, 1991.

Fortes, Alexandre, and Antônio Luigi Negro. "Historiografia, Trabalho, y Cidadanía no Brasil." *Trajetos: Revista de História [Universidade Federal de Ceará]* 1, no. 2 (2002): 25–49.

Fortes, Alexandre, Antônio Luigi Negro, Fernando Teixeira da Silva, Hélio da Costa, and Paulo Fontes. *Na Luta por Direitos: Estudos Recentes em História Social do Trabalho*. Campinas: Editora da Universidade Estadual de Campinas, 1999.

French, John D. *Afogados em Leis: A CLT e a Cultura Política dos Trabalhadores Brasileiros*. São Paulo: Fundação Perseu Abramo, 2001.

———. *The Brazilian Workers' ABC: Class Conflicts and Alliances in Modern São Paulo*. Chapel Hill: University of North Carolina Press, 1992.

———. "The Laboring and Middle-Class Peoples of Latin America and the Caribbean: Historical Trajectories and New Research Directions." In *Global Labour History*, edited by Jan Lucasen. Forthcoming.

———. "The Latin American Labor Studies Boom." *International Review of Social History* 45 (2000): 279–310.

———. "The Metalworkers of ABC, 1950–1980: Linking Consciousness and Mobilization in Brazil." Forthcoming.

——. "The Origin of Corporatist State Intervention in Brazilian Industrial Relations, 1930–1934: A Critique of the Literature." *Luso-Brazilian Review* 28, no. 2 (1991): 13–26.

——. Review of *Working Women, Working Men: São Paulo and the Rise of Brazil's Industrial Working Class, 1900–1955*, by Joel William Wolfe. *Business History Review* 69, no. 2 (1995): 238–41.

——. " 'They Don't Wear Black-Tie': Intellectuals and Workers in Modern São Paulo, 1958–1981." *International Labor and Working-Class History*, no. 59 (2001): 60–80.

French, John D., and Alexandre Fortes. *Urban Labor History in Twentieth Century Brazil*. Albuquerque: Latin American Institute/University of New Mexico, 1998.

French, John D., and Joann C. Pavilack. "What Workers Want and What Union Leaders Do: Analyzing a 1961 Diary from São Paulo, Brazil." Paper presented at the Ninth Latin American Labor History Conference, State University of New York at Stony Brook, 10–11 April 1992.

Fry, Peter. *Para Inglês Ver: Identidade e Cultura na Sociedade Brasileira*. Rio de Janeiro: Zahar, 1982.

Füchtner, Hans. *Os Sindicatos Brasileiros: Organização e Função Política*. Rio de Janeiro: Edições Graal, 1980.

Fuller, Linda. *Work and Democracy in Socialist Cuba*. Philadelphia: Temple University Press, 1992.

Furtado, Celso. *Diagnosis of the Brazilian Crises*. Berkeley: University of California Press, 1965.

Gacek, Stanley Arthur. "Revisiting the Corporatist and Contractualist Models of Labor Law Regimes: A Review of the Brazilian and American Systems." *Cardozo Law Review* 16 (1994): 21–110.

Geddes, Barbara. "Building 'State' Autonomy in Brazil, 1930–1964." *Comparative Politics* 22 (1990): 217–35.

Genro, Tarso Fernando. *Contribuição à Crítica do Direito Coletivo do Trabalho*. São Paulo: Editora LTr, 1988.

Giglio, Wagner D. *Direito Processual do Trabalho*. São Paulo: Suggestões Literárias, 1972.

Gomes, Orlando. "A Justiça do Trabalho." *Revista Brasileira de Estudos Políticos*, no. 34 (1972): 155–209.

Goodman, Louis Wolf. "Legal Controls on Union Activity in Latin America." In *Workers and Managers in Latin America*, edited by Stanley M. Davis and Louis Wolf Goodman, 231–34. Lexington, Mass.: D. C. Heath, 1972.

Gordon, Lincoln, and Engelbert L. Grommers. *United States Manufacturing Investment in Brazil: The Impact of Brazilian Government Policies 1946–1960*. Cambridge: Division of Research, Graduate School of Business Administration, Harvard University, 1962.

Grez Toso, Sergio, ed. *La "Cuestión Social" en Chile: Ideas y Debates Precursores, 1804–1902*. Santiago de Chile: Dirección de Bibliotecas, Archivo, y Museos, Centro de Investigaciones Diego Barros Araña, 1995.

Grinberg, Keila. *O Fiador dos Brasileiros: Cidadania, Escravidão, e Direito Civil no Tempo de Antônio Pereira Rebouças*. Rio de Janeiro: Civilização Brasileira, 2002.

Grossi, Yonne de Souza. *Mina de Morro Velho: A Extração do Homem. Uma História de Experiência Operária*. Rio de Janeiro: Paz e Terra, 1981.

Guilherme dos Santos, Wanderley. *Cidadania e a Justiça: A Política Social na Ordem Brasileira*. Rio de Janeiro: Campus, 1979.

Gusmão, Cupertino de. *Do Bojo do Estado Novo: Memórias de um Socialista na República de Trinta e Sete*. Rio de Janeiro: n.p., 1945.

——. *Recursos na Justiça do Trabalho: Teoria e Prática dos Recursos na Justiça do Trabalho*. Rio de Janeiro: n.p., 1944.

Haider, Carmen. *Capital and Labor under Fascism*. 1930; reprint, New York: AMS, 1968.

Hall, Michael M. "Corporativismo e Fascismo." In *Do Corporativismo ao Neoliberalismo: Estado e Classe Trabalhadora no Brasil e na Inglaterra*, edited by Angela Maria Carneiro Araújo, 13–28. São Paulo: Boitempo, 2002.

——. "Labor and the Law in Brazil." In *The Rise and Development of Collective Labour Law*, edited by Marcel van der Linden and Richard Price, 79–95. Bern: Peter Lang, 2000.

Hall, Michael M., and Marco Aurélio Garcia. "Urban Labor." In *Modern Brazil: Elites and Masses in Historical Perspective*, edited by Michael L. Conniff and Frank D. McCann, 161–91. Lincoln: University of Nebraska Press, 1989.

Hall, Michael M., and Paulo Sérgio Pinheiro. "O Grupo Clarté no Brasil: Da Revolução nos Espíritos ao Ministério do Trabalho." In *Libertários no Brasil: Memória, Lutas, Cultura*, edited by Antônio Arnoni Prado, 251–87. São Paulo: Brasiliense, 1986.

Herrup, Cynthia B. *A House in Gross Disorder: Sex, Law, and the Second Earl of Castlehaven*. New York: Oxford University Press, 1999.

Hippólito, Lúcia. *De Raposas e Reformistas: O PSD e a Experiência Democrática Brasileira, 1945–64*. Rio de Janeiro: Paz e Terra, 1985.

Hobsbawm, Eric. *The Age of Extremes: A History of the World, 1914–1991*. New York: Pantheon, 1994.

Holston, James. "The Misrule of Law: Land and Usurpation in Brazil." *Comparative Studies in Society and History* 33, no. 4 (1991): 695–725.

Huntington, Samuel P. *Political Order in Changing Societies*. New Haven: Yale University Press, 1968.

Ianni, Octavio. *Industrialização e Desenvolvimento Social no Brasil*. Rio de Janeiro: Editora Civilização Brasileira, 1963.

Instituto Brasileiro de Geografia e Estatística. *Anuário Estatístico do Brasil*. Rio de Janeiro: Fundação IBGE, 1947–77.

Instituto Histórico e Geográfico de São Paulo. *Washington Luis (Visto pelos Contemporâneos no Primeiro Centenário de Seu Nascimento)*. São Paulo: Instituto Histórico e Geográfico de São Paulo, 1969.

International Labour Office. "Labor Legislation and Collective Bargaining in the Americas." In *Workers and Managers in Latin America*, edited by Stanley M. Davis and Louis Wolf Goodman, 217–29. Lexington, Mass.: D. C. Heath, 1972.

Jácome Rodrigues, Iram. *Sindicalismo e Política: A Trajetória da CUT*. São Paulo: Scritta/Fundação de Amparo à Pesquisa no Estado de São Paulo, 1997.

Jaguaribe, Hélio. *Political Development: A General Theory and a Latin American Case Study*. New York: Harper and Row, 1973.

Jesus, Carolina Maria de. *Antologia Pessoal*. Edited by José Carlos Sebe Bom Meihy. Rio de Janeiro: Editora Universidade Federal de Rio de Janeiro, 1996.

——. *Meu Estranho Diário*. São Paulo: Xamã, 1996.

Junqueira, Eliane Botelho. "O Bacharel do Direito no Século XIX: Herói ou Anti-Herói." *Luso-Brazilian Review* 34, no. 1 (1997): 77–93.

Kahil, Raouf. *Inflation and Economic Development in Brazil, 1946–1963*. Oxford: Clarendon, 1973.

Kant de Lima, Roberto. "Bureaucratic Rationality in Brazil and in the United States: Criminal Justice Systems in Comparative Perspective." In *The Brazilian Puzzle: Culture on the Borderlands of the Western World*, edited by David J. Hess and Roberto A. DaMatta, 241–69. New York: Columbia University Press, 1995.

Kirkendall, Andrew J. *Class Mates: Male Student Culture and the Making of a Political Class in Nineteenth-Century Brazil*. Lincoln: University of Nebraska Press, 2002.

Knight, Alan. "Populism and Neo-Populism in Latin America, Especially Mexico." *Journal of Latin American Studies* 30, no. 2 (1998): 223–48.

Kornis, Mônica, and Ivan Junqueira. "Segadas Viana." In *Dicionário Histórico-Biográfico Brasileiro, 1930–1983*, edited by Israel Beloch and Alzira Alves de Abreu, 343–54. Rio de Janeiro: Forense-Universitaria/Centro de Pesquisa e Documentação de História Contemporânea do Brasil/Fundação Getúlio Vargas, 1984.

Koval, Boris. *História do Proletariado Brasileiro: 1857 a 1967*. Translated by Clarice Lima Avierina. São Paulo: Alfa-Omega, 1982.

Lacerda, Maurício de. *Evolução Legislativa do Direito Social Brasileiro*. Rio de Janeiro: Ministério do Trabalho, Indústria, e Comércio, Serviço de Documentação, 1960.

——. *História de uma Covardia*. 1927; reprint, Rio de Janeiro: Editora Nova Fronteira, 1980.

——. *Segunda República*. Rio de Janeiro: Freitas Bastos, 1931.

Lahuerta, Milton. "Intelectuais e Resistência Democrática: Vida Acadêmica, Marxismo, e Política no Brasil." *Cadernos AEL [Arquivo Edgard Leuenroth]*, no. 14–15 (2001): 57–93.

Lara, Silvia Hunold. "Escravidão, Cidadania, e História do Trabalho no Brasil." *Projeto História*, no. 16 (1998): 35–38.

La Rochefoucauld, François, and Irwin Primer. *Moral Maxims*. Translated by Irwin Primer. Newark, Del./Cranbury, N.J.: University of Delaware Press/Associated University Presses, 2003.

Leite Lopes, José Sérgio. *A Tecelagem dos Conflitos de Classe na Cidade das Chaminés*. São Paulo/Brasília: Marco Zero/Editora Universidade de Brasília, 1988.

Leme, Marisa Saenz. *A Ideologia dos Industriais Brasileiros, 1919–1945*. Petrópolis: Vozes, 1978.

Lenharo, Alcir. *Sacralização da Política*. Campinas: Papirus/Editora da Universidade Estadual de Campinas, 1986.

Lessa, Orígenes. *Getúlio Vargas na Literatura de Cordel*. Rio de Janeiro: Editora Documentário, 1973.

Levenson-Estrada, Deborah. *Trade Unionists against Terror: Guatemala City, 1945–1985*. Chapel Hill: University of North Carolina Press, 1994.

Levine, Robert M. *Father of the Poor? Vargas and His Era*. New York: Cambridge University Press, 1998.

Levy, Herbert Victor. *A Batalha da Produção e Outras Problemas Nacionais*. São Paulo: Livraria Martins, 1948.

Lima, Jacob Carlos. *Trabalho, Mercado, e Formação de Classe: Estudo sobre Operários Fabris em Pernambuco*. João Pessoa: Editora Universitária/Universidade Federal de Paraíba, 1996.

Lima, Maria Emília A. T. *A Construção Discursiva do Povo Brasileiro: Os Discursos do Primeiro de Maio de Getúlio Vargas*. Campinas: Editora da Universidade Estadual de Campinas, 1990.

Lima, Mário de Almeida. "A Proteção ao Trabalho e a Contribuição de Lindolfo

Collor." In *Origens da Legislação Trabalhista Brasileira: Exposições de Motivos*, edited by Mário de Almeida Lima, 9–102. Porto Alegre: Fundação Paulo do Couto e Silva, 1990.

Lima, Valentina da Rocha, ed. *Getúlio: Uma História Oral*. Rio de Janeiro: Record, 1986.

Linden, Marcel van der, and Richard Price, eds. *The Rise and Development of Collective Labour Law*. Bern: Peter Lang, 2000.

Lobo, Eulália Maria Lahmeyer, Antônio Oliveira, Bernardo Kocher, Eduardo Navarro Stotz, Fátima Sebastiana Gomes Lisboa, Pedro Tórtima, Mariza Simões, and Luiza Mara Braga Martins. *Rio de Janeiro Operário: Natureza do Estado e Conjuntura Econômica, Condições de Vida e Consciência de Classe*. Edited by Eulália Maria Lahmeyer Lobo. Rio de Janeiro: Access, 1992.

Lobo, Eulália Maria Lahmeyer, and Eduardo Navarro Stotz. *Tira o Retrato do Velho, Põe o Retrato do Velho: O Movimento Sindical Contemporâneo e o Fim da Era Vargas: Uma Avaliação*. Occasional Paper 24. Miami: Center for Labor Research and Studies, 1998.

Lobos, Júlio Alejandro. *Manual de Guerilla Trabalhista para Gerentes e Supervisores*. São Paulo: Melhoramentos, 1986.

———. *Sindicalismo e Negociação*. Rio de Janeiro: José Olympio, 1985.

Loewenstein, Karl. *Brazil under Vargas*. New York: Macmillan, 1942.

Lopes da Silva, Zélia. *A Domesticação dos Trabalhadores nos Anos 30*. São Paulo: Editora Marco Zero, 1990.

Lopes de Almeida, Fernando. *Política Salarial, Emprego, e Sindicalismo 1964–1981*. Petrópolis: Vozes, 1982.

Lothian, Tamara. "The Political Consequences of Labor Law Regimes: The Contractualist and Corporatist Models Compared." *Cardozo Law Review* 7, no. 4 (1986): 1001–73.

———. "Reinventing Labor Law: A Rejoinder." *Cardozo Law Review* 16 (1995): 1749–63.

Löwy, Michael, and Sarah Chucid. "Opinões e Atitudes de Líderes Sindicais Metalúrgicos." *Revista Brasileira de Estudos Políticos*, no. 13 (1962): 132–69.

Loyola, Maria Andréa. *Os Sindicatos e o PTB: Estudo de um Caso em Minas Gerais*. Petrópolis: Vozes/Centro Brasileiro de Análise e Planejamento, 1980.

Lucas, Fábio. *Conteúdo Social nas Constituições Brasileiras*. Estudos Economicos, Políticos, e Sociais 14. Belo Horizonte: Faculdade de Ciências Economicas da Universidade de Minas Gerais, 1959.

Macedo, Jozé Norberto. *Fazendas de Gado no Vale do São Francisco*. Documentário da Vida Rural 3. Rio de Janeiro: Ministério da Agricultura Serviço de Informação Agrícola, 1952.

Machado da Silva, Luiz Antônio. "O Significado do Botequim." *América Latina* 12, no. 3 (1969): 160–82.

Macieira, Anselmo. "Oliveira Viana: Historiador Social a Serviço do Brasil." *Sociologia* 14, no. 3 (1952): 223–43.

Mackinnon, María Moira, and Mario Alberto Petrone. *Populismo y Neopopulismo en America Latina: El Problema de la Cenicienta*. 1st ed. Buenos Aires: Editorial Universitaria de Buenos Aires, 1998.

Maram, Sheldon Leslie. *Anarquistas, Imigrantes, e o Movimento Operário Brasileiro, 1890–1920*. Rio de Janeiro: Paz e Terra, 1979.

Marçal, João Batista. *Comunistas Gaúchos: A Vida de 31 Militantes da Classe Operária*. Porto Alegre: Tchê! 1986.

Marcondes, J. V. Freitas. *Radiografia da Liderança Sindical Paulista*. Série de Monografias Trabalhistas 2. São Paulo: Instituto Cultural do Trabalho, 1964.

——. "Social Legislation in Brazil." In *Brazil: Portrait of a Half a Continent*, edited by T. Lynn Smith and Alexander Marchant, 382–400. New York: Dryden, 1951.

Marcondes Filho, Alexandre. *Trabalhadores do Brasil!* Rio de Janeiro: Edição da Revista Judiciária, 1943.

Martinho, Francisco Carlos Palomanes. "O Populismo Sindical: Um Conceito em Questão." In *Política e Cultura: Visões do Passado e Perspectivas Contemporâneas*, edited by Elisa Reis, Maria Hermínia Tavares de Almeida, and Peter Fry, 30–49. São Paulo: Associaçao Nacional de Pós-Graduação e Pesquisa em Ciências Sociais/Editora Hucitec, 1996.

Martins, Eloy. *Um Depoimento Político (55 Anos de PCB)*. Porto Alegre: Gráfica Pallotti, 1989.

Martins, Luciano. "A Gênese de uma Inteligentsia: Os Intelectuais e a Política no Brasil 1920 a 1940." *Revista Brasileira de Ciências Sociais* 2, no. 4 (1987): 65–87.

Martins Rodrigues, Leôncio. *Industrialização e Atitudes Operárias (Estudo de um Grupo de Trabalhadores)*. São Paulo: Brasiliense, 1970.

——. "Sindicalismo e Classe Operária (1930–1964)." In *História Geral da Civilização Brasileira*. Book 3, *O Brasil Republicano*. Vol. 3, *Sociedade e Política (1930–1964)*, edited by Boris Fausto, 507–55. São Paulo: Difusão Européia do Livro, 1981.

——. *Trabalhadores, Sindicatos, e Industrialização*. São Paulo: Brasiliense, 1974.

Martins Rodrigues, Leôncio, and Fábio Antônio Munhoz. "Bibliografia sobre Trabalhadores e Sindicatos no Brasil." *Estudos CEBRAP*, no. 7 (1974): 151–71.

Maurette, Fernand. *Some Social Aspects of Present and Future Economic Development in Brazil*. Studies and Reports, Series B (Social and Economic Conditions), 25. Geneva/London: International Labour Office/P. S. King and Sons, 1937.

Maybury-Lewis, Biorn. *The Politics of the Possible: The Brazilian Rural Workers' Trade Union Movement, 1964–1985*. Philadelphia: Temple University Press, 1994.

McMillan, Claude, Jr. "The American Businessman in Brazil: Contrasting Cultural Backgrounds, Business Practices, and Management Philosophies." *Business Topics* 2 (1963): 68–80.

Medeiros, Jarbas. *Ideologia Autoritária no Brasil, 1930–1945*. Rio de Janeiro: Fundação Getúlio Vargas, 1978.

Medeyros, J. Paulo de. *Getúlio Vargas: O Reformador Social*. Rio de Janeiro: n.p., 1941.

Mello, Arnon de. *Legislação Social e Desenvolvimento, 1930–1964*. Maceío: Gazeta de Alagoas, 1969.

Mendonça, Joseli Maria Nunes. *Entre a Mão e os Anéis: A Lei dos Sexagenários e os Caminhos da Abolição no Brasil*. Campinas: Editora da UNICAMP, 1999.

Mericle, Kenneth S. "Corporatist Control of the Working Class: Authoritarian Brazil since 1964." In *Authoritarianism and Corporatism in Latin America*, edited by James M. Malloy, 303–38. Pittsburgh: University of Pittsburgh Press, 1977.

Merry, Sally Engle. *Getting Justice and Getting Even: Legal Consciousness among Working-Class Americans*. Chicago: University of Chicago Press, 1990.

Merton, Robert K., David L. Sills, and Stephen M. Stigler. "The Kelvin Dictum and Social Science: An Excursion into the History of an Idea." *Journal of the History of the Behavioral Sciences* 20 (1984).

Middlebrook, Kevin J. *The Paradox of Revolution: Labor, the State, and Authoritarianism in Mexico*. Baltimore: Johns Hopkins University Press, 1995.

Ministério do Trabalho, Indústria, e Comércio. *Dez Anos de Legislação Social:*

Ementário dos Atos Oficiais Expedidos de 1930 a 1940. Rio de Janeiro: Imprensa Nacional, 1940.

Moraes, Evaristo de. *Apontamentos do Direito Operário*. 1904; reprint, São Paulo: Editora LTr, 1971.

——. *O Anarquismo no Tribunal do Júri [Processo de Edgar Leuenroth]*. Rio de Janeiro: Grupo Editor La Vero, 1918.

Moraes, Josino. *A Indústria da Justiça do Trabalho*. Campinas: Editora Komedi, 2001.

Moraes Filho, Evaristo de. "Introdução." In *O Batismo do Trabalho: A Experiência de Lindolfo Collor*, by Rosa Maria Barbosa de Araújo, 13–22. Rio de Janeiro: Civilização Brasileira, 1981.

——. *O Problema do Sindicato Único no Brasil: Seus Fundamentos Sociológicos*. 1952; reprint, São Paulo: Alfa-Omega, 1978.

——, ed. *O Socialismo Brasileiro*. Brasília: Universidade de Brasília, 1981.

Moreira Cardoso, Adalberto. *Sindicatos, Trabalhadores, e a Coqueluche Neoliberal: A Era Vargas Acabou?* Rio de Janeiro: Editora da Fundação Getúlio Vargas, 1999.

Moreira de Carvalho, Inaiá Maria. "Droits Légaux et Droits Effectifs: Enfants, Adolescents, et Citoyenneté au Brésil." *Cahiers des Ameriques Latines* 22 (1998): 5–22.

——. *Operário e Sociedade Industrial na Bahia*. Estudos Baianos 4. Salvador: Universidade Federal da Bahia, 1971.

Morel, Regina Lúcia de Moraes. "Empresa Estatal e Gestão da Força da Trabalho: Trabalhadores da Companhia Siderúrgica Nacional Entre a 'Dádiva' e os 'Direitos.'" In *Anais do Seminário Internacional Padrões Tecnológicos e Organização do Trabalho na Indústria Brasileira*, 257–83. São Paulo: Departamento de Sociologia, Universidade de São Paulo, 1988.

Morel, Regina Lúcia de Moraes, and Wilma Mangabeira. "'Velho' e 'Novo' Sindicalismo e Uso da Justiça do Trabalho: Um Estudo Comparativo com Trabalhadores da Companhia Siderúrgica Nacional." *Dados* 37, no. 1 (1994): 103–24.

Morris, James O. *Elites, Intellectuals, and Consensus: A Study of the Social Question and the Industrial Relations System in Chile*. Ithaca: New York State School of Industrial and Labor Relations, Cornell University, 1966.

Morris, James O., and Efrén Córdova, eds. *Bibliography of Industrial Relations in Latin America*. Ithaca: New York State School of Industrial and Labor Relations, Cornell University, 1967.

Morse, Richard M. "The Heritage of Latin America." In *Politics and Social Change in Latin America: The Distinct Tradition*, edited by Howard J. Wiarda, 25–69. Amherst: University of Massachusetts Press, 1974.

Motta, Alberico. *Classes Sociais e Poder Político*. Salvador: Universidade Federal da Bahia, Instituto de Ciências Sociais, 1966.

Munakata, Kazumi. *A Legislação Trabalhista no Brasil*. São Paulo: Brasiliense, 1981.

Murilo de Carvalho, José. *A Formação das Almas: O Imaginário da República no Brasil*. São Paulo: Companhia das Letras, 1990.

Nascimento, Amauri Mascaro. "História do Direito do Trabalho no Brasil." In *História do Trabalho, do Direito do Trabalho, e da Justiça do Trabalho: Homenagem a Armando Casimiro Costa*, edited by Irany Ferrari, Amauri Mascaro Nascimento, and Ives Gandra da Silva Martins Filho, 75–163. São Paulo: Editora LTr, 1998.

Needel, Jeffrey D. "History, Race, and the State in the Thought of Oliveira Viana." *Hispanic American Historical Review* 75, no. 1 (1995): 1–30.

Negro, Antônio Luigi. "Nas Origens do 'Novo Sindicalismo': O Maio de 59, 68, e 78 na Indústria Automobílistica." In *O Novo Sindicalismo Vinte Anos Depois*, edited by Iram Jácome Rodrigues, 9–31. Petrópolis: Editora Vozes, 1999.

———. "A 'Via Willyana': Industrialização e Trabalhadores do Setor Automobilístico." *Tempo (Revista do Departamento de Historia da Universidade Fluminense)*, no. 7 (1999): 71–98.

Negro, Antônio Luigi, and Paulo Fontes. "Trabalhadores em São Paulo: Ainda um Caso de Polícia." In *No Coração das Trevas: O DEOPS/SP Visto por Dentro*, edited by Maria Aparecida de Aquino, Marco Aurélio Vannucchi Leme de Matos, and Walter Cruz Swensson Jr., 157–97. São Paulo: Arquivo do Estado de São Paulo/Edições Imprensa Oficial, 2001.

Neves Delgado, Lucília de Almeida. *PTB: Do Getulismo ao Reformismo (1945–1965)*. São Paulo: Marco Zero, 1989.

———. "Trabalhismo, Nacionalismo, e Desenvolvimentismo: Um Projeto para o Brasil (1945–1964)." In *O Populismo e Sua História: Debate e Crítica*, edited by Jorge Ferreira, 205–71. Rio de Janeiro: Civilização Brasileira, 2001.

Nogueira, Danilo. "Working in Brazil." *Translation Journal* 3, no. 2 (1999), <http://accurapid.com/journal/08legal1.htm>, 7 November 2003.

Noronha, Eduardo. *Entre a Lei e a Arbitrariedade: Mercados e Relações de Trabalho no Brasil*. São Paulo: Editora LTr, 2000.

Nosella, Paolo [interviewer]. *Por Que Mataram Santos Dias? Quando os Braços se Unem à Mente*. São Paulo: Cortez, 1980.

Nunes, Antônio Carlos Felix. *PC Linha Leste*. São Paulo: Livramento, 1980.

Oliveira, Francisco de. "A Economia Brasileira: Crítica a Razão Dualista." *Seleções CEBRAP*, no. 1 (1977): 5–78.

Oliveira, Jaime A. de Araújo, and Sonia M. Fleury Teixeira. *(Im)Previdência Social: 60 Anos de História da Previdência no Brasil*. Petrópolis: Editora Vozes, 1986.

Oliveira Vianna, Francisco José de. *Direito do Trabalho e Democracia Social (O Problema da Incorporação do Trabalhador no Estado)*. Rio de Janeiro: José Olympio, 1951.

———. *Problemas do Direito Corporativo*. Rio de Janeiro: José Olympio, 1938.

Pacheco, José Aranha de Assis. *Prevenção de Dissidios Trabalhistas*. São Paulo: Imprensa Gráfica da Revista dos Tribunais, 1945.

Paoli, Maria Célia. "Os Trabalhadores Urbanos na Fala dos Outros: Tempo, Espaço, e Classe na História Operária Brasileira." In *Cultura e Identidade Operária: Aspectos da Cultura da Classe Trabalhadora*, edited by José Sergio Leite Lopes, 53–101. Rio de Janeiro: Universidade Federal de Rio de Janeiro/Museu Nacional/Marco Zero, 1988.

Paranhos, Adalberto. *O Roubo da Fala: Origens da Ideologia do Trabalhismo no Brasil*. São Paulo: Boitempo, 1999.

Pazzianotto Pinto, Almir. "Sindicatos, Corporativismo, e Política." In *21 Anos de Regime Militar*, edited by Gláucio Ary Dillon Soares and Maria Celina Soares D'Araújo, 89–122. Rio de Janeiro: Editora Fundação Getúlio Vargas, 1994.

Peixoto, Alzira Vargas do Amaral. *Getúlio Vargas, Meu Pai*. Rio de Janeiro: Editôra Globo, 1960.

Pena, Eduardo Spiller. *Pajens da Casa Imperial: Jurisconsultos, Escravidão e a Lei de 1871*. Campinas: Editora da Universidade Estadual de Campinas/Centro de Pesquisa em História Social da Cultura/Fundação de Amparo à Pesquisa no

Estado de São Paulo/Centro Nacional de Desenvolvimento Científico y Tecnológico, 2001.

Pereira, Osny Duarte. *Quem Faz as Leis no Brasil?* Cadernos do Povo Brasileiro 3. Rio de Janeiro: Editôra Civilização Brasileira, 1963.

Pereira de Souza, Romulo Augustus. *Memórias de um Pelego*. Rio de Janeiro: Gryphus, 1998.

Pessanha, Elina Gonçalves da Fonte, and Regina Lúcia de Moraes Morel. "Gerações Operárias: Rupturas e Continuidades na Experiência de Metalúrgicos no Rio de Janeiro." *Revista Brasileira de Ciências Sociais (Rio de Janeiro)* 6, no. 17 (1991): 68–83.

Phelps, Dudley Maynard. *Migration of Industry to South America*. New York: McGraw-Hill, 1936.

Pimenta, Joaquim. *Sociologia Jurídica do Trabalho*. 3d ed. Rio de Janeiro: Imprensa Nacional, 1948.

Pimpão, Hirosê. *Getúlio Vargas e o Direito Social Trabalhista*. Rio de Janeiro: n.p., 1942.

Pinheiro, Paulo Sérgio. *Estratégias da Illusão: A Revolução Mundial e o Brasil, 1922–1935*. São Paulo: Companhia das Letras, 1991.

——. *Política e Trabalho no Brasil (dos Anos Vinte a 1930)*. Rio de Janeiro: Paz e Terra, 1977.

——. "Trabalho Industrial no Brasil: Uma Revisão." *Estudos CEBRAP*, no. 14 (1975): 123–29.

——. "Violência do Estado e Classes Populares." *Dados-Revista de Ciências Sociais*, no. 22 (1979): 15–24.

——, ed. *Crime, Violência, e Poder*. São Paulo: Brasiliense, 1983.

——, ed. *Escritos Indignados: Polícia, Prisões, e Política no Estado Autoritário*. São Paulo: Brasiliense, 1984.

Pinheiro, Paulo Sérgio, and Michael M. Hall. *A Classe Operária no Brasil: Documentos (1889 a 1930)*. 2 vols. São Paulo: Alfa-Omega, 1979.

Pochmann, Márcio. "Mudança e Continuidade na Organização Sindical Brasileira no Período Recente." In *Crise e Trabalho no Brasil: Modernidade ou Volta ao Passado?* edited by Carlos Alonso Barbosa de Oliveira and Jorge Eduardo Levi Mattoso, 269–301. São Paulo: Scritta, 1996.

Polícia do Estado de São Paulo. *Código Telgráfico para Uso das Autoridades Policiais*. São Paulo: Tipografia do Gabinete de Investigações, 1939.

Pompeu de Campos, Reynaldo. *Repressão Judicial no Estado Novo: Esquerda e Direita no Banco dos Réus*. Rio de Janeiro: Achiamé, 1982.

Population Reference Bureau. *2003 World Population Data Sheet*. 2003. <http://www.prb.org>. 13 October 2003.

Prado Júnior, Caio. "É Preciso Deixar o Povo Falar [Entrevista com Caio Prado Júnior]." In *A História Vivida*, edited by Lourenço Dantas Mota, 1:301–19. São Paulo: O Estado de São Paulo, 1981.

Puech, Luiz Roberto de Rezende. *Direito Individual e Coletivo do Trabalho (Estudos e Comentários)*. São Paulo: Editora Revista dos Tribunais, 1960.

Quartim de Moraes, João. "Oliveira Vianna e a Democatização Pelo Alto." In *O Pensamento de Oliveira Vianna*, edited by Elide Rugai Bastos and João Quartim de Moraes, 87–130. Campinas: Editora da Universidade Estadual de Campinas, 1993.

Ramalho, José Ricardo. *Estado-Patrão e Luta Operária: O Caso FNM [Fábrica Nacional de Motores]*. Rio de Janeiro: Paz e Terra, 1989.

Ramalho, José Ricardo, and Marco Aurélio Santana, eds. *Trabalho e Tradição Sindical no Rio de Janeiro: A Trajetória dos Metalúrgicos*. Rio de Janeiro: Fundação Carlos Chagas Filho de Amparo à Pesquisa do Estado do Rio de Janeiro, 2001.

Rebouças, Antônio José de Arruda. *Insalubridade: Morte Lenta no Trabalho: A Insalubridade no Brasil*. São Paulo: Oboré, 1989.

Rego, Alcides Marinho. *A Vitória do Direito Operário no Governo Getúlio Vargas*. Rio de Janeiro: Departamento de Imprensa e Propaganda, 1942.

Reis Filho, Daniel Aarão. "O Colapso do Colapso do Populismo ou a Propósito de uma Herança Maldita." In *O Nome e a Coisa: Populismo na Política Brasileira*, edited by Jorge Ferreira, 319–77. Rio de Janeiro: Civilização Brasileira, 2001.

Ribeiro, A. Varella. *O Problema da Greve*. Rio de Janeiro: Lito-Tipo Guanabara S.A.-Editora, 1959.

Ribeiro Costa, Vanda Maria. "Corporativismo e Justiça Social: O Projeto de Oliveira Vianna." In *O Pensamento de Oliveira Vianna*, edited by Elide Rugai Bastos and João Quartim de Moraes, 131–43. Campinas: Editora da Universidade Estadual de Campinas, 1993.

Rodrigues, Aluísio. *O Estado e o Sistema Sindical Brasileiro*. São Paulo: Editora LTr, 1981.

Romão, Frederico Lisbôa. *Na Trama da História: O Movimento Operário de Sergipe 1871 a 1935*. Aracaju: Sindimina, Sindipema, Sindisan, Sindicato dos Bancários, Advocacia Operária, 2000.

Rose, R. S. *One of the Forgotten Things: Getúlio Vargas and Brazilian Social Control, 1930–1954*. Westport, Conn.: Greenwood, 2000.

Rowland, Robert. "Classe Operária e Estado de Compromisso (Origens Estruturais da Legislação Trabalhista e Sindical)." *Estudos CEBRAP*, no. 8 (1974): 5–40.

Rugendas, João Maurício. *Viagem Pitoresco Através do Brasil*. Translated by Sérgio Millïet. 8th ed. Reprint, Belo Horizonte: Itatiaia, 1979.

Sady, João José. *Direito Sindical e Luta de Classes*. São Paulo: Instituto Cultural Roberto Morena, 1985.

Santana, Marco Aurélio. *Homens Partidos: Comunistas e Sindicatos no Brasil*. Campinas/Rio de Janeiro: Boitempo/Universidade do Rio de Janeiro, 2001.

———. "Partido e Militancia Sindical: A Atuação Comunista no Sindicato dos Metalúrgicos do Rio de Janeiro (1947–1964)." *Revista de Sociologia e Política*, no. 8 (1997): 73–94.

———. "Política e História em Disputa: O 'Novo Sindicalismo' e a Idéia da Ruptura com o Passado." In *O Novo Sindicalismo Vinte Anos Depois*, edited by Iram Jácome Rodrigues, 133–61. Petrópolis: Editora Vozes, 1999.

———. "Trabalhadores e Militância Sindical: A Relação Partido/Sindicato/Classe no Sindicato dos Metalúrgicos do Rio de Janeiro (1947–1964)." In *Trabalho e Tradição Sindical no Rio de Janeiro: A Trajetória dos Metalúrgicos*, edited by José Ricardo Ramalho and Marco Aurélio Santana, 165–212. Rio de Janeiro: Fundação Carlos Chagas Filho de Amparo à Pesquisa do Estado do Rio de Janeiro, 2001.

Santana, Marco Aurélio, and Regina Malta Nascimento. " 'Trabalhadores do Brasil' e 'Peões': Passado e Presente na Fala de Duas Gerações de Militantes Operárias." *Tempo (Revista do Departamento de Historia da Universidade Fluminense)*, no. 7 (1999): 99–128.

Santos, Raimundo N. "Una Historia Obrera de Brasil: 1888–1979." In *Historia del Movimiento Obrero en América Latina*, edited by Pablo González Casanova, 9–72. Mexico City: Instituto de Investigaciones Sociales de la Universidad Nacional Autónoma de México, 1984.

Santos, Roberto. *Leis Socias e Custo da Mão-de-Obra no Brasil*. São Paulo: Editora da Universidade de São Paulo, 1973.

Santos, Theotonio dos. *Brasil: La Evolución Histórica y la Crisis del Milagro Económico*. Mexico City: Editorial Nueva Imagen, 1978.

Scarmuzzi, Olyntho V. *Memórias de um Ex-Polícia Especial (Obsessão ao Poder)*. Rio de Janeiro: Revista Continente Editorial, 1981.

Schmitter, Philippe Charles. *Interest Conflict and Political Change in Brazil*. Stanford: Stanford University Press, 1971.

——. "Still the Century of Corporatism?" In *The New Corporatism: Social-Political Structures in the Iberian World*, edited by Frederick B. Pike and Thomas Stritch, 84–131. Notre Dame, Ind.: University of Notre Dame Press, 1974.

Schwartzman, Simon, ed. *Estado Novo, um Auto-Retrato (Arquivo Gustavo Capanema)*. Brasília: Editora Universidade de Brasília com o Apoio Fundação Roberto Marinho, 1983.

Schwarz, Roberto. *Misplaced Ideas: Essays on Brazilian Culture*. London: Verso, 1992.

Seidman, Gay W. *Manufacturing Militance: Workers' Movements in Brazil and South Africa, 1970–1985*. Berkeley: University of California Press, 1994.

Shearer, John C. *High-Level Manpower in Overseas Subsidiaries: Experience in Brazil and Mexico*. Princeton: Industrial Relations Section, Princeton University, 1960.

——. "The Underdeveloped Industrial Relations of U.S. Corporations in Underdeveloped Countries." *Proceedings of the Seventeenth Annual Meeting, Industrial Relations Research Association* 17 (1964): 1–11.

Sigaud, Lygia. *Os Clandestinos e os Direitos: Estudos sobre Trabalhadores da Cana-de-Açucar de Pernambuco*. São Paulo: Duas Cidades, 1979.

——. "Direito e Coerção Moral no Mundo dos Engenhos." *Revista Estudos Históricos* 18 (1997): 361–88.

Silva, Hélio. *1954: Um Tiro no Coração*. Rio: Civilização Brasileira, 1978.

Silva, Hélio, and Maria Cecília Ribas Carneiro. *Os Presidentes: Getúlio Vargas: A 2a Deposição 3a Parte, 1946–1954*. São Paulo: Grupo de Comunicação Três, 1983.

Silva Martins Filho, Ives Gandra da. "Breve História da Justiça do Trabalho." In *História do Trabalho, do Direito do Trabalho e da Justiça do Trabalho: Homenagem a Armando Casimiro Costa*, edited by Irany Ferrari, Amauri Mascaro Nascimento, and Ives Gandra da Silva Martins Filho, 167–221. São Paulo: Editora LTr, 1998.

Silvert, Kalman. "The Politics of Social and Economic Change in Latin America." In *Politics and Social Change in Latin America: The Distinct Tradition*, edited by Howard J. Wiarda, 159–69. Amherst: University of Massachusetts Press, 1974.

Simão, Azis. *O Sindicato e o Estado*. 1966; reprint, São Paulo: Dominus/Editora da Universidade de São Paulo, 1981.

——. "O Sindicato na Vida Política do Brasil." *Revista de Estudos Sócio-Econômicos* 1, no. 9 (1962).

Simões, Carlos. *Direito de Trabalho e Modo de Produção Capitalista*. São Paulo: Símbolo, 1979.

Simonsen, Roberto. "A Indústria e o Ensino Profissional." In *O Pensamento Industrial no Brasil, 1880–1945*, edited by Edgard Carone, 273–84. Rio de Janeiro: Difusão Européia do Livro, 1977.

Siqueira Neto, José Francisco. *Direito do Trabalho e Democracia: Apontamentos e Pareceres*. São Paulo: Editora LTr, 1996.

Sitrângulo, Cid José. *Conteúdo dos Dissídios Coletivos de Trabalho (1947 a 1976)*. São Paulo: Editora LTr, 1978.

Skidmore, Thomas E. *Politics in Brazil, 1930–1964*. 1976; reprint, Oxford: Oxford University Press, 1986.

———. *The Politics of Military Rule in Brazil, 1964–1985*. Oxford: Oxford University Press, 1988.

Sodré, Fábio. "As Necessidades dos Operários Brasileiros." *Estudos Brasileiros* 1, no. 1 (1938).

Souza Martins, Heloisa Helena Teixeira de. *O Estado e a Burocratização do Sindicato no Brasil*. São Paulo: Hucitec, 1979.

Souza Martins, José de. *A Chegada do Estranho*. São Paulo: Hucitec, 1993.

Souza Netto, F. de A. *Legislação Trabalhista: Collectanea Completa das Leis, Decreto-Leis, Decretos, Regulamentos, Instrucções, Portarias, Circulares, Modelos e Tabellas Referentes à Legislação do Trabalho, Actualmente em Vigor, com as Devidas Notas Explicativas*. 2d ed. São Paulo: Livraria Acadêmica, 1939.

Spalding, Hobart A., Jr. *Organized Labor in Latin America: Historical Case Studies of Urban Workers in Dependent Societies*. New York: Harper and Row, 1977.

Springer, Joseph Frank. *A Brazilian Factory Study 1966: Working Class Conditions and Attitudes during a Political-Economic Crisis*. CIDOC Cuaderno 33. Cuernavaca, Mexico: Centro Intercultural de Documentacion, 1969.

Suriano, Juan, ed. *La Cuestión Social en Argentina, 1870–1943*. Buenos Aires: Editorial La Colmena, 2000.

Teixeira da Silva, Fernando. *A Carga e a Culpa: Os Operários das Docas de Santos: Direitos e Cultura de Solidaridade 1937–1968*. São Paulo/Santos: Editora Hucitec/Prefeitura Municipal de Santos, 1995.

———. *Operários sem Patrões: Os Trabalhadores de Santos no Entreguerras*. Campinas: Editora Universidade Estadual de Campinas, 2003.

———. Review of *Afogado em Leis*, by John D. French. *Labor History* 44, no. 1 (2003): 127–28.

Teixeira da Silva, Fernando, and Hélio Costa. "Trabalhadores Urbanos e Populismo: Um Balanço dos Estudos Recentes." In *O Populismo e Sua História: Debate e Crítica*, edited by Jorge Ferreira, 205–72. Rio de Janeiro: Civilização Brasileira, 2001.

Tejo, Aurélio de Limeira. *Jango: Debate sobre a Crise dos Nossos Tempos*. Rio de Janeiro: Editorial Andes, 1957.

Tenório de Brito, Luis. "Washington Luis e a Questão Social." In *Washington Luis (Visto pelos Contemporâneos no Primeiro Centenário de Seu Nascimento)*, 85–90. São Paulo: Instituto Histórico e Geográfico de São Paulo, 1969.

"Tópicos do Manifesto da Aliança Liberal, de 20 de Setembro de 1929, Referentes ao Programa Político-social." In *História dos Partidos Brasileiros*, edited by Vamireh Chacon, 321–27. Brasília: Editora da Universidade de Brasília, 1981.

Torre Villar, Ernesto de la, and Jorge Mario García Laguardia. *Desarrollo Histórico del Constitucionalismo Hispanoamericano*. Mexico City: Universidad Nacional Autônoma de México, Instituto de Investigaciones Jurídicas, 1976.

Touraine, Alain, and Daniel Pécaut. "Working Class Consciousness and Economic Development in Latin America." In *Masses in Latin America*, edited by Irving Louis Horowitz, 65–94. New York: Oxford University Press, 1970.

Trigueiro do Vale, Osvaldo. *O Supremo Tribunal Federal e a Instabilidade Político-Institucional*. Rio de Janeiro: Civilização Brasileira, 1976.

Unger, Roberto Mangabeira. *Knowledge and Politics*. New York: Free Press, 1975.

Vargas, Getúlio. *As Diretrizes da Nova Política no Brasil*. Rio de Janeiro: José Olympio, 1943.

——. *A Campanha Presidencial*. Rio de Janeiro: José Olympio, 1951.

——. *A Nova Política do Brasil*. Vols. 1, 3–5. Rio de Janeiro: José Olympio, 1938.

——. "The Suicide Letter of Getúlio Vargas." In *A Documentary History of Brazil*, edited by E. Bradford Burns, 368–71. New York: Knopf, 1966.

——. "Vargas's Labor Day Address to Workers in Vasco da Gama Stadium, 1951 [Excerpt]." In *Father of the Poor? Vargas and His Era*, edited by Robert M. Levine, 150. Cambridge: Cambridge University Press, 1998.

——. "Vargas's Suicide Letter, August 24, 1954." In *Father of the Poor? Vargas and His Era*, edited by Robert M. Levine, 150–52. Cambridge: Cambridge University Press, 1998.

Velasco, Marilton. *Cativos na Liberdade: Hipocrisia e Farsa nas Relações de Trabalho*. Petrópolis: Editora Vozes, 2001.

Verucci, Florisa, and Daphne Patai. "Women and the New Brazilian Constitution." *Feminist Studies* 17, no. 3 (1991): 551–68.

Viotti da Costa, Emília. *The Brazilian Empire: Myths and Histories*. 1985; reprint, Chapel Hill: University of North Carolina Press, 2000.

Wanderly Reis, Fábio. "Apresentação." In *Elites Industriais e Democracia: Hegemonia Burguesa e Mudança Política no Brasil*, by Renato Raul Boschi. Rio de Janeiro: Graal, 1979.

Weffort, Francisco Corrêa. "Democracia e Movimento Operário: Algumas Questões para a História do Período 1945–1964. [Primeira Parte]." *Revista da Cultura Contemprânea* 1, no. 1 (1978): 7–13.

——. "New Democracies and Economic Crisis in Latin America." In *What Kind of Democracy? What Kind of Market? Latin America in the Age of Neoliberalism*, edited by Philip Oxhorn and Graciela Ducatenzeiler, 219–26. University Park: Pennsylvania State University Press, 1998.

——. "Origens do Sindicalismo Populista no Brasil (A Conjuntura do Após Guerra." *Estudos CEBRAP* 4 (1973): 65–105.

——. *O Populismo na Política Brasileira*. Rio de Janeiro: Paz e Terra, 1978.

——. "Raízes Sociais do Populismo em São Paulo." *Revista Civilização Brasileira*, no. 2 (1965): 39–60.

Weinstein, Barbara. *For Social Peace in Brazil: Industrialists and the Remaking of the Working Class in São Paulo, 1920–1964*. Chapel Hill: University of North Carolina Press, 1996.

Welch, Cliff. *The Seed Was Planted: The São Paulo Roots of Brazil's Rural Labor Movement, 1924–1964*. University Park: Pennsylvania State University Press, 1999.

Werneck Sodré, Nelson. *História da Burguesia Brasileira*. 2d ed. Rio de Janeiro: Editôra Civilização Brasileira, 1967.

Werneck Vianna, Luiz Jorge. *Liberalismo e Sindicato no Brasil*. 4th ed. Belo Horizonte: Editora Universidade Federal de Minas Gerais, 1999.

Whyte, William F., and Allan R. Holmberg. "Human Problems of U.S. Enterprise in Latin America." *Human Organization* 15 (1956): 1–40.

Wiarda, Howard J. "The Corporative Origins of the Iberian and Latin American Labor Relations Systems." *Studies in Comparative International Development* 13, no. 1 (1973): 3–37.

——. "Law and Political Development in Latin America: Toward a Framework for Analysis." In *Politics and Social Change in Latin America: The Distinct Tradition*, edited by Howard J. Wiarda, 199–229. Amherst: University of Massachusetts Press, 1974.

———. "Social Change and Political Development in Latin America: Summary, Implications, Frontiers." In *Politics and Social Change in Latin America: The Distinct Tradition*, edited by Howard J. Wiarda, 269–92. Amherst: University of Massachusetts Press, 1974.

Williams, Daryle. *Culture Wars in Brazil: The First Vargas Regime, 1930–1945*. Durham: Duke University Press, 2001.

Wimmer, Franz, ed. *Michaelis Diccionário Ilustrado*. Vol. 2, *Português-Inglês*. São Paulo: Melhoramentos, 1999.

Winston, Colin M. *Workers and the Right in Spain, 1900–1936*. Princeton: Princeton University Press, 1985.

Wolfe, Joel William. *Working Women, Working Men: São Paulo and the Rise of Brazil's Industrial Working Class, 1900–1955*. Durham: Duke University Press, 1993.

Wolkmer, Antônio Carlos. *Constitucionalismo e Direitos Socias no Brazil*. São Paulo: Acadêmica, 1989.

Wright, Angus, and Wendy Wolford. *To Inherit the Earth: The Landless Movement and the Struggle for a New Brazil*. Oakland, Calif.: Food First Books, 2003.

index

ABC region of greater São Paulo, 46, 50, 105, 111–12, 134, 149, 158, 192 (n. 41). *See also* Santo André, São Paulo; São Bernardo de Campo, São Paulo
Abel, Christopher, 23, 182 (n. 48)
Adorno, Sérgio, 69
Aguiar Walker, Neuma Figueiredo de, 105, 190 (n. 17)
Alba, Victor, 56
Albertino Rodrigues, José, 2
Alberto, João, 202 (n. 99)
Alexander, Robert, 186 (n. 17), 193 (n. 54)
Almeida, Fernando Lopes de, 51
Alves, Maria Helena Moreira, 58
Amadeo, Edward J., 104
Andrade, Doutel de, 92
Andreotti, Marcos, 46–48, 98–99, 104, 112–20, 134–36, 138, 149–50, 152, 175–76 (nn. 32, 45), 189 (n. 4), 194 (n. 73), 199–200 (nn. 71, 73)
Anticommunism, 12, 15, 32, 65, 81–82, 84, 90, 136–37, 139, 145, 162 (n. 18), 185–86 (nn. 16, 17), 200 (n. 81). *See also* Police repression; Political culture
Avelar, Sonia, 102, 190 (n. 13)

Baer, Werner, 1, 159 (n. 2)
Bahia, 193 (n. 62)
Barbosa, Rui, 163 (n. 34)
Barbosa de Araújo, Rosa Maria, 20
Barreto, Antônio, 44, 174 (n. 16)
Barros, Adhemar de, 68, 74, 99
Barros, Alberto da Rocha, 44
Barsted, Dennis, 88
Basbaum, Leôncio, 25–26, 30, 199 (n. 64)
Bello, José Maria, 32
Bergquist, Charles, 38, 164 (n. 1)
Bernardes, Arthur da Silva, 196 (n. 26)
Bernardo, Antonio, 33
Besouchet, Lídia, 143
Bezerra de Menezes, Geraldo, 21

Blanco, Merida H., 193 (n. 62)
Boito, Armando, Jr., 85
Bonfante, Emílio, 88, 188 (n. 56)
Bosísio, Carlos Eduardo, 175 (n. 32)
Bourdieu, Pierre, 22, 106
Brandão Lopes, Juarez Rubens, 112, 114
Braz, Philadelpho, xii, 45, 106–8, 110–11, 113–20, 145–47, 149, 158, 191 (n. 36), 192–93 (nn. 43, 50)
Brazilian Workers' ABC, xii, 59–60, 98, 182 (n. 53)
Burlamaqui, Paulo, 21

Café Filho, João, 75, 184 (n. 81)
Camargo, José Márcio, 104
Campista, Ary, 164 (n. 40)
Campos, Francisco, 15
Cancelli, Elizabeth, 136, 199 (n. 68)
Cardoso, Adalberto Moreira, 178 (n. 3)
Cardoso, Fernando Henrique, 24
Carteira do trabalho, 2, 48, 96, 107, 119, 128, 152, 157, 176 (nn. 44–45), 191 (n. 39). *See also* Consolidaçao das Leis do Trabalho; Grievances
Carvalho, Daniel de, 68, 170 (n. 68), 201 (n. 98)
Castro Gomes, Angela Maria de, 2, 5, 7, 171–72 (n. 1), 185–86 (n. 2), 188 (n. 68)
Catholic church, 65, 162 (n. 18), 163 (n. 34), 179 (nn. 11, 12), 186 (n. 16)
Cavalcanti, Rodolfo, 93
Ceará, 94
Cerqueira Filho, Gisálio, 20, 70, 131, 167 (n. 29)
Chagas, Francisco, 93
Chaves Neto, Elias, 140
Coelho, Danton, 75–77, 79, 86, 185 (n. 8)
Collier, David and Ruth, 164–65 (n. 2), 168 (n. 42)
Collor, Lindolfo, 12, 17, 19, 34–35, 62, 122, 127–28, 132–33, 135–36, 163–64

(n. 38), 170 (n. 75), 181 (n. 39), 196
(n. 28)

Communism, 98, 107, 133–34, 138, 148,
155–56, 162 (n. 15), 185–86 (n. 16), 199
(n. 64), 200 (n. 81). *See also* Anticommunism; Police repression

Consolidaçao das Leis do Trabalho (Consolidation of Labor Laws), 1–5, 10, 25–
26, 30, 39–42, 44, 52, 54–56, 57–65,
71–73, 89, 97–98, 100, 106–7, 116, 119,
140–41, 148, 151–53, 155, 157–58, 159
(n. 2), 171–72 (nn. 1, 5, 7, 8), 175
(n. 36), 181 (n. 37); *dissídios coletivos*,
41, 48, 50, 57, 59, 172 (n. 5); *dissídios
individuais*, 41, 101–4; enforcement of,
34–35, 39, 42, 44–45, 54, 71, 77, 83, 88–
89, 157, 159 (n. 2), 165 (n. 2), 170
(n. 73), 171 (n. 83), 173 (n. 9), 177
(n. 56); Fascist inspiration, charges of,
4, 10, 14, 16, 20, 58, 134, 161 (n. 11), 162
(nn. 15, 17), 163 (n. 36); *pelegos*, 78, 80,
125–26, 164 (n. 40), 201 (n. 98); union
elections, 16, 75, 78–80. *See also* Delegacia Regional do Trabalho; Estado
Novo; Labor courts; Labor law; Ministério do Trabalho, Indústria, e Comércio; Oliveira Vianna, Francisco José
de; Segadas Vianna, José de; Tribunal
Regional do Trabalho; Tribunal Superior do Trabalho

Constitution: of 1824, 61; of 1891, 127, 196
(n. 27); of 1934, 12, 135, 137, 162 (n. 16);
of 1937, 13–14, 15, 20, 69, 139, 161
(n. 8), 162 (n. 16); of 1946, 2, 69, 77,
90, 183 (n. 66), 188 (n. 65); of 1988, 4,
5, 71, 181 (n. 33). *See also* Labor law;
Law, Brazilian; Legal consciousness;
Legal culture; Political culture

Córdova, Éfren, 4, 159 (n. 5)

Corporatism, 4, 7, 11, 14–17, 19–20, 24,
29, 36, 38, 56–59, 65–67, 118, 161
(n. 11), 163 (n. 36), 164–66 (nn. 2, 24),
168 (n. 42), 172 (n. 1), 180 (n. 28), 190
(n. 15)

Corrêa dos Santos, Hercules, 192 (n. 45)

Couto, Mário, 98

D'Araújo, Maria Celina Soares, 85–86

Delegacia/Departamento de Ordem

Política Social (Social and Political
Order Department or Delegacy), 78–
79, 81, 83, 95, 135, 137, 145, 186 (n. 17),
199 (n. 71); *atestado de ideologia*, 16,
78–79. *See also* Police repression; Political culture

Delegacia Regional do Trabalho
(Regional Labor Delegacy), 44–45, 49,
77, 83–84, 92, 174 (n. 16), 177 (n. 56),
184 (n. 75). *See also* Ministério do Trabalho, Indústria, e Comércio

Dias, Everardo, 132

Dias, Santos, 151–52

Drummond, Herberto de Magalhaes, 47

Dutra, Eurico, 50, 65, 67–68, 75, 77–
78, 91, 95, 144–46, 183 (n. 66), 201
(n. 98)

Erickson, Kenneth, 26, 165 (n. 2), 166
(n. 24), 187 (n. 51), 189 (n. 13)

Estado Novo, 1, 3, 12–16, 19, 25, 27, 38–
39, 62, 64–65, 67, 69, 74, 77–78, 81–
82, 94, 97, 107, 123, 125–26, 135–42,
159 (n. 9), 161 (n. 8), 162 (n. 14), 166
(n. 24), 171 (n. 76), 174 (n. 21), 182
(n. 48), 197 (n. 40), 201 (n. 92)

Europe, influence of, 57–58, 62, 128–29,
131, 140–41, 163 (nn. 36, 37), 167
(n. 32), 178 (n. 2), 181 (n. 38), 184
(n. 81), 194 (n. 3), 198 (n. 44); immigrants, 128–31, 140–41; *para Inglés ver*
(for the English to see), 60–61, 180
(n. 25). *See also* Communism; International Labour Organization/Office;
Labor law; Legal culture; Positivism

Falcão, Waldemar, 123

Faoro, Raimundo, 30

Ferreira, Jorge, 95, 184 (n. 2)

Figueiredo, Morvan Dias de, 30, 51, 86

Fischer, Brodwyn, 176 (n. 44)

Flory, Thomas, 144

Flynn, Peter, 33

Fontes, Amando, 69, 79

Fontes, Lourival, 90

Forbath, William, 6

Fry, Peter, 180 (n. 25)

Fuerstenthal, Achim, 52, 177 (n. 59)

Furtado, Celso, 31

Garcez, Lucas Nogueira, 82
Garcia, Marco Aurélio, 19
Geddes, Barbara, 177 (n. 60)
Giglio, Wagner, 46–47, 175 (n. 36)
Gomes, Orlando, 175–76 (n. 40)
Gonzaga, Gustavo, 104
Goodman, Louis, 56
Goulart, João "Jango," 63, 84–92, 145,
    177 (n. 60), 181 (n. 40), 187 (n. 51), 188
    (nn. 56, 62). *See also* Trabalhismo; Par-
    tido Trabalhista Brasileiro; Populism
Grandi, Carlos, 49
Grievances, 13, 41, 94, 104, 118, 120, 161
    (n. 7), 192 (nn. 40, 50), 193 (n. 71);
    assiduidade integral, 48, 75, 201
    (n. 98); wages and working condi-
    tions, 49–50, 86, 90, 106, 177 (n. 56).
    See also Consolidaçao das Leis do
    Trabalho; Labor courts; Labor
    mobilization
Gudin, Eugênio, 21, 164 (n. 41)
Guilhen, Miguel, 107, 158
Guilherme dos Santos, Wanderley, 2
Gusmão, Cupertino de, 125–26, 195
    (n. 17)

Hall, Michael, 19–20
Hammond, Henry S., 77, 185 (n. 8)
Herrup, Cynthia, 6
Historiography, 10–11, 14, 16–17, 19, 23–
    39, 54–60, 85–86, 123–24, 159 (n. 5),
    160 (nn. 15, 20), 164–65 (nn. 2, 9), 166
    (n. 23), 167 (n. 31), 184–85 (n. 2); artifi-
    ciality thesis, 29–32, 36, 168 (n. 47);
    corporatist consensus, 5, 25–26, 33–34,
    58, 60, 95, 166 (n. 15); culturalist thesis,
    56–59, 178–79 (nn. 10–12); *trabalhista*
    thesis, 7, 89, 184–85 (n. 2). *See also* Cor-
    poratism; Methodology
Holanda de Cavalcanti, Deocleciano, 53
Holston, James, 63
Humor, 2, 13, 40, 54, 72, 98, 159 (n. 9),
    161 (n. 7), 172 (n. 6), 180 (n. 29), 183–
    84 (nn. 72, 81), 195 (n. 19). *See also*
    Legal consciousness; Political culture
Huntington, Samuel, 28

Industrialists, 24, 32–35, 37, 43, 58, 66–
    67, 71, 77, 83, 105, 134, 143, 147, 159

(n. 5), 169–70 (nn. 65, 66, 68), 177
    (n. 59), 178–79 (nn. 2, 15), 190 (n. 15),
    201 (n. 96, 98); Serviço Social da
    Indústria, 78, 114
International Confederation of Free
    Trade Unions, 4
International Labour Organization/
    Office, 4, 21, 54–55, 89, 127, 129, 160
    (n. 13), 163 (n. 38), 170 (n. 73), 198
    (n. 44). *See also* Maurette, Fernand

Jaguaribe, Hélio, 165 (n. 5), 169–70
    (n. 66)
Jesus, Carolina Maria de, 94–95
Julião, Francisco, 175 (n. 36)

Kubitschek, Juscelino, 30

Labor courts, 40–41, 43, 45–52, 57, 59,
    101–11, 114–20, 127, 139, 174 (nn. 31,
    32), 188 (n. 65), 189–90 (nn. 9, 13),
    190 (nn. 20, 22), 193 (n. 62); *juizes
    classistas*, 46–47, 175–76 (n. 40), 191
    (n. 37). *See also* Consolidaçao das
    Leis do Trabalho; Tribunal Regional
    do Trabalho; Tribunal Superior do
    Trabalho
Labor law: comparative, 20–21, 23–24,
    38, 41, 54–56, 59–60, 72, 159 (n. 5),
    160 (n. 17), 163 (n. 37), 164–65 (n. 2),
    167 (n. 31), 169 (n. 65), 171 (n. 81), 178
    (n. 2), 179 (n. 15), 182 (n. 48); *direitos*,
    45–46, 48–49, 53, 107, 111, 191–92
    (n. 39), 192 (n. 40); justice at a dis-
    count, 45, 120–21, 174 (n. 24); origins
    of, 6, 11–12, 14–22, 25, 28, 63–64, 127–
    28, 133, 160 (n. 18), 163 (n. 34), 169
    (n. 63), 196 (n. 29); unionization
    Decree 19,770 of 1931, 17, 161 (n. 12),
    163 (n. 34), 166 (n. 24); workers and,
    8, 98, 100, 158, 191 (n. 39), 193 (n. 62);
    workers' views of as fraud, 44–46, 49,
    51–53, 72, 78, 83, 93, 98–99, 116, 120,
    135, 152, 174 (n. 28), 175 (n. 32), 180
    (n. 25), 189 (n. 4); workers' views of as
    ideal, as Bible, 8, 54, 61, 88, 94–99,
    107, 151–52, 155, 157–58. *See also* Cath-
    olic church; Collor, Lindolfo; Consol-
    idaçao das Leis do Trabalho; Europe,

influence of; Labor courts; Law, Brazilian; Lawyers; Legal consciousness; Legal culture; Moraes, Evaristo de; Moraes Filho, Evaristo de; Positivism; Social question

Labor mobilization, 98, 105, 112–21, 173 (n. 14)

Lacerda, Maurício de, 19–20, 133, 198 (n. 49)

Law, Brazilian: general, xi, 53, 55, 61, 71–73, 120–21, 153, 175 (n. 36), 181 (n. 33), 184 (n. 72); law as *outorga* or gift, 3, 4, 8, 10, 13, 16, 26–33, 36–38, 63, 106, 153, 161 (n. 5). *See also* Consolidaçao das Leis do Trabalho; Constitution; Labor law; Lawyers; Legal consciousness; Legal culture; Political culture; State intervention

Lawyers (*bacharéis/bacharelismo*), 21–22, 39, 60–64, 67, 69–70, 76–77, 107, 140–41, 143, 156, 172–73 (n. 7), 175–76 (nn. 36, 40), 180 (n. 27), 183 (n. 67), 189 (n. 9), 191 (n. 36), 200 (nn. 74, 81). *See also* Legal culture

Legal consciousness, 8–9, 97, 100, 116–17, 148–49, 191–92 (n. 39), 193 (n. 62). *See also* Political culture

Legal culture, 6, 21–22, 60–63, 67, 69–71, 127–28, 142, 161 (n. 8), 163 (n. 34), 172 (n. 7), 180 (n. 28); preference for "advanced" laws, 1, 54–57, 72, 128, 178 (nn. 2, 3), 181 (n. 38), 184 (n. 81). *See also* Europe, influence of; Lawyers; Legal consciousness; Oliveira Vianna, Francisco José de; Political culture; Segadas Vianna, José de; Slavery

Leite Lopes, José Sérgio, 98–99, 117

Lepage, Enio, 77, 83

Lessa, Orígenes, 94–95

Leuenroth, Edgard, 19

Levy, Herbert, 201 (n. 97)

Lewis, Colin, 23, 182 (n. 48)

Liberal Alliance, 11, 127, 163 (n. 38), 198 (n. 44)

Lima, Jacob Carlos, 117

Lima, Maria Emília A. T., 85

Lins de Barros, Antônio Luis, 177 (n. 56)

Lobos, Júlio Alejandro, 40, 54, 72, 184 (n. 81)

Loewenstein, Karl, 2, 159 (n. 6), 167 (n. 24), 178 (n. 3), 182 (n. 48)

Lothian, Tamara, 59

Luis, Washington, 11, 95, 122–24, 126–29, 131–32, 136–37, 139, 144, 195–98 (nn. 22–23, 29, 36, 44)

Lula da Silva, Luis Inácio, 5, 134, 149–52, 158

Macedo, Jozé Norberto, 96

Maia, Deodato, 181 (n. 38)

Mangabeira, João, 185–86 (n. 16)

Mangabeira, Vilma, 190 (n. 20)

Maram, Sheldon, 131

Marçal, João Batista, 155–57

Marcondes, J. V. Freitas, 55

Marcondes Filho, Alexandre, 30, 125, 140–41, 173 (n. 8), 181 (n. 37), 195 (n. 14). *See also* Consolidaçao das Leis do Trabalho; Ministério do Trabalho, Indústria, e Comércio

Martins, Eloy, 98

Martins Rodrigues, Leôncio, 111, 114, 160 (n. 18), 182 (n. 49)

Marxism, 58, 63

Maurette, Fernand, 127, 170 (n. 73), 197 (n. 35)

McMillan, Claude, 43, 173 (n. 10)

Medeiros, Borges de, 127, 196 (n. 28)

Mello, Oswaldo Trigueiro de Albuquerque, 69

Mericle, Kenneth, 14, 29, 47, 56, 100–101, 104–5, 118, 175 (n. 36), 189 (n. 13)

Merry, Sally, 100, 117

Methodology, xi, 6, 7, 71, 105–6, 124, 160 (n. 21). *See also* Historiography; Legal consciousness

Military dictatorship (1964–85), 3, 90, 202 (n. 99)

Minas Gerais, 1, 47, 94, 102, 170 (n. 68), 171 (n. 83), 184 (n. 75), 191 (n. 36), 201 (n. 98)

Ministério do Trabalho, Indústria, e Comércio (Ministry of Labor, Industry, and Commerce), 12, 18, 30–31, 35, 39, 45, 64–65, 67, 74–78, 80–83, 88, 90, 125, 133, 143, 161 (n. 2), 170–71 (nn. 70, 83), 181 (n. 37), 185–86 (nn. 12, 22), 188 (nn. 56, 57), 198 (n. 45); inspection

services, 44–45, 174 (n. 16); Instituto de Aposentadorias e Pensoes dos Industriários, 52–53, 177 (n. 60). *See also* Collor, Lindolfo; Consolidaçao das Leis do Trabalho; Delegacia Regional do Trabalho; Labor law; Marcondes Filho, Alexandre; Oliveira Vianna, Francisco José de; São Paulo, state and city of: Departamento Estadual do Trabalho; Segadas Vianna, José de
Monteiro, Rego, 21
Montenegro, Pedro de Albuquerque, 69, 100
Moraes, Evaristo de, 19, 21–22, 196 (n. 28), 198 (nn. 45, 46)
Moraes Filho, Evaristo de, 14, 21, 29, 126, 128, 131–32, 135, 144, 161 (nn. 11, 12), 195–96 (nn. 20, 28), 198 (nn. 45–46)
Moreira Junior, Delfim, 46
Morel, Regina Lúcia de Moraes, 190 (n. 20)
Morena, Roberto, 62
Morse, Richard, 56, 179 (n. 11)
Mota, João Dirceu, 151, 155–58
Moura, Paulo de Campos, 62
Müller, Filinto, 135–36
Munakata, Kazumi, 25

Nascimento, Amaury Mascaro, 172 (n. 7)
National Democratic Union, 132, 198 (n. 46)
Nazareth, Agripino, 19–20
Neves Delgado, Lucília de Almeida, 86
New Left, 24–26, 171 (n. 79), 171–72 (n. 1). *See also* Spalding, Hobart; Weffort, Francisco
Nogueira, Danilo, 107
Noronha, Eduardo, 174 (n. 24), 190 (n. 15)

Oliveira Vianna, Francisco José de, 21–22, 27, 32–33, 36, 64–66, 139, 167 (n. 32), 168 (n. 47), 182 (n. 58)

Pacheco, José Aranha de Assis, 143–44
Paoli, Maria Célia, 5, 8, 73, 97, 106
Paranhos, Adalberto, 27, 140
Partido dos Trabalhadores, 5, 149
Partido Trabalhista Brasileiro (Brazilian Labor Party), 3, 48, 62–63, 74–77, 81–82, 84–86, 88–89, 147, 181 (n. 40), 184–85 (n. 2). *See also* Goulart, João "Jango"; Populism; Trabalhismo
Pazzianotto Pinto, Almir, 30, 172 (n. 8)
Pereira de Souza, Romulo, 45, 153
Pernambuco, 69, 100, 96, 98, 116–17, 151, 177 (n. 56), 191 (n. 39)
Perón, Juan, 38
Phelps, Dudley Maynard, 34–35, 170 (n. 70)
Pimenta, Joaquim, 19–21, 123, 143, 172 (n. 7), 195 (n. 18)
Pinheiro, Paulo Sérgio, 20, 24, 196 (n. 30)
Poletto, Henrique, 48
Police repression, 8, 16, 48, 68–70, 78, 83–84, 90, 92, 122, 128, 130, 133–40, 141–42, 144–49, 151, 153, 176 (n. 44), 185–86 (nn. 16, 17), 195 (n. 17), 197 (nn. 37, 40), 198–99 (nn. 44, 52), 199 (n. 64), 200 (nn. 73, 81), 201–2 (nn. 92, 99). *See also* Anticommunism; Delegacia/Departamento de Ordem Política Social; Political culture; Strikes; Tribunal de Segurança Nacional
Political culture, xi–xii; authoritarianism, 8, 10, 14–16, 24–25, 31, 64–65, 68, 70–71, 81–82, 87, 96, 129–30, 142, 153, 166 (n. 24), 173 (n. 14), 202 (n. 99); dominant class, 5, 21, 60, 197 (n. 36), 201 (nn. 96, 98); paternalism, 2, 8, 25, 27, 56–57, 70–71, 86–89, 136, 142, 144, 148, 197 (n. 36); patronage, 47, 53, 61, 76–78, 86, 95–96, 125–26, 182 (n. 48), 185 (n. 12), 195 (nn. 18, 19). *See also* Anticommunism; Humor; Law, Brazilian; Legal consciousness; Legal culture; Oliveira Vianna, Francisco José de; Segadas Vianna, José de; Working-class consciousness
Populism, 24–26, 31, 58, 60, 85–87, 91, 169–70 (n. 66), 184 (n. 2), 187 (n. 51); demagoguery, charges of, 62–63, 67, 87, 126, 170 (n. 68), 201 (n. 98). *See also* Historiography; Partido Trabalhista Brasileiro; Trabalhismo
Positivism, 127, 157, 196 (n. 28), 202 (n. 105). *See also* Medeiros, Borges de

Prado Júnior, Caio, 188 (n. 62), 200
(n. 81)
Prestes, Júlio, 123
Puech, Luiz Roberto, 49

Quadros, Jânio, 82, 99
Quartim de Moraes, João, 67

Rego, Alcides, 135
Revolution of 1930, 11, 29, 38, 122. *See
also* Collor, Lindolfo; Liberal Alliance
Ribeiro Costa, Vanda Maria, 67, 183
(n. 66)
Riberão Preto, São Paulo, 200 (n. 81)
Rio de Janeiro, 19, 36–39, 45, 48, 81, 84,
92, 99, 102, 129–30, 133, 136, 145, 153,
168 (n. 47), 170 (n. 73), 171 (n. 83), 181
(n. 40), 185 (n. 16), 192 (n. 45), 195
(n. 19), 201–2 (n. 99)
Rio Grande do Sul, 11, 36, 64, 75, 85–87,
98, 102, 127, 138, 152, 155–58, 171
(n. 83), 187 (n. 52), 196 (n. 28), 200
(n. 73)
Rochefoucauld, Duc de La, 59
Rodrigues, Aluísio, 29
Rodrigues Alves, Francisco de Paula,
130–31
Rose, R. S., 199 (n. 68)
Rural workers, 75, 96, 128, 159 (n. 2), 173
(n. 14), 175–76 (nn. 36, 44), 180
(n. 29), 191 (n. 39), 196 (n. 29)
Rusticci, Nelson, 83

Saad, Eduardo Gabriel, 31
Sady, João José, 63
Salert, Irving, 44, 82–84, 88–89, 92
Sales Filho, Francisco Antonio, 136
Salgado Filho, Joaquim Pedro, 135
Santana, Marco Aurélio, 185 (n. 16)
Santo André, São Paulo, 48, 50–52, 134,
191–92 (nn. 36, 43). *See also* ABC
region of greater São Paulo
Santos, João Oliveira, 92
Santos, São Paulo, 93
Santos, Theotonio dos, 24
São Bernardo de Campo, São Paulo, 111,
114, 192 (n. 43). *See also* ABC region of
greater São Paulo
São Paulo, state and city of, 7, 11–12, 30–
31, 34, 36–39, 42–52, 63, 67, 71–72,
74–75, 77–78, 82–84, 91, 94–96, 99,
101–2, 123, 126–31, 134, 137–49, 151,
170 (n. 73), 171 (n. 83), 172 (n. 5), 173
(n. 9), 174 (n. 16), 177 (n. 56), 178
(n. 4), 183 (n. 66), 185 (n. 8), 188
(n. 57), 189 (nn. 9, 13), 196 (nn. 29,
30), 197 (n. 37), 200 (nn. 73, 81), 201
(n. 97); Departamento Estadual do
Trabalho (State Labor Department),
77, 83, 196 (n. 30). *See also* Luis, Washington; Ministério do Trabalho, Indústria, e Comércio
Scarmuzzi, Olyntho, 135, 201 (n. 99)
Schmitter, Philippe, 61, 163 (n. 36), 168
(n. 42), 180 (n. 28)
Segadas Vianna, José de, 30, 36, 62–64,
68, 71–72, 81–90, 92, 172–73 (n. 8), 181
(nn. 37, 40), 182 (n. 50), 185 (n. 12)
Sergipe, 69, 163 (n. 34)
Shearer, John, 43
Siguad, Lygia, 117, 191 (n. 39)
Silva, Delarme Monteiro da, 94–96
Silvert, Kalman, 56, 66, 118, 178 (n. 10)
Simão, Azis, 111, 171 (n. 81)
Simonsen, Roberto, 62, 169 (n. 66)
Siqueira Neto, José Francisco, 71
Skidmore, Thomas, 30, 167 (n. 24)
Slavery, 60, 142–43, 151, 183 (nn. 67, 72),
196 (n. 28), 201 (n. 96)
Social question, 12, 15, 19–20, 26, 29–30,
55, 65, 71, 122–29, 131–34, 140–41, 159
(n. 5), 163–64 (nn. 34, 38), 168 (n. 47),
169 (n. 65), 170 (n. 75), 195 (n. 19), 197
(nn. 35, 40), 201 (nn. 92, 97); *caso de
polícia* aphorism, 3, 8, 26, 30, 122–24,
126, 131–34, 136, 139, 141, 144, 147–49,
170 (n. 75), 194 (n. 3), 197 (n. 40), 198
(n. 44), 201 (nn. 92, 97). *See also* Consolidaçao das Leis do Trabalho; Labor
law; Luis, Washington; Moraes, Evaristo de; Oliveira Vianna, Francisco
José de
Souza, Amaury de, 14
Souza Martins, Heloisa Helena Teixeira
de, 183 (n. 66)
Spalding, Hobart, 32–33, 164–65 (n. 2),
169 (n. 61)
Springer, Joseph, 49, 120, 189 (n. 9)

State intervention, 3, 8, 14, 23–30, 32–34, 37–38, 56–59, 65–67, 99, 101, 122, 124, 139, 143–44, 164 (n. 41), 166 (n. 17), 168 (n. 42), 178 (n. 2), 182 (n. 48). *See also* Labor law; Legal culture

Strikes, 11, 111–12, 126–28, 131, 138–40, 145, 147–48, 159 (n. 5), 190 (n. 21), 201 (n. 98); antistrike Decree Law 9,070, 69, 183 (n. 66); maritime workers (1953), 84, 88, 188 (n. 56); São Paulo, 187 (n. 31); of 1917, 197 (n. 37); of 1953, 82–83, 91; of 1957, 51–52, 69, 181 (n. 40); of 1979, 202 (n. 2). *See also* Police repression

Talarico, José Gomes, 68, 76, 81–84
Tavares de Almeida, Maria Hermínia, 64
Tejo, Aurélio de Limeira, 86, 89
Tenório de Brito, Luis, 126, 129, 132
Thomas, Albert, 129
Trabalhismo, 3, 62–63, 74, 84–88, 147, 167 (n. 25), 184–85 (n. 2). *See also* Goulart, João "Jango"; Partido Trabalhista Brasileiro; Vargas, Getúlio
Tribunal de Segurança Nacional (National Security Court), 16, 137, 199 (n. 72)
Tribunal Regional do Trabalho (Regional Labor Court), 47, 51, 69, 100
Tribunal Superior do Trabalho (Supreme Labor Court), 21, 46, 51–52, 172 (n. 8), 174 (n. 31), 176 (n. 52)

Unger, Roberto Mangabeira, 153

Vargas, Alzira, 13
Vargas, Getúlio, 1–3, 6–8, 10–15, 24–26, 28, 31, 38–39, 48, 60, 62, 65, 72, 74–76, 79–82, 84–86, 88–96, 120, 122–28, 133–36, 142, 145, 148–49, 159 (n. 9), 160 (n. 11), 165 (n. 5), 168 (n. 44), 178 (n. 3), 184 (n. 2), 186 (n. 19), 194 (n. 3), 195 (n. 18), 199 (n. 68). *See also* Estado Novo; Goulart, João "Jango"; Populism; Trabalhismo
Velasco, Marilton, 184 (n. 75)
Ventura, Alvaro, 135
Viotti da Costa, Emília, 36, 60

Wanderley Reis, Fábio, 31
Weffort, Francisco, 25–26, 33, 37, 95, 106, 161 (n. 11), 162 (n. 15), 171 (nn. 79, 1)
Weinstein, Barbara, 169 (n. 66)
Welch, Cliff, 93, 190 (n. 13), 193 (n. 66)
Werneck Sodré, Nelson, 135, 168 (n. 47), 201 (n. 92)
Werneck Vianna, Luiz Jorge, 24, 122
Wiarda, Howard, 56–58
Winston, Colin M., 57
Wolfe, Joel, 85, 192 (n. 47)
Working-class consciousness, 7–8, 36, 53, 93–96, 98–100, 111–17, 124, 148–53, 189 (n. 9), 191–92 (n. 39), 192 (n. 40), 193 (nn. 57, 62). *See also* Legal consciousness; Rural workers; Trabalhismo